Semiotics of the Christian Imagination

Bloomsbury Advances in Semiotics

Semiotics has complemented linguistics by expanding its scope beyond the phoneme and the sentence to include texts and discourse, and their rhetorical, performative, and ideological functions. It has brought into focus the multimodality of human communication. *Advances in Semiotics* publishes original works in the field demonstrating robust scholarship, intellectual creativity, and clarity of exposition. These works apply semiotic approaches to linguistics and non-verbal productions, social institutions and discourses, embodied cognition and communication, and the new virtual realities that have been ushered in by the internet. It also is inclusive of publications in relevant domains such as socio-semiotics, evolutionary semiotics, game theory, cultural and literary studies, human-computer interactions, and the challenging new dimensions of human networking afforded by social websites.

Series Editor: Paul Bouissac is Professor Emeritus at the University of Toronto (Victoria College), Canada. He is a world renowned figure in semiotics and a pioneer of circus studies. He runs the SemiotiX Bulletin [www.semioticon.com/semiotix] which has a global readership.

Titles in the series include

Computable Bodies, Josh Berson
Cognitive Semiotics, Per Aage Brandt
Critical Semiotics, Gary Genosko
Music as Multimodal Discourse, edited by *Lyndon C. S. Way*, Simon McKerrell
Peirce's Twenty-Eight Classes of Signs and the Philosophy of Representation, Tony Jappy
Semiotics and Pragmatics of Stage Improvisation, Domenico Pietropaolo
The Languages of Humor, edited by Arie Sover
The Semiotics of Caesar Augustus, Elina Pyy
The Semiotics of Clowns and Clowning, Paul Bouissac
The Semiotics of Che Guevara, Maria-Carolina Cambre
The Semiotics of Emoji, Marcel Danesi
The Semiotics of Light and Shadows, Piotr Sadowski
The Semiotics of X, Jamin Pelkey
The Social Semiotics of Tattoos, Chris William Martin

Semiotics of the Christian Imagination

Signs of the Fall and Redemption

Domenico Pietropaolo

BLOOMSBURY ACADEMIC
LONDON • NEW YORK • OXFORD • NEW DELHI • SYDNEY

BLOOMSBURY ACADEMIC
Bloomsbury Publishing Plc
50 Bedford Square, London, WC1B 3DP, UK
1385 Broadway, New York, NY 10018, USA
29 Earlsfort Terrace, Dublin 2, Ireland

BLOOMSBURY, BLOOMSBURY ACADEMIC and the Diana logo are trademarks
of Bloomsbury Publishing Plc

First published in Great Britain 2021
This paperback edition published in 2022

Copyright © Domenico Pietropaolo, 2021

Domenico Pietropaolo has asserted his right under the Copyright, Designs and Patents Act, 1988, to be identified as Author of this work.

For legal purposes the Acknowledgements on p. xi constitute an extension of this copyright page.

Cover image © The temptation of Adam and Eve by the devil. Pedestal of the statue of Madonna with Child, western portal (of the Virgin), of Notre-Dame de Paris, France © Jebulon/Wikimedia commons

All rights reserved. No part of this publication may be reproduced or transmitted in any form or by any means, electronic or mechanical, including photocopying, recording, or any information storage or retrieval system, without prior permission in writing from the publishers.

Bloomsbury Publishing Plc does not have any control over, or responsibility for, any third-party websites referred to or in this book. All internet addresses given in this book were correct at the time of going to press. The author and publisher regret any inconvenience caused if addresses have changed or sites have ceased to exist, but can accept no responsibility for any such changes.

A catalogue record for this book is available from the British Library.

A catalog record for this book is available from the Library of Congress.

ISBN: HB: 978-1-3500-6412-6
PB: 978-1-3501-9692-6
ePDF: 978-1-3500-6413-3
eBook: 978-1-3500-6414-0

Series: Bloomsbury Advances in Semiotics

Typeset by Deanta Global Publishing Services, Chennai, India

To find out more about our authors and books visit www.bloomsbury.com and sign up for our newsletters.

For Laura

Contents

List of figures	viii
Preface	ix
Acknowledgements	xi
1 The centrality of signs in the Christian imagination	1
2 Gendering the serpent	23
3 Cajetan on the fall of Eve	47
4 Workers of evil	67
5 The fall from harmony	89
6 Passiontide drama	105
7 Signs of the Passion and signs of compassion	131
8 Imitatio Christi	153
9 Signum magnum	165
10 The starry saints	181
Notes	201
Bibliography	221
General Index	233
Index Locorum	242

Figures

1. Jacopo della Quercia, The Temptation, San Petronio, Bologna. Creative Commons (Public Domain). 28
2. The Temptation, Portal of the Virgin, Notre-Dame Cathedral, Paris. Creative Commons (Public Domain). 32
3. The Temptation, Michelangelo, Sistine Chapel, Vatican. Mondadori Portfolio / Getty Images. 39
4. The Temptation, Raffaello, Stanza della Segnatura, Vatican. Pascal Deloche / Getty Images. 43
5. The Crucifixion, Pacino da Bonaguida. Creative Commons (Public Domain). 142
6. Jesus Mounting the Cross, Chapel of Monastero di Sant'Antonio in Polesine, Ferrara (author's photograph of a wooden reproduction). 145
7. Christ Nailed to the Cross by Fra Angelico and Workshop. Monastero di San Marco, Florence Vincenzo Fontana / Getty Images. 148
8. Orbita Probitatis by Theodoor Galle. Engraving in Veridicus Christianus by Jan David, 1606, p.351. ETH-Bibliothek Zürich, Rar 8222, https://doi.org/10.3931/e-rara-34430 / Public Domain. 162
9. Judith and Holofernes, 1599, by Michelangelo Merisi da Caravaggio (1571-1610), oil on canvas, 145x195 cm. Photo by DeAgostini/Getty Images. 178
10. Constellation of the Archangel Michael (Ursa Minor). Engraving in *Coelum Stellatum Christianum* by Julius Schiller, 1627. Used with permission from Felice Stoppa (www.atlascoelestis.com/) 185

Preface

The semiotics of the Christian imagination consists of a repertory of signs and a logic of signification through which the Christian community of faith is encouraged to envision spiritual truths, in accordance with conventional readings of Scripture under the tutelage of the church. After reviewing the theory of signs and signification developed for this purpose in the later Middle Ages and Renaissance, the present book analyses various examples of the imaginative semiotization of the fall of Adam and Eve from their original state of innocence and of the church's perception of God's plan for the redemption of mankind, as expressed by representative playwrights, artists, scholars and theologians from late medieval, Renaissance and baroque culture. In an age that, on the one hand, exalted the dignity of man on earth and, on the other hand, experienced a profound and long crisis of faith that undermined that dignity, the ideas of the fall and redemption were fundamental concerns of theological anthropology and shaping principles of the Christian imagination. The early modern vision of man in the cosmos is a product of both.

The present book explores a few aspects of that vision, focusing on the consilience between theology and the arts at its base. It includes an introductory chapter on the centrality of signs in the Christian culture of the time, offering a close reading of a selection of primary sources on the theory of signs that enjoyed official status and exercised great influence in all fields. This chapter is followed by nine chapters on the ideas of the fall and redemption of mankind filtered through, and given material representation by, the semiotic paradigms of various fields of culture, including biblical exegesis, the verbal and visual arts, music appreciation and science.

The method adopted is to look for the semiotic strategies used by authors and artists to focus on their object of contemplation and to give that object a rhetorically and aesthetically captivating form for their readers or viewers, whose understanding they wished to guide. The object of contemplation is frequently a Scriptural passage or a point of doctrine, decoded and recoded by imaginative theology. The philosophical principle that informs this approach is based on Giambattista Vico's concept of poetic logic in the creative operations of culture, namely the idea that the metaphysical semiotics by means of which we contemplate the essence of things as theologians or metaphysicians is identical with the poetic semiotics by which we signify that essence perceptibly in all areas of culture as authors, artists, performers or even scientists. The main argument of the present book is that the structure of the Christian imagination, as displayed in its contemplation of the fall and redemption of mankind, comprises both versions of semiotics as inseparable aspects of its operation, which is always simultaneously cognitive and creative.

Acknowledgements

In working on this project, I have incurred a debt of gratitude to various people. At Bloomsbury, I would like to thank Andrew Wardell, commissioning editor for Linguistics, and Paul Bouissac, editor of the Advances in Semiotics series, for their strong support of the project and their friendly encouragement along the way. I am also grateful to Becky Holland for her valuable assistance throughout the process, especially in the final stages of the manuscript preparation, to Brian Wallace for overseeing the production and to Joseph Gautham and Aditya Selvaraj for their careful reading of the text and expert editorial assistance. I am also grateful to the four anonymous scholars commissioned by Bloomsbury to review my original proposal and final manuscript. I thank them for their careful reading of the text and their thoughtful comments.

Parts of Chapters 6, 9 and 10 originally appeared in somewhat different forms in volumes of conference proceedings and essays published respectively by Gruyter, Dovehouse editions and Legas and are here published with kind permission, for which I am most grateful.

I would also like to express my gratitude to Anne Anderson, with whom I discussed various themes of the book when we were revitalizing the Christianity and Culture Programme at the University of St. Michael's College during her term as president and mine as principal and vice-president academic. I am also grateful to Ada Testaferri for her valuable suggestions and stimulating conversation on various topics. My greatest debt, however, is to Laura Pietropaolo, my wife. I am deeply grateful to her not only for her patience and enduring support throughout the process but also for her intellectual companionship and her enlightened understanding of all the issues contemplated in the book.

1

The centrality of signs in the Christian imagination

Signa dantur hominibus, quorum est per nota ad ignota pervenire.[1]

In recent years the relationship between theology and the liberal arts has given rise to a view of biblical exegesis that, in addition to conventional commentaries, includes sculpture, art, music, drama, literature and science as semiotic paradigms for explicating fundamental passages of Scripture and for illustrating related principles of doctrine and faith.[2] The present book is a study of how the culture of the early modern period, with its profound interest in the idea of imaginative representations, lent itself to such an expanded view of biblical reading and to an ongoing transformative dialogue with theology, in a period marked by a severe crisis of faith. Central to this concern of early modern culture was the development of a semiotics of the imagination, by means of which to understand in a concrete manner, and to give material expression to, abstract principles of official doctrine pertaining to the ideas of the fall and redemption of mankind. The concept of sign behind this development was generally grounded in the doctrine of analogy, viewed as the only reliable cognitive link between the immanence of the thinking subject as a fallen creature and the transcendence of salvation through redemption.

This introductory chapter is an outline of the semiotic apparatus through which the Christian imagination of the early modern period related the world of immanence to the world of transcendence, with special reference to the fall and redemption of mankind. It argues that, with respect to these themes, the concepts of sign and signification, considered both as instruments of cognition and as means of expression, occupy a central role in the Christian imagination from the later Middle Ages to the turn of the seventeenth century. Among the many possible examples that can be adduced from the contemporary reflection on signs, we will focus on three, which, on account of the authority that their authors enjoyed, are a good indication of the church's institutional views and clear testimony of the semiotic orientation of its culture. They include a recapitulative statement on the nature of signs by the late medieval pope Lothario Conti, who reigned as Innocent III, various pronouncements on biblical signs by an authoritative theologian of the Renaissance, Cardinal Tommaso de Vio, originally from Cajeta (modern Gaeta) and hence commonly known as Cajetan, and the discussion of sacred signs in the Catechism of the Council of Trent, authored by a committee appointed by Pius V.[3] These sources have hitherto received no attention in standard accounts of the history of semiotics, though they are without doubt representative of mainstream thought on the subject in this period of history. Throughout the Middle Ages, signs were theorized in the context of the theology of the sacraments, understood as rituals that both signify and give real presence to divine grace, though not all theologians agreed on the relative importance of the signifying and efficacious functions of the words and gestures of the rituals. In their own theorization of signs and of the dynamics of signification, Innocent III, Cajetan and the authors of the Roman Catechism brought together various medieval sources and built upon their union with considerable sophistication.

Innocent III

'Only in God does the life of the intellect make no use of signs,' remarked Jacques Maritain in an essay on the nature of signs and symbols. Steeped as Maritain's philosophical perspective was in the culture of Scholasticism, this statement calls attention to the pervasive presence of signs in the culture of the later Middle Ages and Renaissance.[4] God creates and knows, simultaneously and immediately, and does not need signs to do either; human beings, on the other hand, know that creation proclaims the work of God (Ps. 19.1) and must interpret the signs of that proclamation in order to come into cognitive contact with God. Maritain's view is particularly relevant to the field of sacramental theology, since the concept of sacrament, in St Augustine's classical definition of it, is totally grounded in the idea of sign, and sacraments are needed only by fallen creatures seeking salvation, which is why God instituted them for the benefit of humanity. St Augustine's clear understanding of signs on this front remains a focal point of theological reflection in the period contemplated in the present study. Though it was elaborated by Augustine in the context of sacramental theology, the theory of signs enters easily into other areas of intellectual and spiritual life that need to confront the notion of symbolic representation. Only God has no need of signs in the life of His own intellect, but the analysis of all forms of communication and representation, including communication addressed by God to man and vice versa, would be next to vacuous without the notion of signs. The legacy of much of the medieval reflection on the nature of signs is neatly summed up by Innocent III in the brief chapter on *De distinctione signorum* (On the Distinction of signs) of his treatise *De Sacro Altaris Mysterio*,[5] written in 1198 and first issued in print in 1534:

> Signorum autem alia sunt naturalia, et alia positiva. Naturalia sunt, quae secundum naturam significant. Quorum quaedam sunt quae per antecedens significat subsequens, ut rubore vespertino significatur serenitas matutina. Alia sunt quae per consequens significant antecedens ut fumo vel cinere significatur ignis. Positiva sunt quae secundum impositionem significant, quorum alia sunt signum rei sacrae, ut serpens aeneus erectus in eremo (Num. XXI) . . . Alia sunt rei non sacrae, ut arcus triumphalis erectus in bivio. Signorum rei sacrae, alia sunt sacra, ut baptismus; alia non sacra, ut agnus paschalis. Sacra sunt signa Novi Testamenti, non sacra Veteris.[6]
>
> (Some signs are natural and others are positive. Natural signs are those that signify in accordance with nature. Among these are signs that signify a consequent by its antecedent, as when fair weather in the morning is signified by red sky the previous evening, and signs that signify the antecedent by means of its consequent, as when fire is signified by smoke or ashes. Positive signs signify by imposed meaning, and among these we find signs of sacred things, such as the brazen serpent erect in the desert (Num. 21). Other signs, such as a triumphal arch erected at a crossroads, signify things that are not sacred. Some signs of sacred things, such as baptism, are themselves sacred. Others, such as the paschal lamb, are not sacred. Sacred signs are found in the New Testament; non-sacred signs are in the Old Testament.)

Innocent III begins his reflection on the nature of signs by reminding the reader of the distinctive feature of medieval semiotics as outlined by St Augustine, namely that the term *signum* covers both natural and artificial signs, a distinction that assigns to the same category of being signs that occur in nature, or the world created by God, and signs that occur in culture, which is the product of man's creation. This inclusive conception of the sign, which is strikingly different from the one inherited from classical discussions of σημεῖον in antiquity, remained foundational in the Renaissance and beyond, though not without controversy.[7] Innocent refines the category of *signum* by using the conceptual framework of jurisprudence to distinguish natural from artificial signs. In analogy with positive and natural law, he separates natural from positive signs, from which we infer that, just as by adhering to natural law we participate in the moral order of the cosmos, by reading natural signs we participate in the network of signifying relations that underlies the whole of reality. Innocent III interprets natural signs by means of a principle of logic that regards the structure of reasoning as a relationship between an antecedent and a subsequent. Antecedence may indicate a form of material causation (fire causes smoke and ashes), in which case the signifying process is necessarily true, or else it may imply simple temporal precedence without causal determination (the redness of the sky in the evening and fair weather the morning after), and in that case signification may or may not be true. By contrast, positive signs are artificial: they are not found in nature as signs, and they signify by imposed definition.

All signs of sacred things, whether they are themselves sacred or not, are positive. In analogy with a positive law, which has no natural reference to cosmic morality, a positive sign has no intrinsic element of signification, theological or otherwise. All meaning is the result of a defined valence imposed on the sign, in analogy with the practice of *legem ponere* of which the imposition of meaning reminds us etymologically. Precisely how such meaning is imposed, Innocent does not say, but it is clear that the meaning of signs is not merely a matter of mere convention or habitual practice. Signs are positive when their meaning is consciously assigned to them, *secundum impositionem*. An important implication of Innocent's view is that meaning comes from a source of authority accepted as such by the community using the signs. The meaning of these signs is normative, binding the community of sign users, which is the church, to a clearly defined interpretation. Such signs exert a clear illocutionary force on their interpreters because they seek to shape their attitude of mind and to reorient their moral conduct, and that force is strong, coming as it does from an acknowledged source of superior authority. This analysis of the sign is preliminary to a discussion of the word 'sacrament', which, under specific circumstances, Innocent treats virtually as a synonym of sign. Underlying his approach is St Augustine's definition of sacrament as a 'sacrum signum' (*De Civ. Dei*, 10.5). Innocent observes that the word 'sacrament' itself has a narrow and a general meaning. In the narrow sense, a sacrament is a sacred sign, whereas in the wider application of the term, a sacrament is simply a sign of a sacred thing. The difference between a sacred sign and the sign of a sacred thing is that only a sacred sign has the power to justify the person receiving it. Sacraments that justify are found only in the New Testament; the Old Testament includes many more sacraments (*legalia sacramenta*), but these were never endowed with justifying efficacy.

The reference to the presence of signs in the Old and New Testaments suggests the possibility of an exegesis from a semiotic perspective and argues, indirectly, that signs may be ubiquitous in the Christian imagination, which views reality through a prism of faith warranted by the Bible. Innocent also considers sacraments from the perspective of the semiotic agency involved in them, classifying them as either active or passive signs. A sacrament, he says, is to be understood *quasi sacrum signans, vel sacrum signatum*, depending on whether it signifies (*signans*) a sacred thing or is itself a signified (*signatum*) sacred thing or event. The concept of an active sacrament is well represented by the Eucharistic bread, which is a sacrament in so far as it signifies something sacred, while that of a passive sacrament is exemplified by the unity of the church, which is called a sacrament because it is a signified rather than a signifying entity. Only the body of Christ, Innocent adds, is a sacrament in both senses, a sacred signifier and the sacredness that it signifies.

In making these observations, Innocent III introduces a conspicuous social element into the picture by indicating that the fundamental concepts of his summary enjoy currency in the Christian community. He does this by formulating salient aspects of sacred signs with direct reference to the expression of common views in contemporary sacramental culture: *dixerunt* (they said), *dicitur* (it is said), *dicuntur* (they are called), *nuncupatur* (they are called). Such echoes of shared beliefs and preoccupations are witness to the semiotic self-awareness of contemporary culture, of which the pontiff is the highest representative, indirectly citing only those views that he is willing to sanction with his authority.

Innocent's strong declaration of the theological foundation of the sign, seen here in its dual structure of signifier and signified, is also a statement of its centrality in the culture of the centuries that followed it, in which, with the conceptual framework of signs, the theology of the sacrament continued to be taught, reaffirmed and debated. The culture of the Renaissance, on various fronts profoundly different from Innocent's, resonates with echoes of the motifs and themes mentioned by Innocent – including Innocent's own echoes of Augustine and the various motifs that he developed from those echoes. The printed edition of *De Sacro Altaris Mysterio* in 1534 and the presence of echoes of its theory of signs in William Durand's *Rationale divinorum officiorum* (7.23-25), itself issued in print already in 1459 and frequently after that, are material markers of the continuity of Latin culture *sub specie semioticae*. From this perspective, as John Deely has argued, the Renaissance may be regarded as the silver years of the Latin age of understanding, an age in the history of thought that began with Augustine and ended at the turn of the seventeenth century.[8]

Cajetan on God's mode of speaking

A key figure in the development of semiotic awareness in this period was the Dominican Cardinal Thomas de Vio, more commonly known in English-language scholarship by his toponymic adjective Cajetan. Distinguished theologian, philosopher and exegete, Cajetan was a prolific scholar whose views exercised considerable influence in the Latin age, and, consequently, will play a considerable role in the present study. Here, however, it is sufficient to call attention to a couple of passages from his large oeuvre in order to show his contribution to the development of 'semiotic consciousness' (Deeley) in Renaissance theology.

In his commentary on St Paul's Epistle to the Hebrews, Cajetan observes that God speaks to man *vel intelligibiliter, vel imaginabiliter, vel sensibiliter*,[9] through his intellect, his imagination and his senses, using, we may add, different kinds of signs.[10] St Augustine had taken into consideration only signs that we perceive with our senses, but in the later Middle Ages a number of theologians, starting with St Thomas Aquinas, revised the Augustinian conception of the sign to include signs that are not perceivable *sensibiliter*. Such mental entities are images and ideas that may occur to us, not as the end points of our thinking but as signs that redirect our understanding towards something that is other than they are, functioning in a manner analogous to that of material signs except that they are not themselves sensible. In this revised concept of sign, images, recollections and ideas are signs that operate silently on the intellect and the imagination. The revision was not without debate and controversy. The Thomists, building on Aquinas's notion that terms signify a general quality abstracted from concrete individuals called by a certain name, understood ideas as mental signs, in contrast with Roger Bacon, who famously maintained that names signify objects and not concepts of objects. The Thomistic view was that spoken words signify concepts directly and objects indirectly, through the mediation of concepts.[11] Concepts are not in themselves different forms of knowledge but aids that the mind uses to focus on the object of which it seeks knowledge. They are intentional signs, says Maritain, in that they anchor the mind to the object we want to intend, and they have this peculiar characteristic, that as the mind grasps the object through them, they disappear from consciousness, from which they are displaced by our understanding of the object that they signify.¹² God, says Cajetan, can speak to us by means of external sensible signs, such as the words of the Bible and the elements of nature. But He can also do so by means of internal signs, speaking directly to the intellect and the imagination, generating in us a mode of thinking that we may variously perceive as inspiration, prophetic visions and the like, all forms of apprehension governed by the signifying intentionality of internal signs.

In order to make that intentionality intelligible, God presents himself in anthropological terms, assuming a mode of speaking that is commensurate with the capacity of the human intellect. God, in other words, encodes his messages in ways that can be easily decoded by human beings. In interpreting such passages in the Bible, exegetes frequently have tacit recourse to the theological concept of divine accommodation.¹³ In his communication with human beings, God achieves revelation by imitating their mode of thinking and speech, which is tantamount to saying that in reporting such cases the text exhibits what, in terms of modern accommodation theory, may be called a semiotic strategy of convergence, that is to say a rhetorical tactic followed by the speaker to bring his approach to communication closer to his interlocutor's in order to achieve greater nearness and fuller understanding.¹⁴

Cajetan calls this type of divine accommodation speaking *humano more*. In his commentary on the episode of the book of Genesis (9.12-16) in which God says to Noah that henceforth the rainbow in the sky shall be a sign of their covenant, Cajetan remarks that by saying that the rainbow will be for him a reminder of his promise not to cause another flood, God allows himself to be imagined speaking *humano more*, like a human being. God speaks as if he had the human faculty of memory, a faculty that could be activated by the sight of a material phenomenon, which, in turn, was meant to protect the covenant from any potential loss of memory on his part. Cajetan says:

> Hominibus enim humano more se describit ad similitudinem hominis qui ex sensibili signo excitatur ad memoriam promissi.¹⁵
>
> (He describes himself to human beings in a human manner, in the likeness of a man stimulated to remember a promise by a sensible sign.)

The special significance of this passage – among others that mention signs – is that here God himself, quoted as a speaker, explicitly points to the crucial role of signs in the history of salvation when he defines the rainbow as a sign (*hoc signum*) of his covenant relationship (*foederis*) with humanity. Since the covenant is universal and salvation is the ultimate goal, the semiotic of the covenant is located at the very heart of the life of mankind on earth.

However simple signs of God's revelation may be, their interpretation is fraught with difficulties for most men. In his commentary on the episode in the Gospel of St Matthew (16.2-4) – in which Jesus reproaches the crowd for being unable to see the signs of the coming of the Messiah and yet have learnt to interpret weather signs – Cajetan observes that a special disposition is required to discern the signs of revelation, and that is righteousness or the absence of malice. He paraphrases the words of Jesus this way:

> ex praecedentibus signis didicistis iudicare futuram pluuiam, vel serenitatem, & signa praesentia temporum Messiae non solum nescitis, sed non potestis scire ob vestram maliciam. Et dixit hoc, quod signa, temporum Messiae certiora & clariora erant, quam signa pluuiae & serenitatis, ad significandum eorum inexcusabilitatem.[16]
>
> (From the preceding signs you have learned to predict future rainy or fair weather and yet, on account of your wickedness, you do not know the signs of the times of the Messiah. And in order to signify their inexcusability, he said that the signs of the times of the Messiah were clearer and more certain than signs of rainy and fair weather.)

Malicia prevents man from interpreting divine signs correctly. This is because in order to hear God speaking to him, man must first be in the right frame of mind to receive his signs. According to Aquinas, the nature of man's mind is such that man has the natural aptitude to understand and love God (ST 1a, q.93, a.4) and hence is well equipped to understand his signs. Yet *malicia* can cloud his mind and prevent him from understanding God's signs without making himself ready to receive them. The attitude described by Cajetan represents a creaturely version of communicational accommodation, a mode of sign discernment that involves his will as well as his intellect. Sins of *malicia* create distance between man and God and are primarily a result of a deliberate decision to do something reprehensible. *Malicia* is like a source of noise that deforms the signs making them unrecognizable and keeping man wilfully ignorant of their message. Such wilful ignorance is a most reprehensible action, and Cajetan appropriately describes it with the highly charged term of *inexcusabilitas* (without excuse), a term used by St Paul to condemn persisting unbelief in God when the signs of his existence are easy to read.[17]

In the Gospel story, God was speaking to the unbelievers by means of the words of Jesus, spoken directly by him to them, as well as by his deeds, both of which are recorded in the Gospel. The text thus involves a double manner of signification, since the words of the narratives signify the events, which in turn signify the will of God. This manner of signification distinguishes the Bible from all human forms of writing. In his commentary on the *Summa Thelogica*, Cajetan writes:

> Auctor huius doctrinae est Deus, ceterarum homo: ergo in potestate huius auctoris est accommodatio et vocum et rerum ad significandum, et non in potestate auctoris aliarum. Ergo in ceteris scientiis voces tantum significant: in hac vero et voces et res.[18]
>
> (God is the author of this doctrine, whereas man of others. Hence it is within the power of this author to use words and things in order to signify, but it is not in the power of authors of other sciences. In other sciences, therefore, only words signify, while in this one words as well as things signify.)

This brief statement and others like it represent Cajetan's approach to the interpretation of the Bible on the basis of the doctrine of signs. The primary sense of the text is the literal meaning of the words, namely the narrative of the events and the words spoken by the characters, including Jesus; the secondary meaning is the spiritual meaning signified by the events that make up the narratives, which are themselves signs operating at a different level of signification. Revelation occurs through language but also through things *simpliciter* and things signified by the language of the narratives. An important implication of this semiotic view of meaning is that visualizations – that is, depictions in the mind – are themselves signs without being materially perceivable. They belong to Maritain's class of intentional signs, which fix the cognitive gaze of the reader onto the aspect of divine revelation that the text has been designed to impart at that point. Cajetan's formulation of the concept of a sign may have a surprisingly modern ring for students of semiotics, especially if they are coming to the subject by way of Saussurean linguistics. In modern semiotic theory, the signifier and the signified are both mental entities, though, for the sake of convenience, the signifier is frequently considered a sensible entity. But a word does not need to be pronounced to function as a signifier, nor does its meaning need to have graphic existence.

As mental entities, the signifier and the signified are ontologically distinct from the referent, which normally belongs to the extra-mental and material order of reality. Cajetan makes this point using the logical vocabulary of Scholasticism in his continuation of Aquinas's commentary on Aristotle's *Peri hermeneias*. The quiddity of a word, considered as a species of the genus sign, is the meaning that it has for users of the language to whose vocabulary it belongs. Its semantic content, that which it signifies, is not an object present in external reality, but a concept or an image present in consciousness. The sign does not signify something rather than something else on account any of its intrinsic properties. It does so because of its particular relationship to that object whose properties it represents. Signification is a relational concept. A word and its meaning are related in the same way as a sign and the object that it signifies. These are two different ways of saying the same thing, except that the one using the vocabulary of the doctrine of signs is more inclusive, covering as it does non-verbal as well as verbal signs.

The signifier–signified relationship must be determined by considering the properties of the signified mental image as a reflection of those of the external referent. In *De ente et essentia*, Cajetan explains that the relationship can be established *per accidentalia illius signati, per communia, per essentialia, per nutus, et quibusvis aliis modis*.[19] This is tantamount to saying that the relationship between signifier, signified and referent is arbitrary. Cajetan illustrates the arbitrariness of signs by moving to another language, in which what the Latins call *homo* the Greeks call *anthropos*.[20] The intelligibility of a sign is restricted to the community that uses the same object as a sign for the same thing. Here we encounter a sociological dimension to the argument: signs presuppose a community of people linked by them. Nor are all the signs available to a community exclusively verbal. Cajetan does not specify, but it is clear that the common and essential properties of the thing signified in many cases can be expressed in the silent languages of painting, sculpture and mime.[21] As soon as we move from the realm of verbal language to one that also includes non-verbal communication, the community of sign users becomes immediately larger.

Signs in the Roman Catechism

The key text on the centrality of semiotics in the Renaissance is the *Catechism of the Council of Trent*, a work whose significance in the semiotic culture of the seventeenth century and beyond appears to have eluded historians of semiotic thought. Yet it was one of the most frequently consulted, authoritative and official publications of the church. Conceived as a comprehensive manual for the use of priests in the spiritual formation of their parishioners, the *Catechismus ex decreto SS. Concilii tridentini ad parrochos* was first published in 1566 and was designed to exercise great influence throughout the Catholic world, ideally reaching every single member of the church.[22] In this context, it is significant that the section on the sacraments begins with the statement that the priest should first educate his parishioners about the theory of signs, thus enabling them to achieve the minimum semiotic competency needed to understand the doctrine of the sacraments. The social dimension of signs to which Innocent III alluded in his introduction to the sacraments is expanded exponentially by the *Catechism*, both in space and in time, its horizon of potential application being the horizon of the entire Catholic world. Whatever else he may accomplish with his homilies and direct teaching, the parish priest contributes in hitherto unknown ways to the creation and enhancement of a semiotic consciousness in the Catholic world.

A quick summary of the rudiments of the doctrine of signs represents an unavoidable preliminary step for parishioners who intend to give serious thought to the sacrament they are about to receive or whose celebration they witness in church. To make sure that the faithful truly grasp the essential idea of sacrament, the pastor must begin with the most basic principle of the semiotic tradition, namely the principle that many of the sensible objects by which we are surrounded in our daily lives are signs. Consequently, our relationship with external reality is one of continuous discrimination between objects that we perceive as signs, or objects that redirect our minds to a transcendent elsewhere, and objects that we perceive as non-signs, which anchor the focus of our gaze to their own immanence. Raising awareness of this approach to our perception of reality is the pastor's main pedagogical objective prior to introducing his listeners to the theology of the sacraments:

> Atque in primis docere oportebit, rerum omnium, quae sensibus percipiuntur, duo esse genera. aliae enim ob id inuentae sunt, ut aliquid significent: aliae non alterius rei significandae, sed sua tantum causa effectae sunt.[23]
>
> (He should first observe that sensible objects are of two sorts: some have been invented precisely to serve as signs; others have been established not for the sake of signifying something else, but for their own sakes alone.)

By starting his pedagogical exercise with a reference to sensible signs, the pastor uses a model of sign that his parishioners would find easy to grasp. At the same time, he attaches his lesson to a venerable medieval tradition, rooted in St Augustine's *De doctrina Christiana*, from which the dual category of sensible objects entered the semiotic arena, soon becoming formulaic and commonplace. The *Catechism*'s introduction to the doctrine of signs is restricted to sensible signs because it is meant as a point of access to the sacraments, which are visible signs of a spiritual reality. For St Augustine, a sign is a sensible object which, in addition to its effect on the senses of the perceiver, brings to the mind the thought of an object different from the object of perception: *aliud ex se faciens in cogitationem venire*.[24] Once the Augustinian approach to signs entered Peter

Lombard's *Sentences*, it became a focal point of sacramental theology, aptly called by Deely the 'high semiotics' of theology, especially with reference to the Renaissance, when St Augustine stood astride Catholicism and Protestantism 'as a kind of governing figure over the thinking of both sides'.[25] To be sure, by the time of the *Catechism*, the general doctrine of signs had been developed to much greater sophistication, with far-reaching distinctions in both logic and metaphysics not found in St Augustine.[26] But such a rigorous exposition of the nature of signs from the perspective of the general doctrine, appropriate though it would be in technical treatises in those branches of philosophy, would not serve a useful function in an educational homily on sacramental theology.

A similar observation may be made concerning the distinction between natural and artificial signs. Natural signs are such things as smoke, understood as a sign of fire, or the appearance of the sky, interpreted as a sign of a certain type of weather to come. The meaning that natural signs have for a community of users is not the result of a collective agreement to interpret them in a particular way rather than in another but the result of an independent pattern in the appearance of natural phenomena, learnt from experience. A natural phenomenon may be called a sign of another phenomenon if it is materially or causally linked to it, in what modern semiotic theory calls an indexical relationship. Such a relationship may be inferred even when the signified phenomenon is not available to perception. A person who sees smoke in external reality will see the underlying fire in his mind, though as a perceivable phenomenon it may still be hidden from view (*qui adhuc latet*). Signs can reveal the presence of things that are not themselves visible – a concept that, as we shall see, plays a fundamental role in the judiciary semiotics of witchcraft. The signification of natural signs, the pastor should explain, has nothing to do with an arbitrary decision (*voluntate*) to signify this or that, but is based entirely on our experience of the world.

Conventional signs, on the other hand, have everything to do with arbitrary decisions. There is nothing in their nature that necessarily implies their meaning, which is instead the result of a consensus among the community of users who first devised them:

> Quaedam uero signa natura non constant, sed constituta, atque ab hominibus inuenta sunt, ut et colloqui inter se, et alijs animi sui sensa explicare, uicissimque aliorum sententiam, et consilia possent cognoscere.[27]
>
> (Other signs are not natural, but conventional, and are invented by men to enable them to converse one with another, to convey their thoughts to others, and in turn to learn their opinions and receive the advice of other men.)

Conventional signs enable us to express our thoughts and to communicate with others. They are instruments for the creation and exchange of meaning. Their semiotic intentionality is to fulfil the need for self-expression and communication, including communication with God. The consensus at the basis of this conception of signs is that the signs themselves are shared by their community as a code, without which neither the signification of ideas nor the communication of opinions would be possible.

Codes that use primarily the sense of hearing include speech, which consists of signs especially suitable for the manifestation of human thought, *quae ad experimendas intimas animi cogitationes maximam uim habent*, most powerful in expressing the innermost cognitive activity of the mind.[28] The fact that language can be so efficient in the semiotic externalization of ideas in human communication should not be taken in absolute terms: there are situations in which a flag and a trumpet can convey with much greater clarity and efficiency than speech the messages for which they were designed. But there can be no doubt that words are the most powerful signs, and the pastor leaves no room for feelings of uncertainty: *verba enim inter omnia signa maximam uim habere perspicuum est.*[29] Words are semiotic objects that exemplify the concept of conventional sign in the clearest possible terms. Without its semiotic function, the water of baptism would be simple water, and fulfilling the non-symbolic function of ordinary water would be its reason for existence. The same thing is not true of words. If they were suddenly to lose their power to signify and communicate ideas, words would have no reason for existence, since they were invented precisely for that purpose:

> Nam si ex uocabulis uim significandi detraxeris sublata
> uidetur esse causa, quamobrem uocabula instituerentur.[30]
>
> (Thus, with regard to words: take away their power of expressing ideas, and you seem to take away the only reason for their invention.)

By expressing this view of conventional signs, the authors of the *Catechism* echo the doctrine of language outlined by St Thomas Aquinas. Jakobson rightly regards this doctrine as a highly sophisticated analysis of the concept of sign, indeed as 'the most subtle treatment' available to the student of semiotics as such and not only to scholars interested in the history of the discipline. Language, says Jakobson with the help of Scholastic terminology, consists of signs 'which serve *ad significandum*', but which, beyond that intentionality and the social consensus that makes it possible, signify nothing in themselves.[31] The statement just quoted from the *Catechism* may remind us of a modern principle of European semiotics, born in the context of structuralism. Lévi-Strauss famously observed that language is the most complete and sophisticated semantic system, pointing out that 'it cannot but signify, and [that it] exists only through signification'.[32] The semiotics of Jakobson, Lévi-Strauss and other European scholars is based on the concept of language as a system of elements whose only function is to signify. The semiotic function of language is extended by them to other cultural systems that involve the creation of objects that signify, though signification may not be their primary function. The primary function of architectural creations is not semiotic but utilitarian. The primary purpose of a church building is to serve the community as a place of worship; the secondary purpose is to make a theological statement that may contribute to the spiritual formation of the community, signifying ideas by its configuration of space and its decorative details. Take away the signifying character of sacred architecture, and you are left with a building that may well continue to have a utilitarian function. The same thing, however, would not be true of language, which, without its capacity to signify the thoughts of one person for another, would be both useless and worthless.

For the authors of the catechism, then, words illustrate well the fact that the signifying function of conventional signs is the inalienable part of their essence as signs, whatever other uses the same objects may be put to in the life of a community. Their semiotic core is also independent of the senses through which signs may be materially perceived: they are not affected by the eye that sees them or the ear that hears them. The semiotics of the *Catechism*, however, is by no means limited to the senses of sight and hearing involved in language. The theological foundation of the doctrine of signs necessarily includes all the senses, because all the senses are involved in the liturgy, though the senses of sight and hearing remain the primary ones. As the pastor expands on the objects that have a semiotic intentionality built into them, he lists various examples of signs, from verbal signs to visual and acoustic signs of all kinds. There are many conventional signs: *nonnulla ad oculorum, pleraque ad aurium sensum, reliqua ad ceteros sensus pertinent*, which is to say that while some signs belong to the sense of sight, many others pertain to hearing, and the rest to the other senses.[33] The *Catechism* does not go into any detail on this point, probably because the pastor is expected to know that the liturgical experience of his parishioners is replete with repeated examples of signs based on the entire sensorium: the sense of smell in the burning of incense that signifies the rising of prayers to heaven, the sense touch so central to the rituals of baptism, ordination and last rights, the sense of taste involved in receiving Holy Communion on the tongue rather than in the hands, the senses of sight and hearing, without which the faithful could have no awareness of the liturgy or benefit from its salvific function.

Beyond the perception of written and spoken language, the *Catechism* does not say much about sight and hearing as semiotic domains, though there is some stress on hearing, focusing especially on musical instruments:

> quemadmodum tubarum, tibiarum, aut citharae sonus, qui non solum delectandi sed plerumque significandi causa funditur, ad aurium iudicium spectat: quo quidem praecipue sensu verba etiam accipiuntur.[34]
>
> (And it is equally obvious that the sound of trumpets, flutes and lyres, produced not only to cause pleasure but sometimes also to signify – in which sense we especially take words – pertains to the ear.)

With respect to the ability to signify, the difference between music and language is one of degree, language being endowed with the power to express thoughts of much greater complexity. In contrast with modern language-based semiotics, the concept of signification assumed by the authors of the *Catechism* covers a much larger domain than the ideas of semantics and syntax involved in verbal signification, an idea already clearly present in the multi-sensorial concept of sign presupposed by sacramental theology. Musical sounds are signs that can both give rise to a sense pleasure and signify ideas in the manner of language. The two aspects of its activity were not always clearly distinguished, as we see in the council's prohibition not only of singing but also of organ music if it signified anything 'lascivious or impure', concepts that can refer just as well to the arousal of a felling by sense impressions and to the designation of ideas that arise concomitantly in the mind without arousing the senses. Admissible music produces sense impressions and signifies ideas that are fully in conformity with the theological tradition, which makes use of musical concepts, such as harmony, to symbolize spiritual realities. Nicholas of Cusa explained that 'sensuous impressions are beautiful only insofar as they reflect spiritual ideas'.[35] Such an approach allowed one to conceive of music, at least in part, as a semantic art that could be employed in the creation and communication of meaning.

Though they are central to worship, acoustical signs have no sacramental significance if they are not part of a sacramental ritual. As components of sacraments, they contribute to both the signification and the realization of sanctity, but in other contexts – as in sacred music and drama, for example – they can only signify it. The same is true of visual signs. Hence it is clear, the *Catechism* explains, why such things as crosses and pictorial representations of saints are all signs of sacred things but have no sacramental significance: *quamuis sacrarum rerum signa sint, non ideo tamen sacramenta dicenda esse.*[36] Signs of sacred things account for most of the spiritual and cultural life of the Christian community, so much so that it may not be possible for us to imagine a community that is not everywhere surrounded by such signs. The reason for our inability to do so is clear: all communities, Christian or otherwise, presuppose the existence of a body of signs held in common by their members, signs which bind them into a community. The Christian community is identified by the symbols that articulate the spiritual life of its members. The principle is a fundamental one, and the *Catechism* leaves no doubt on the matter, quoting once again St Augustine:

> cum praesertim nullus hominum coetus queat, ut etiam a D. Augustino traditum est, siue uerae, siue falsae religionis nomine quasi unum corpus coagmentari, nisi aliquo uisibilium signorum foedere coniungantur.[37]
>
> (As St. Augustine observes, no society of men, professing a true or a false religion, can be, so to speak, consolidated into one body, unless united and held together by some bond of sensible signs.)

Individual members of society see the same symbols around them as an articulation of their beliefs. Hence it is the signs and symbols of their spirituality that unite each member of society to the others, incorporating them all into the symbolic body that is their community of faith. This principle of social cohesion and spiritual affirmation, through the acceptance and cultivation of the semiotic code of a common spirituality, is presented in the *Catechism* as a fundamental truth, the validity of which is meant to be recognized by all. A bond of sensible signs is the distinct sine qua non of the Christian community. The authors of the Catechism do not present this principle as an idea derived solely from St Augustine, as the usual English translation may suggest (*as St Augustine observes*), but as the result of an independent observation that was also (*ut etiam*) noted by St Augustine.[38] They merely add the authority of St Augustine to what ought to be a normal perception of the community itself, expecting the principle to appear self-evident to all. For the *Catechism*, the very idea of a community without the binding force of a shared symbolic system is simply inconceivable. If a community exists, then it is by virtue of its shared symbolism.

It is through the mediation of this symbolism that the members of the community can become acquainted with the will of God, and through this symbolism God reveals himself to the community. All sacred signs are crucial to the corporate unity of the community, but they do not all operate in the same way on the collective imagination. In the semiotic ritual of the sacraments, man comes into contact with God in an act that weaves together 'God's dispensation of grace and man's response to it'.[39] The signifying process is performative in both directions, and it is in this compound performance that the sacraments enact what they signify.

We may perceive this process of signification and enactment of divine grace by considering our perception of dramatic mimesis. Aristotle (*Poetics* 1448b17) says that our experience of imitation, in which we know that what we perceive on stage signifies something other than itself, can fall in one of two categories. It refers either to our observation of the signifying stage action or to our visualization of the real action that is so signified. The first type occurs when our focus remains anchored to the material signifier because we have no real consciousness of the object signified, whose existence we do not recognize or acknowledge. The consequence in such cases is that our experience of signification by mimesis is almost entirely limited to the signifier and the signifying process itself, and is less concerned with the signified ideas that transcend them both. The second type occurs when we are able to acknowledge without difficulty the existence of the signified object, because we believe in it or because we have prior experience of it. In cases of this type, our intellectual focus shifts from the representing to the represented action, with the result that our experience of semiosis is focused on the invisible action signified rather than the stage action that signifies it. Aristotle's reflection, however, invites a further distinction among the different types of actions and ideas that elicit a signified-centred response from the audience. For, as Gregory Nagy has argued, when that object is a particular aspect of reality, mimesis results in the creation of a copy, rather than in the re-enactment of reality, but when the object of representation is the absolute, such as we find expressed in myth, the process of imitation results in the re-enactment of the absolute itself.[40] In this case, performance enables the absolute to come to presence again and to be received by the spectators, not as a mere likeness but as an actual recurrence in the here and now of their spiritual lives.

This argument is valid a fortiori for the Christian sacramental rituals, which were not instituted in order to signify something other than themselves but to bring God into the life of the recipient and to signify the very process by which this occurs. Sacraments are signs that both signify and mediate sanctification, leaving traces of the touch of God on the soul. The *Catechism* is very clear on this point, asking the pastor to help his congregation visualize the sanctifying touch of God by means of a highly graphic analogy. Echoing Augustine's analysis of signs in *De doctrina Christiana* (2.1), the *Catechism* likens the efficacious action of the sacraments to the impression of footprints on the ground by someone walking upon it. The sanctity acquired by means of sacramental signs is itself a sign of the operation of God in man's soul, whose action it makes known to us:

> Sicut et vestigio, quod terrae impressum intuemur, transisse aliquem, cujus vestigium apparet, facile cognoscimus.[41]
>
> (Just as from a footprint, which we see impressed on the ground, we easily know that someone, whose footprint appears, has walked there.)

In order to explain the nature of the sacraments, the pastor has recourse to this visual analogy, likening the soul to the ground and its sanctity to footprints, but he makes it clear that the semiosis of divine action is not based on any similarity between man and God but on their direct connection. The sanctifying action of the sacrament is a transformative operation that leaves impressed upon the soul a trace of its invisible contact with God, in a manner that can be analogically represented as footprints on the ground. Walking and footprints are only the elements of a modelling system. The signifying function is fulfilled, says the *Catechism*, by a 'certain kind' of resemblance (*specie quadam et similitudine*), a phrase in which the qualifier (*quadam*) reminds us that we are dealing with analogy rather than resemblance. The modelling system suggests that for the authors of the *Catechism* the sacraments are a special case of what modern semiotic theory knows as indexical signs, that is signs that, among other things, signify the agent that produced them by inducing us to infer a relationship of causal contact. Analogy is what makes the inference possible. Just as footprints are related to the foot by the continuity of cause and effect, so the sanctity of the soul figures as an effect of God's grace. Sacramental semiotic theory privileges indexicality because indexicality offers the theological imagination a model for both the sanctifying and the signifying operations of sacramental signs, treating the two operations as a single and indivisible activity. For this reason alone, indexicality is without doubt the most prominent semiotic aspect of the sacramental imagination.

The sacramental imagination

The indexical characterization of the sacraments in the *Catechism* is rooted in the theological tradition of *vestigia Dei*, which views the elements of creation as material traces of the causality of God. As signs, *vestigia* are primarily indexical, and as such they elicit a response to their materiality in a way that signs which are primarily iconic do not. For the latter immediately direct the mind to the resemblance of their referents and fix our cognitive gaze on it, whereas indexical signs induce us to infer their referents by asking us to contemplate first the material expression of their effect, even if there is no similarity of form between effect and cause, as there is none between smoke and fire. It is the special trait of such signs, says St Thomas, that they may function as material representations of the causality of which they are the result and to which they direct the mind.[42] This is true even when it is not possible to visualize the cause, as in the sacraments. Sacramental indexicality links semiotic immanence to causal transcendence and calls for a bifocal mode of understanding, equally sensitive to the significative and the causative side of the relationship, namely its logic and its metaphysics.

Logic and metaphysics concern all branches of knowledge and all the arts – metaphysics as the fund of ideas that validate the concept of reality presupposed by the premises of each art, and logic as the set of significative processes that validate the ways in which those premises generate discourse, verbal or physical as the case may be, and lead us to an understanding of reality. St Thomas observes that the same process that enables the drawing of conclusion inheres in both metaphysics and logic. They are both needed in the study of every other branch of knowledge, *eo quod utraque scientia communis est et circa idem subjectum quodammodo* ('for the reason that both sciences are common and in some way concern the same object').[43] For St Thomas metaphysics and logic, the latter understood as the art that governs representation in thought and language, are ultimately concerned with the same object from different perspectives. Metaphysics concerns the nature of things, whereas logic concerns the ways of representing their nature to the mind.

An analogous view of the relationship between metaphysics and logic, as the two sciences that consider the same object from different perspectives, was reformulated in the early eighteenth century by Giambattista Vico in the context of a process of understanding in which the main instrument of thought is the imagination. In a memorable passage of the *Scienza nuova*, Vico observes:

> Or – perché quella ch'è metafisisca in quanto contempla le cose per tutti i generi dell'essere, la stessa è logica in quanto considera le cose per tutti i generi di significarle – siccome la poesia è stata sopra da noi considerata per una metafisica poetica, per la quale i poeti teologi immaginarono i corpi essere per

lo piú divine sostanze, cosí la stessa poesia or si considera come logica poetica, per la qual le significa.

(That which is metaphysics insofar as it contemplates things in the forms of their being, is logic insofar as it considers things in all the forms by which they may be signified. Accordingly, as poetry has been considered by us above as a poetic metaphysics in which the theological poets imagined bodies to be for the most part divine substances, so now the same poetry is considered as poetic logic, by which it signifies them.)[44]

By 'poetry' Vico means both ancient mythology and the works of art of all ages, in so far as they are all products of the imagination. A poem or, more generally, a work of art is both a poetic metaphysics and a poetic logic. Rational metaphysics and logic are related to their imaginative counterparts by simple analogy. For Vico, poetic logic and poetic metaphysics are the basis of all discourse that is generated concretely rather than abstractly, making use of imaginative universals. Imaginative universals are images whose presence is recognizable in many individual things of the same type, without the aid of abstractions and rational analysis. In an imaginative and pre-rational apprehension of types of Hercules, it is not the abstract concept of strength that we see manifested in the actions of different men that enables us to say that they are different versions of the original Hercules but the same concrete image of the hero, recurring in all of them, though with a different appearance. Under that imaginative guise, all the different exemplars of the hero can be called Hercules because each of them is in fact identical with the original Hercules and can be used to predicate things about him. Imaginative universals are to the arts what abstract concepts are to philosophy.

The notion of poetic signification raises the question of resemblance with the original, so prominent in all mimetic approaches to art and so central to the visual culture of the Renaissance. Artists and poets immerse themselves in a reality – either through direct observation or by research in historical texts – and construct their discourse by means of imaginative universals, through which they signify metaphysical truths that transcend the realistic representations of historians and the abstract representations of philosophers. That is why, Vico argues, the character of Goffredo da Buglione in Tasso's *Jerusalem Delivered* is a better expression of the essence of a crusader captain than Tasso's historical referent, the real Godefroy de Bullion.[45] The poetic character of Godefroy is an imaginative universal that signifies the metaphysical essence of a military leader in a way and to a degree that the real one cannot.

Poetic metaphysics is the doctrine of being as signified to and in the imagination through the operation of poetic logic, regarded as the logic of concrete signs. Originally elaborated by Vico as a tool for understanding the workings of the human mind in the mythical ages of civilization, poetic logic remained for him the logic of the imagination even in the ages of reason and science. In the period of history contemplated in the present study, poetic logic is the logic of the Christian imagination, while the poetic metaphysics to which it is linked is a poetic theology of the Christian faith.

2

Gendering the serpent

In one of his sermons in a Piazza of Siena in 1427, Saint Bernardine offered the crowd that had gathered to listen to him a brief commentary on the story of the fall, in which he said that, before the creation of the world, the devil was already excogitating a way of being adored like a god. As soon as God created animals and human beings in their two genders, the devil, a genderless spirit, chose the body of a serpent and the face of woman in order to tempt Eve, thereby causing the fall of mankind.[1] The female gender seemed to the devil the appropriate one for his evil plan, and so it was by the hybrid creature that Eve was approached and from whom she heard the words *Eritis sicut Dii* (you shall be like God). By giving this summary of the narrative of the fall, Saint Bernardine was making use of a reading of Genesis that had long entered the theological and popular imagination, becoming quickly an integral part of the proclamation of the Word of God by verbal, pictorial and sculptural means.

The honour of having first proposed this fantastic commentary on the narrative of the fall has been at times attributed to Bede, but that is without foundation. The tradition of the maiden-faced serpent can be traced back only to Peter Comestor, who in the *Historia scholastica*, completed around 1173, characterized the serpent of Eden as a maiden-faced reptile (*virgineum vultum habens*) in a potent expression of misogyny.[2] The *Historia scholastica* was a paraphrase of the Bible that enjoyed great currency in late medieval and Renaissance culture. Comestor does not say anything about the rest of the serpent's body, which he presumed to be reptilian, but he leaves the reader with the impression that this image is actually described in the text of Genesis, which instead says nothing of the sort. Those who did not read the Bible themselves or who read it on their own but had confidence in Comestor's authoritative interpretation automatically visualized the serpent of Eden as an innocent-looking woman (*virgineum*). The consequence that now a misogynist might easily be reminded of the serpent of Eden by an innocent-looking woman and, furthermore, might feel authorized by the Bible to delve into the nature of that association seems inevitable. By means of a single image, the *Historia scholastica* both demonizes woman, potentially as evil and as duplicitous as Lucifer, and suggests that even before Eve fell prey to the serpent's deception, the female gender, which Eve shared with the devil, was an instrument of the fall.

After Comestor, the serpent's human femaleness was variously elaborated, varying from the femininity of a young girl to that of a mature woman, and it was extended to include not only the face but the entire upper part of the body, frequently with fully exposed breasts in a prominent position. In the reading of the book of Genesis behind such pictorial glosses on the episode, the divine author of the Sacred Scriptures inspired the collaborating human author to visualize the devil in the episode of the fall as a hybrid woman-serpent and to articulate that vision verbally in the sacred text. Those who did not or could not read the text on their own had no way of knowing, or any reason to suspect, that the human gendering and sexualization of the serpent had absolutely no basis in the sacred text, that it was a pure fantasy invented to give theological authority to the idea that femaleness is a biological window through which the devil has access to the world.

Not everyone was in agreement, of course, but the vast majority of those who wanted to give the serpent a human face chose without difficulty the female gender. In his examination of sacred art in *Il riposo* (1584), the scholar and playwright Raffaello Borghini begs to differ with the majority, finding that the conventional gendering of the serpent by recent and contemporary artists is nothing less than an attack on women. Granted, the image of a hybrid creature is more disturbing than that of a simple snake and hence more interesting to depict, but if painters and sculptors wanted to depict a scene with greater measure of horror in it, 'why not make it the head of a man instead?' The artists who continue to decorate churches with maiden-faced serpents in the Garden of Eden do much harm to women, so much so that, in Borghini's view, when they recalled the book of Genesis, most people now imagined the serpent with the face of a woman that they saw in sacred art. This 'malignant invention' at times goes as far as to give the serpent 'the face of a young girl to show that great deceptions and betrayals are often hidden under a beautiful and delicate face'.[3] Borghini's criticism is a rational and valiant defence of women from the misogyny of art and theology, surprisingly modern for a man of so patriarchal a period as the Counter-Reformation, but his was a lonely and, for that reason, feeble voice that did not generate echoes or reverberations.

In the different forms in which it was elaborated, the visual interpretation of the maiden-headed serpent found its way into highly influential works, like the sermons of Saint Bernardine, and the decorative artworks of important churches, such as the Basilica of San Petronio in Bologna, Notre-Dame Cathedral in Paris and the Vatican itself, where it became part of the church's semiotic apparatus for the enculturation of viewers. There is a sense in which it is useful to think of a church building as an active school, continuously reaching out to the imagination of the people that admire its decorations, on the outside as well as on the inside. The church uses the edifice not only as a place of worship but also as a tool for the edification of the faithful. In this perspective, architecture, sculpture and painting are channels of communication and semiotic tools of enculturation, used by the church to speak to the faithful, in a systematic effort to ensure that they embrace fundamental principles of doctrine and recall the biblical narratives on which the doctrine is based. To this effect, the church places at the disposal of the artists that it employs a vast repertory of visual signs, whose communicative effectiveness is validated by the classical principle, reinvigorated in the Middle Ages, according to which the impact that visual signs exert on the imagination of the viewer is much greater than that of verbal signs.

With respect to church buildings, the liturgist William Durand, bishop of Mende, stated the principle in probably its most sophisticated form in his *Rationale divinorum officiorum* (c. 1285), a rightly famous medieval treatise that remained highly influential throughout the early modern period:

> Pictura namque plus uidetur mouere animum quam scriptura. Per picturam quidem res gesta ante oculos ponitur quasi in presenti generi uideatur, sed per scripturam res gesta quasi per auditum, qui minus animum mouet, ad memoriam reuocatur.
>
> (Indeed, pictures seem to move the soul more than texts. Through pictures certain deeds are placed before the eyes, and they seem to be happening in the present time, but with texts, the deeds seem to be only a story heard, which moves the soul less, when the thing is recalled by the memory.)[4]

Ironically the expression *ante oculos ponere* (to place before the eyes), a formula by which classical rhetoric frequently represented the iconic vividness of speech (cf. Cicero, *Pro Marcello* 30), is here invoked to establish the superiority of the figurative arts over language. The vividness of mental images generated by words remains inferior to the vividness of painted or sculpted images, which appear to place under the subject's gaze the real objects that they depict. Whether painted or sculpted, material images of the fall belong to a more powerful semiotic code than the mental images generated by speech and poetry. A crucial part of that power concerns the immediate impact that material images have on the mind of their beholder, an impact manifested as an emotional and participative response to the message that they carry. The visual signs on church walls, Durand explicitly observes, stir up the mind more forcefully than the verbal signs of written texts. The physical language of vision has a much higher capacity to engage than the mental language of visualization activated by speech. In an age in which most reading was still carried out in the form of an oral performance, the reading of biblical passages took place as a vocalized communal event, as is always the case anyhow when a passage is part of the liturgy. In this type of reading, the mental images of the verbal text can reach its receivers only through the sense of hearing (*per auditum*) through the proxy of language heard from another's voice.[5] But material images, Durand is careful to say, give us the impression that the events depicted are happening in the present just as they are perceived in the work of art, and that is why every time that we look at them, they stir us up, and we feel as if we were witnessing their occurrence, or their recurrence, at that very moment.

It is through such visual representations of Adam, Eve and the serpent in church that people could most easily acquire the habit of visualizing the narrative of Genesis in alignment with the anti-feminist biblical theology of the fall that tacitly enjoyed the official sanction of the church. The examples that follow have been selected on account of the significance of their institutional settings. The Basilica of San Petronio, the major church of Bologna, was meant to be the largest and most important in the state outside Rome, in a city that had deep historical roots of loyalty to the papacy. Bologna was the location of a very famous university with scholars and students of distinction from the other Italian states and beyond, many of whom were likely to visit San Petronio routinely for spiritual or aesthetic reasons. Notre-Dame Cathedral was the centre of Christian spirituality associated with the prestigious faculty of theology of the University of Paris, and hence a place whose authority was to remain unchallenged for centuries. The Vatican was the heart itself of Catholicism and the seat of its governing authority. The figurative representation of the fall is analogous to a verbal statement of the same subject, only it has a much more powerful impact on the imagination and intellect of its viewers. As a statement of the church's position on the matter, a visual representation of crucial verses from the book of Genesis comes with an extraordinary illocutionary force, like the thundering voice of an inspired preacher, because it speaks with the authority of the institution on whose doors, walls and ceilings it is depicted.

The visual language of the church building, with its internal and external decorations, carried great weight, not only for the unschooled populace but also for the clergy. All those who view its pictures and shapes habitually, on a continuing basis, are likely to let what they see inform their thinking and shape their imagination. Medieval theologians from Bede to Durand were fully aware of the conditioning power of the church's physical language and took seriously the idea that its messages gave the impression of coming directly from God, whose house the church building is. Frequently liturgists, as Christiania Whitehead has shown, referred to the physical imagery of the church in terms 'that reveal ecclesiastical thinking upon the divisions and interdependencies of Christian society'.[6] Ecclesiastical thinking could have a profound influence on society, especially when its images also purported to be visual translations of passages in the Bible, conveying the thought of God.

Jacopo della Quercia

Jacopo della Quercia's panel of the fall on the portal of San Petronio, carved in the period 1429–34, is in very low relief and therefore heavily dependent on lines to demarcate contours and to give the impression of perspective.[7] The elements of the composition project out from the background plane by a very small amount, insufficient to show significant curving in of the rear of the protruding masses where they join the surface from which the figures emerge in relief. Such a high degree of dependence on design places the composition closer to a two-dimensional painting than a three-dimensional sculpture and invites its perusal as if it were a page of visual text.

The scene itself consists of four pictorial elements on a plain background: Eve on the left, Adam on the right and the serpent in a fig tree in the centre. The serpent has the face of a maiden and is located lower than the human characters, reaching with its head just above their waist line. So positioned in the composition, the eyes of the three characters form a downward-oriented isosceles triangle, with Eve looking down at the serpent with which she shares an understanding, while Adam looks sternly at her. The high relief point of the picture, to which the eye of the viewer is naturally drawn, includes the thighs and torso of both Adam and Eve and the head of the serpent.

From a semiotic point of view, we can remark that the centrality of the serpent in the tree signifies its pivotal role in the drama. However, the picture is not organized in chronological order and is not a literal rendering of the biblical text. In the Bible we first meet the serpent, described as cleverer than all other animals, but without any indication that it had a human face. By the time that

Figure 1 Jacopo della Quercia, The Temptation, San Petronio, Bologna. Creative Commons (Public Domain).

Jacopo della Quercia designed his panel, the tradition of representing the serpent as a maiden was already well established.

Jacopo della Quercia turned the motif into a bas-relief, as one of a series of panels decorating the left pilaster of the portal of the Basilica of San Petronio in Bologna. It was installed at shoulder height and could be easily contemplated, in every detail, by all who entered the church. The location of the panel has considerable signifying force, for the door, in the interpretation that Durand gave of church architecture, was a sign for Christ himself, in accordance with his own words in the fourth Gospel: *ego sum ostium per me si quis introierit salvabitur* ('I am the door, and whoever enters through me shall be saved') (Jn 10.9). The Christological interpretation of the door sets the context against which Jacopo's depiction of the fall should itself be interpreted, namely Christ's reversal of the evil work of the Antichrist. The faithful who enter the church are thus reminded of both the fall and redemption, and are instructed that the journey from one to the other is paralleled by their own transition from the world outside the church to the one inside, understanding 'church' as both the edifice and the mystical body of Christ. According to a theory that went back at least as far as Irenaeus, the tree of knowledge of good and evil was also a sign for the cross on which Christ was sacrificed. The tree through which sin entered the world could symbolically point the faithful to the tree on which Jesus was crucified, 'so that as by means of a tree we were made debtors to God, [so also] by means of a tree we may obtain the remission of our debt'.[8]

Partly wrapped around the trunk of the tree, the serpent signifies Christ by a process of reverse polarity, in which negative orients the mind towards positive, redirecting the beholder from the fall to redemption. In the exegetical culture inherited by Jacopo, it was common to interpret signs both *in bono* and *in malo*, choosing the favourable or the unfavourable signification of a sign on the basis of the context in which it occurs.[9] Japoco della Quercia draws on this tradition to posit the redemption of mankind as the polarity to which all else is subordinated. In an unusual graphic interpretation of this realignment of the mind, Jacopo adds a detail that calls attention to itself. In Jacopo's depiction of the fall, the snake is shown as having pierced the tree trunk with its tail, and now appears to emerge from it, using the hole for support as it raises itself upwards in the direction of Eve. While reinforcing the idea that the serpent, as both an animal and the devil, comes from the world below to tempt mankind with the power of sin, this extraordinary detail suggests an attempt to wound the cross as the main symbol of the church. The intimation recalls by allusion a famous scene in Dante's depiction of the earthly paradise, in which the cart symbolizing the church, pulled by Christ in the guise of a griffin and flanked by the authors of the Gospels, is violently attacked by a dragon emerging from the earth, who pierces it with its tail, in an attempt to destroy it, and manages to turn it into a monster of corruption.[10] Endowed as it is with a feminine *virgineum vultum*, Jacopo's serpent is less monstrous but not less potent than Dante's, since he pierces not the church figured as a cart but the cross itself, visually asserting himself as the Antichrist and positing the female gender as his instrument of deception. Under a contemplative male gaze, the panel could only teach the suspicion that the body of woman was the conduit through which the ancient serpent could reach out from the abyss (Rev. 20.2), ready to strike again.

Its strike is sweet, and therein lies its power. Against the dominant exegetical tradition, which identified the tree of the knowledge of good and evil as an apple tree, Jacopo represents it as a fig tree, drawing on a respectable but less popular interpretation. By doing so, he adds a mark that is semiotically charged, both *in bono* and *in malo*, with a wealth of associations from various other codes in which it appears in exegetical and theological literature. Thus, to mention only the most relevant examples – examples that the faithful would probably hear about in homilies – the fig tree of Genesis suggests forbidden eroticism, while the fig tree in the Song of Songs (2.13) suggests the joy of unreproachable love. Whereas under the fig tree of Genesis, Adam and Eve turned away from God, burdening all of future humanity with original sin, it was precisely under a fig tree that Augustine opened his soul to God's love and illumination (*Conf.* 8.12.28). And it was under a fig tree that Jesus saw Nathanael, who believed in him and became a disciple as a result of that (Jn 1.50), but on his way to Bethany Jesus cursed a fig tree because it was without fruit, and caused it to wither away (Mk 11.12-14). These and other associations indicate that the pragmatic value of the fig tree in the panel, for the homiletic material and the occasions for personal reflection that it offered, was commensurate with the range of themes that it covered by allusion. In the journey of faith, which for some may well begin as a simple walk from the exterior to the interior of the church, the faithful are called upon to reflect on the sense *in malo* as well as *in bono* that the fig tree of Eden can have in their own pilgrimage to redemption.

As the only inanimate element of the composition, the fig tree gives form to the space in which Eve, the serpent and Adam interact, like the characters of a brief dramatic scene. As if on the stage of such a scene, Eve stands in a one-quarter position to the left, bending her body a little towards her left so as to position herself almost frontally with respect to the serpent, towards which it advances, and yet be fully visible to the viewer outside the panel. On the other side of the snake–tree combination, Adam also stands in a one-quarter left position, placing his body in a parallel stance to Eve's but giving the impression that he is attempting to walk offstage, while turning to look reprovingly at her over his right shoulder. This is a surprising posture for him to assume. In a symmetrical and equal sharing of the scene, we would expect him to stand one-quarter right, that is, turning his body slightly to his right, advancing, like Eve, towards the centre. In giving a dramatic form to his panel, Jacopo destabilized the viewer's expected positioning of the characters and thereby invests the picture with a new semiotic valence. Adam's posture is a sign of his initial reluctance to accept Eve's invitation to share the forbidden fruit. This automatically transfers onto the human characters in the scene the misogynistic attitude made explicit by the female gendering of the serpent. The theological message that it conveys is that Adam was less responsible than Eve, not only because Eve was the one that succumbed to craftiness of the devil but also because, unlike Eve, Adam initially gestured to walk away from it all, reproving his companion for her weakness.

This positioning of the characters in the panel enables Jacopo to exhibit their sexuality in full, omitting the loincloth of fig leaves mentioned in the text of Genesis (3.7). Adam and Eve here are totally naked, and their sexuality is flaunted by the artist. Eve holds a fig in her right hand in the same line of sight as her breasts, all three in high relief and in a configuration that enables the breasts to eroticize the fig, and vice versa. At the same time, with his left hand, also on the relief plane, Adam calls attention to his genitals while making a gesture to cover them up. There are no signs that Adam has already accepted a fruit from Eve, or indeed that a fruit has even been offered to him, and yet he has started to feel ashamed of his exposed sexuality. His consciousness has taken this pudendal turn without any visible signs of active participation by him, almost as if his contiguity to Eve were by itself sufficient to cause his fall.

Eve is clearly the more active of the two characters. We note that the snake has no hands, a fact that calls attention to the way Eve uses her hands. Albeit under the influence of the serpent, Eve grasps the fruit herself with her right hand, performing an act that signifies her readiness to sin and makes the beholder first aware of the role of the sense of touch in the artist's visualization of the fall, since the prohibition was that they could not even touch the fruit of the forbidden tree. The sense of touch, however, is stressed that much more by Eve's left hand, which she spreads on the serpent's chest in a gesture indicating anything but resistance. Jacopo's carving of Eve's hand on the serpent is a sign of remarkable force, possibly the viewer's point of empathic access to Eve's sensuality. Haptic images, as Jacopo knew intuitively and modern scholars and philosophers know analytically and scientifically, automatically trigger in their beholders mechanisms of empathic response that enable them to experience in their own bodies feelings analogous to those presumably experienced by the subject depicted, even if they consciously resist the experience.[11] Jacopo's bas-relief is designed to activate such a response, predisposing the viewers to an empathic recognition of Eve's sensuality by awakening in them awareness of the presence of analogous sensuality in their own bodies, of which Eve is but an empathic sign.

As a sculptural gloss on Gen. 3.1-7, the panel first of all exercises an exegetical function, telling its viewers that the serpent had the face of a woman, that Eve responded sensually to its advances and that Adam hesitated before yielding to the temptation. The doctrinal lesson imparted by the panel is that there is considerable similarity between the devil and woman, and, indeed, that a woman's face may well be a deceptive sign of the devil working its evil on mankind. But it is through empathic identification that the panel exercises its chief theological function. Sensual empathy is the semiotic key to the personal interpretation of the panel. It is an invisible bridge between an exterior signifier on the pilaster of the portal and a signified in the interior being of its observers, and it operates by changing their reflection into self-reflection, thereby preparing them for homiletic enculturation in the church that they are about to enter.

Notre-Dame Cathedral

The trumeau separating into two the northern portal of the cathedral of Notre-Dame in Paris consists of a large statue of the Virgin Mary, holding the infant

Figure 2 The Temptation, Portal of the Virgin, Notre-Dame Cathedral, Paris. Creative Commons (Public Domain).

Jesus in her arms and resting on a high pedestal, the top part of which includes three panels sculpted in high relief illustrating the creation of Eve, the story of the fall, and the expulsion of Adam and Eve from the earthly paradise. In the middle panel, the serpent is a hybrid creature, with the bottom half of its body as a large snake twirled around the trunk of the tree of knowledge and the upper half the torso of a beautiful young woman. Though the relief is treated by some scholars as an authentic medieval sculpture, examining it as an aesthetic document of thirteenth-century thought, the evidence that the original trumeau was vandalized by angry revolutionaries in 1793 is quite certain, as is the conclusion that the panel of the fall that now graces the pedestal of the Virgin is the product of nineteenth-century restorers working under the artistic and historical vigilance of Eugene Viollet-le-duc.[12] Yet the inclusion of the panel in discussions of early modern spirituality is not as misguided as it may first appear, if the object of the discussion is not the aesthetic finish of the panel but the spiritual imagination to which it is a point of access. For although the artistic merit of the panel – the smooth chiselling, the naturalistic lines and the finished surface – belong to the artistic culture of Medievalism rather than that of the Middle Ages, the imagery that it embodies and the exegetical message that it carries belong to the Christian imagination of the late Middle Ages, some aspects of which we have seen in our outline of the legacy of Peter Comestor.

As an aesthetic object, the panel is indeed a nineteenth-century creation, but as a signifying structure it is no more than a nineteenth-century rendition of a medieval cognitive and artistic form, sustained by the logic, the rhetoric and the idea of the fall in medieval culture. Viollet-le-duc was famously coherent in his application of the principle that to restore the architecture of a building one needs to re-establish its pristine condition, but in a state of completeness that is respectful only of the original cultural context, a state of completeness towards which its architecture tended, independently of the way in which the building may have been completed by others after the time of its original construction.[13] The controversial nature of this concept of restoration derives from the fact that it implies the removal of all additions resulting from previous attempts at restoration. This unearthing of the original style is necessary to allow the building to achieve the appearance that it was meant to have, in accordance with all the material conditions and stylistic aspirations of its age. The original aesthetic features of the building will never be established fully, but that is not a significant factor in the type of investigation with which we are concerned in the present chapter. Our objective is not to assess the aesthetic merit of the panel as a finished work of art but to examine it as a signifying structure of late medieval culture, carved as a restoration on the basis of authentic medieval models in other churches, as a paradigm of perception and theological reflection materially retrieved from medieval culture.

Viewers bring to their encounter with the sculpture the narrative order of the biblical story, recalling the details as they read the panels, like large narrative units: first the creation of Eve, then the fall of Adam and Eve and finally their expulsion from the earthly paradise, sculpted in three different panels arranged sequentially from left to right. The order of panel reading is like that of printed language, from left to right. And each panel is marked by discreteness comparable to verbal language. Vertically the panel is situated on a pedestal, the bottom of which is somewhat higher than the average person's eye level. The panel addresses its viewers from a position of dominance, while they read from a position of guilt. Vertical reading implies that the viewer looks up, sees Adam and Eve succumbing to temptation, then the serpent triumphant in the tree, and finally the foot of the Virgin Mary already above its head, ready to squash it, as in Gen. 3.19 in the text of the Vulgate: *ipsa conteret caput tuum*. In this type of reading the panels are like sequences of discrete signs that function very much like written language.

The overall impression is one of harmony, without apparent tension. The panel is dominated by the image of a hybrid maiden serpent, twirled around the tree of knowledge and emerging at the top through the branches and foliage in the guise of an attractive young woman exposing her breasts and smiling. The serpent is looking down at Eve endearingly, like an angel from above. From this position of pre-eminence, the serpent guides the perception of the panel's viewers, inviting them to read this sculpted version of the story in a clockwise direction. Thus, the focus of perception moves along the serpent's gaze fixed on Eve, and then proceeds along Eve's arm to Adam.

Eve is standing to the serpent's left (the viewer's right) in a one-quarter position with her body almost totally in a frontal attitude with respect to the viewer, but covering her bosom with her left arm, which she raises to bring a fruit to her mouth. Her genital area is covered by leaves from a branch on the lower part of the tree. She has very long hair that reaches all the way down past her waist. Adam is standing to the viewer's left, in a profile position, extending his right arm to accept the fruit that Eve is offering him with her right hand. His genital area is conveniently located behind leaves sprouting from the same branch that covers Eve, but this positioning of their bodies does not appear to be the result of their intention to cover their nakedness from each other and God. There is nothing especially erotic about the way they are represented, though both seem content with what they are about to do. Since they are about to commit their sin but have not yet done so, they do not express shame over their nakedness. The panel thus fuses into one two different stages of the narrative: the first in which Eve succumbs to the serpent's temptation and the second in which Adam follows Eve's invitation. The temptation itself, represented in the Bible as a dialogic exchange between Eve and the serpent, is not included in the sculpture but is presumed present in the viewer's memory. The chronological order of the two stages is sculpted from right to left, inviting the viewer to interpret the panel in a direction that reverses the left-to-right order required by the sequential reading of the three panels in a row as well as the order of the textual narrative that they illustrate.

Since Adam and Eve are not aware of their own sexuality, the leaves covering their genitals can represent only the viewers' expected sense of personal modesty and artistic decorum. The leaves, in other words, take us out of the biblical story and bring us into the social world and psychology of the viewers, for whom the sexual organs are pudenda (parts of the body that must be covered) in depictions as in real life. The detail establishes a bridge between the subject's narrative and the viewers, effectively bringing them into the picture and telling them that the panel is as much about Adam and Eve as it is about them. Their fallen state in the present is itself encoded in the panel as the result of the fall of Adam and Eve. The leaves are proleptic signs whose function is to bring the future into the past or the viewer into the Scriptural text, like a quick flash-forward in cinema, depicting a consequence of the fall as if it had already taken place at the moment when prelapsarian innocence was about to come to an end.

The panel addresses the viewer as one who has already internalized the Scriptural text, visualizing its events through a tradition of interpretation centred on the depiction of the devil as a maiden serpent, pretty and erotically provocative at the same time. The viewers are invited to read the panel horizontally, in an exercise that involves the completeness of their memory of the sequence of events in the book of Genesis. In that reading, they reconstruct in their imaginations the crucial scene in the primeval past of mankind, integrating the visual language of the sculpture and the verbal language of the text, and linking the two sources in a relationship of mutual enrichment as signifying structures.

Genesis may not say anything about the femininity of the devil, but in the viewer's hermeneutical imagination femininity and evil are inextricably linked. However innocent in appearance, the feminine beauty framed by the tree branches is treacherous and can lead to perdition. The viewers are also invited, however, to read the panel vertically, but in this case the reading is subjective as well as objective, incorporating an exercise in self-reflection. Adam, the maiden serpent and Eve do not summon the viewers' attention with any signs, but from their position in front of the pedestal, which invites upward looking simply because the sculptured figures are placed somewhat above their line of sight, the viewers cannot fail to notice that they are already within Mary's field of vision. In raising their heads to meet her eyes, they sweep over the panel, as if palpating it with their gaze, effectively projecting themselves into the narrative and turning the viewing process into a thoroughly personal semiotic experience.

The panel's mode of address, or the way it asks the viewers to position themselves before it, is due partly to the composition itself and partly to its artistic genre. With respect to the genre, we may recall that, in his discussion of the decorative arts of the church, Durand explained that figures sculpted in relief appear to approach their viewers with the message that they carry, almost as if to ensure that the virtues which they teach may seem 'to be naturally inborn in them'.[14] In order to understand how much greater is the concreteness of figures in high relief than that of figures in painting or in low relief, which retains much of painting, we can summon Vico to our aid. He explains that painting requires a higher degree of abstraction than sculpture in order to reduce the three dimensions of reality to a flat surface:

> Perché la fonderia astrae la superficie con qualche rilievatezza, l'intagliatura fa lo stesso con qualche profondità; ma la pittura astrae la superficie assolute, ch'è difficilissimo lavoro d'ingegno.
>
> (For casting abstracts the surface of things along with some relief, and engraving does the same with some depth; but painting abstracts the surfaces absolutely, and this is a labour calling for the greatest ingenuity.)[15]

For that reason, Vico lets us conclude, painted figures are closer to being personified abstractions than real individuals. Sculpture does not rely as much on abstractive procedures, and hence its figures resemble particular individuals more closely: statues and carved figures are concrete images of exterior attributes and can refer to a multitude of individuals by concrete resemblance. Since their viewers may well recognize themselves in that multitude, the impact of high relief representations, which is closer to free-standing sculpture than it is to painting, is extraordinary. The sculpted figures come partly into the spatial, aesthetic and spiritual horizon of individual viewers and address them in a personal way, challenging them to reflect on themselves in their individuality, as if, to paraphrase Durand, the message that they carry were already in them, needing only to be awakened by art.

A significant implication of this mode of address is that the message of the panel as a whole is received as personalized for each individual observer, in the here and now of existence and self-reflection. As a signifier, the Notre-Dame panel of the fall has at least two significations. In one of them it tells us what the characters in the story looked like and how they behaved in the act that led to their commission of original sin. The panel consists of a series of sculpted signs for the visualization of the Genesis narrative, which is what they designate. In the other signification, it signifies for the observer the fall through a woman, both beautiful and innocent in appearance. The implication of this aspect of signification is that every single woman who fits that category will remind the viewer of the devil depicted in the panel, becoming in essence its signifier. Female beauty, compounded of sexuality and innocence, may signify the devil trying to gain access to the minds of the men contemplating it. Female beauty is either actually or potentially a duplicitous sign for evil and must be approached with a hermeneutic of suspicion. In such cases, *signum et signatum convertuntur*, we might say adopting and adapting to our purpose a scholastic formula to indicate that the designate and the sign can change place, reversing the order of signification.[16] The reversal is possible because the signification of iconic signs is reflexive: it is a function of their resemblance alone and not also of their chronology.[17] Iconic signification can be read backwards as well as forwards in time, and it is this attribute that makes the engraving of the fall especially effective at the entrance to the cathedral. It was meant to awaken generations of Catholics to the meaning that the story of Genesis should have for them personally, to condition them to a soul-searching way of visualizing it, and to alert them to the possibility that the devil might be hidden in the erotic radiance of women, perhaps unbeknown to them.

The panel takes the mind of the viewer into two cognitive directions at the same time, in accordance with two approaches to signification inherited from the medieval philosophy of language.[18] In one approach, words were treated intransitively as vocal expressions of concepts in the mind of the speaker. If we generalize words into signs, erotic beauty is the physical expression of the subject's real inner beauty. In the other approach, words were treated transitively as signs of the meanings to which their pronunciation gave rise in the mind of the listener. In our case, the same erotic beauty could be taken as a sign of the turmoil that the appearance of a particular woman may cause in the imagination and conscience of a male viewer.

The transitive treatment of signs, in which the signifier and the signified are embodied by different people and signification entails movement from one to the other, can have profoundly inspiring as well as profoundly tragic social and personal consequences, as we shall see in our chapter on witchcraft. An immediate effect of this outlook on the panel is the implicit suggestion that, given the opportunity and justification to do so, one should look closely at a woman's appearance to see whether her beauty bears any visible marks of the serpent that could serve to justify approaching her with a hermeneutic of suspicion. In the panel, such a mark consists of the claws with which the serpent grasps the branches to support its weight. The serpent's beauty and smile are so captivating that, in our first glance at the panel, we are likely to miss the claws altogether or to pay no attention to them. They are certainly not what first registers in our minds when we look at the panel, but as our field of perception is widened from the centre to the two sides, we notice them right next to the maiden serpent's bosom, like a beastly intrusion into the representation of the sexualized femininity framed by the branches. The effect of the composition is to prolong the act of perception, inviting reflection on and further scrutiny of the torso, hailing the viewers to reconsider with suspicion their initial impression of erotic femininity.

Michelangelo

Michelangelo's panel of the temptation and expulsion of Adam and Eve on the vault of the Sistine Chapel (1508–12) lends itself to a cinematic sort of criticism, in which at first, in a long-shot view, we can see the entire vault and are prompted to ask what relevance has the grand depiction of the book of Genesis to the Christian liturgy celebrated below. In a medium-shot view, we focus on individual panels, considering them in themselves and in relation to the other panels. In a close-up view we focus on details for the purpose of analysis, but only so that we can step back to a medium view, where the details are added together into a unified message, and finally move on to the larger view which is the relevance of the book of Genesis to the liturgy. In the prophetic understanding of the relationship between the two testaments, the Old Testament was regarded as a preparation for the arrival of the New Testament and hence of the Eucharist celebrated in the chapel below.

In an examination of Michelangelo's view of the fall, the medium-shot perspective is crucial. Whereas in the Notre-Dame and Bologna panels, the episode of the temptation is sculpted separately from the expulsion, in his fresco Michelangelo unites them into a single vision, with the temptation on the left and the expulsion on the right. Unless we separate them artificially, we cannot, other than in a close-up view of the details, observe only one of the two sides but must look at both simultaneously, regarding them as two aspects of the same idea. In a medium view, they appear as complementary parts of a single message, in a way that makes Michelangelo's approach to the story eminently theological and only secondarily narrative, as is only appropriate for the Vatican's papal chapel and the location of papal conclaves.

Figure 3 The Temptation, Michelangelo, Sistine Chapel, Vatican. Mondadori Portfolio / Getty Images.

Theologically, the commission of sin and the loss of innocence are simultaneous aspects of the same phenomenon. The rejection of innocence and the loss of innocence are not factually separable, because the punishment for sin occurs as the sin is committed. They are, however, formally separable as objects of thought, and Michelangelo accomplishes this by painting the last prelapsarian instant and the first post-lapsarian instant on either side of the tree of knowledge, which visually marks both the violation of God's prohibition by Adam and Eve and the beginning of their existence under punishment. Thus, when we look at the panel we see in a single view Eve's and Adam's individually yielding to temptation and their expulsion from the garden as simultaneous events, because they occurred in the same instant of time – *statim* (immediately), as later in the century the Fathers of Trent would say, summarizing the theological tradition.[19]

As in the other cases we have already examined, the composition of the panel is structurally dependent on the tree with the hybrid serpent, which marks its centre line, except that in this case it is the centre of the combined panel. In the semiotic economy of the panel, the demonization of femaleness, represented not by abstract symbolism but in concrete biological form, is so prominently conveyed that it dominates the entire picture. The woman part of the creature's body reaches all the way down to the midpoint of her powerful thighs, with which she straddles a branch of the tree of knowledge while she coils her large and long reptilian tails around its trunk. The serpent has blonde hair lightly windblown, in the manner of a Petrarchan image of femininity – *erano i capei d'oro a l'aura sparsi* ('her golden hair was loosed to the breeze')[20] – and rather like the hair of the sword-brandishing angel on the post-lapsarian side of the tree of knowledge. Unlike the angel, however, who is a graceful being, light and airy despite the sword, the serpent, a fallen angel, is massive flesh, exuding earthy sensuality in every part of its body.

The serpent's head in the tree is located at the highest point of the panel and dominates our perception of the human characters on the prelapsarian side, just as, in an analogous pattern, the angel dominates our view of them after the fall. Because it is located so high, it invites a vertical contemplation of its physicality, encouraging us to let our eyes glide down its woman's torso, proceeding spirally along the legs and reptilian lower half until we reach the ground. We note that the thighs turn slowly, almost imperceptibly, into two reptilian tails, which do not have scales but are covered by the same smooth epidermis of the thighs, and hence connote an analogous expression of sensuality. A significant detail in this context is Michelangelo's use of haptic imagery. Given God's command that they should not even touch the fruit (*et ne tangeremus illud*, Gen. 3.3), Adam, who reaches out to pluck a fruit from a branch, and Eve, who stretches her arm to come into physical contact with the serpent's hand, confer on the sense of touch a remarkable semiotic status. Adam's action is a visual sign of his independent and deliberate violation of God's commandment, not as a result of Eve's prompting but on his own initiative and of his own volition, making him equally responsible for the fall of mankind, whereas the serpent's touch of Eve's hand, to which she responds in kind, indicates the sensuality of both and the erotic nature of their disposition, a combined sign of femaleness as the gate through which evil entered the world.

The overall impression that we are left with is that, in the serpent's hybridism, the ratio of woman to reptile is in favour of woman. So much so that we might say we are not before a woman-headed reptile but before a reptile-legged woman, who redeploys the human femaleness of the traditional image from a merely adjectival to a substantive role. The primary signification is the demonic nature ascribed to womanhood under the guise of erotic sensuality, but a secondary suggestion must also be that, in the womanhood chosen by the devil for his physical manifestation, there is aberrant brutishness. In Michelangelo's depiction of the serpent, there is no semblance of simulated youthful innocence to tantalize the intellect of its human interlocutors, but a strong expression of female eroticism to excite their sensual empathy and awaken their erotic imagination. The serpent hands Eve a fig, the symbolic value of which is the disordered desire of lust. Eve, reclining in a sexually provocative pose and alluring in her athletic beauty, raises her left (*sinistra*) arm – on her 'sinister' side, close to evil, as the Latin root suggests – to accept the fig from the serpent, thereby exposing her underarm as a gestural sign of erotic availability.[21] At the same time Adam, vigorous and handsome, gets hold of a branch of the tree with his left hand and reaches out to pluck a fig from another branch with his right. On the post-lapsarian side of the panel, an angel with a sword expels them both from the Garden of Eden. Their previous physical beauty and expressions of delight, signs of their prelapsarian state of innocence, have now become corruptible skin and twisted grimaces, signs of the disorder in soul and body into which they walked by their transgression, in accordance with the official doctrine of the church on original sin since St Augustine.[22]

In his representation of Genesis 3 on the Sistine vault, Michelangelo proceeds in a manner analogous to the way St Augustine recommends reading the Bible. For Augustine, the sacred text is an assemblage of verbal signs, whose literal meaning in the narrative is their semiotic materiality. Through that materiality, the signs send the mind of the reader to moral principles with which to govern his life, which they reveal upon comparison with other signs in the text. The key to the proper interpretation of biblical signs is the relationship that they have with other signs in the vast semiotic universe that is the Bible. Thus, on a large scale, Old Testament signs adumbrate those in the New Testament in a relationship of meaning we call typology. The Sistine Chapel appears to obey the same principle, with the Old Testament on the vault and the New Testament in the liturgy celebrated below, in which the sense that the Old Testament has for Christianity is revealed and enacted. On a smaller scale, we can observe that the panel of the temptation and expulsion is structured on a similar principle. The meaning of each of the two parts is not self-contained but relational. Between large- and small-scale relatedness, we also have the relation of the panel as a whole to the other panels into which the content of Genesis is distributed by the artist.

These connections express the idea that the meaning of the individual signs of the fresco is a matter of their reciprocal dependence, in accordance with one of the fundamental principles of semiotic theory, namely the relativity and interrelation of the signs that constitute a universe of discourse, in which all signs are simultaneously present. As such a universe of signs, the Sistine ceiling flattens out the narrative time of Genesis, from the separation of light and darkness to the drunkenness of Noah, viewing its main episodes *sub specie aeternitatis*, which is the perspective of God, for whom all things are simultaneously present. Though he gives the impression of narrative time by painting the pre- and post-lapsarian aspects of the fall on either side of the Tree of Knowledge, Michelangelo actually paints only the causality and semantic interdependence by which the temptation and the expulsion are related. In a semiotic understanding of this perspective, the arrangement of signs, as we have seen, is itself a sign. In a close-up view of our panel, the fall is signified as the line cognitively separating temptation from expulsion. In a long-range view of the interior of the chapel, the images of our progenitors on the vault, expelled from Eden into history, reflect our gaze back onto the Eucharist as the sacrament, that is, the sacred sign of our redemption, the grandest signifying structure of all.

Raffaello

If Michelangelo flattens out time in order to paint the theology more than the narrative, Raffaello chooses a specific moment in the narrative for his ceiling panel of the temptation in the Stanza della Segnatura, painted in the first year (1508) of the four that Michelangelo worked on the Sistine Chapel. The serpent is youthful and much smaller than Michelangelo's, a little like the one in Notre-Dame. The reptilian part, from bosom down, has a scaly skin and does not connote sensuality. It is not through sex in the earthy way of the Sistine Chapel that the devil reaches Eve. The serpent looks innocent, perfectly at home in the tree, talking to human beings. Eve has already succumbed to the temptation to eat a fruit from the Tree of Knowledge and now tempts Adam to do the same thing. The purpose of the fresco is to focus the mind of the viewer on the temptation itself and on Adam's willing participation in the commission of original sin, and hence on his share of responsibility for the sin and punishment transmitted to mankind.

The Stanza della Segnatura is an official reception room in the Vatican used to meet foreign dignitaries and other important visitors, a room in which treaties and other documents are ceremoniously signed. The setting for the panel of the temptation is thus quite different from the Sistine Chapel, not only because here there is no liturgical function to provide it with typological significance but also

Figure 4 The Temptation, Raffaello, Stanza della Segnatura, Vatican. Pascal Deloche / Getty Images.

because of the considerably more modest architectural base. Yet the context of the Stanza della Segnatura is not without semiotic implications. The setting is by no means a secular one, but it is on the boundary between the church as an institution and the outside world. Here the two worlds meet in non-liturgical events. The Stanza della Segnatura is one of the places where the church can display for visiting dignitaries just where it stands in relation to world culture. The Stanza is dominated by Raffaello's wall fresco depicting the School of Athens, which declares in a grand manner the church's openness to contemporary humanistic culture and its philosophical roots in the classics. Its main function is not to inspire faith and teach doctrine, though these are clearly tasks that the church attempts to carry out in all of its venues. But in a reception hall, where visitors are not likely to spend much time admiring and reflecting on the works of art that decorate its walls and ceiling, it must carry out such tasks directly, with the utmost clarity, relating them to the larger cultural context of its visitors.

As in other depictions of the temptation, in Raffaello's fresco the tree of knowledge marks the central axis of the composition and guides the viewer's focus. Raffaello painted the trunk and the branches of the tree of knowledge the same colour as the flesh of the human characters, with only minimal variation to create the effect of depth and shadows. Indeed, the small shadows designed to give the image of the trunk a sense of texture also resemble those used to suggest the anatomical details of the bodies. This similarity is too exact and too obvious to be dismissed as trivial. The tree of knowledge with the serpent coiled around its trunk is, in the first symbolic instance, a reference to the exegetical tradition for which the image of the tree signified, by reverse typology, the tree of the cross and hence of redemption. As Tertullian had put it in the earliest stage of that tradition, *quod perierat olim per lignum in Adam, id restitueretur per lignum Christi* (what perished by the tree in Adam should be restored by the tree in Christ).[23] But the flesh-coloured surface of the trunk and branches is a subtle reference to the union of the cross as a divine symbol of salvation and the man of real flesh and blood executed on it for the redemption of mankind. The flesh-coloured wood of the tree is a sign for the dual nature of Christ, both divine and human. In this context, the detail of Eve holding onto the branch is an especially significant reference to her redemption by Christ. In a prayer for her salvation included in *De Isaac et Anima*, St Ambrose asks Christ not to leave Eve behind but to take her with him when he goes to the Father, for she is no longer wandering in error but holding onto the tree of life, *jam non errantem, sed arborem vitae tenentem* (now she is not straying but holding on to the tree of life).[24] The iconographic detail of Eve holding onto the tree in the Garden of Eden signifies the tree of the Cross and its saving power.

The leaves and the fruit of the tree of knowledge indicate that it is a fig tree. Whatever else it may allude to, here the fig in Eve's hand is a sexual symbol, an erotic incitement to transgression. Raffaello's tree has a large and thick crown, under which Adam, Eve and the serpent are depicted as if they are having a calm and pleasant conversation, without any signs of tension or consciousness of the transgression against God that Eve has already committed and Adam is about to commit. Raffaello limits himself to depicting instead a scene whose charm was such as to lead Adam to untroubled slippage into sin. Adam is sitting on a grass-covered mound to the left of the tree, and he is also relaxed, without apparent tension. The lack of tension in the depiction of Eve is a sign that Raffaello is not concerned, as Michelangelo was, to paint the theological idea of original sin, according to which the soul and the body plunge into disorder as soon as the violation has been committed. In his fresco, Eve has not lost her beauty and is not tormented by her conscience. She is pleased with herself, and approaches Adam with a radiant expression on her face and in her eyes. Raffaello postpones the consequences of sin to a stage in the narrative beyond the one that is the subject of his fresco.

Eve stands in a classical contrapposto attitude, a posture inherited from Hellenistic statuary in which the weight of the body rests on one leg. To move into this position, Eve twists her torso slightly and, with her left hand, holds on to a branch over her head creating an impression of movement that calls attention to her breasts and her exposed underarm. Eve displays the erotic appeal of her body, while offering Adam a fig with her right hand. Moreover, she has blonde hair, in accordance with a current ideal of feminine beauty, painted as somewhat dishevelled curls, indicating her natural state. The detail may be a subtle sign of the Augustinian theology of sin. As an instrument of temptation, Eve's luminous demeanour may be regarded as an expression of the disordered moral state into which her own nature had been thrust by her disobedience.

This theological underpinning of the fresco is reinforced by the fact that Eve and the serpent resemble each other to a very high degree. Except for the different hue of their skin, the maiden face of the serpent seems to be a slightly smaller version of Eve's face. What is more, they have the same expression, they are tilted at the same angle and they are both looking at Adam, almost as if they are mimicking each other. The resemblance is enough to leave the viewer the impression that, in this particular moment of the narrative, Eve and the serpent form an indivisible semiotic doublet, sharing not only the message of the temptation but also its agency. That is, Eve and the serpent have entered into a partnership in order to tempt Adam. Their resemblance and their shared gaze are a sign of their collaborative intent. The devil is making use not only of femaleness, the biological gender by itself, but also principally of this particular woman, who has already fallen, as the means with which to cause the fall of Adam and of all mankind. This reading of the temptation is corroborated by Adam, who appears eager to accept the gift and is positioned almost as if he were asking for it, looking straight at the woman serpent while he extends his right hand to Eve to accept the fig being offered by her. This attitude indicates that for Adam, the maiden serpent and Eve are presented as the same being and signify two ideas fused into one.

3

Cajetan on the fall of Eve

In the preface to his commentary on the Pentateuch, Cajetan, Cardinal Tommaso de Vio, says that he is aware of the controversial nature of some of his annotations on the literal sense of the text and asks the reader not to reject precipitously any interpretation that may run counter to the exegetical tradition, even if that tradition includes the great doctors of the church. Any interpretation that adheres to the text and respects the context of a passage deserves to be considered attentively if it does not contradict an official doctrine of the church. The major reason why Cajetan's interpretation could occasionally appear less than conventional was the fact that he returned to the Hebrew version of the Pentateuch, comparing it word for word with the Vulgate but limiting his annotations to the Hebrew text, which he examined with the help of experts in the Hebrew language.[1] His goal was to clarify the literal sense of the Hebrew text, to which he frequently referred as the Hebrew verity.

Among the new interpretations that Cajetan proposes in his commentary on Genesis, his reading of the passage on the temptation of Eve by the devil in the guise of a serpent is one of the most provocative. In Cajetan's interpretation of the text, there was no serpent and no external dialogue dramatizing the violation of God's precept against eating from the tree of knowledge.

For Cajetan the serpent is only a figure of thought used by Moses, traditionally regarded as the human author of the Pentateuch, as an expressive stylistic device. Moses's figurative use of language, it seems, was not much different from our own practice, when we say that life is a vale of tears, without thereby intending that it is literally a valley flooded with tears. As a linguistic sign, the serpent is not physically present in the Garden of Eden. That it has been taken as present by scholars and artists is only a testimony to the author's skill in the semiotics of visualization and evidence that the literal sense of the narrative has been misunderstood. For Cajetan, the dialogue between the serpent and Eve is no more than a literary representation of a thought process going on in Eve's mind, following an internal suggestion insidiously planted there by the devil. The image of a corporeal serpent and the dialogue are used by the author as material signs of an immaterial activity taking place in her mind. To read them as verbal signs of a reptile and a real dialogue with it is to misread them. The sin that causes the fall originates entirely within Eve. She does not commit her transgression by listening to an external voice from a reptile controlled by the devil, but to her own inner voice, moving from a source of evil located somewhere within her, where it was planted by the devil as a suggestion. This interpretation leads to the conclusion that the fall of mankind did not come about because an evil being from the outside caused Eve to fall, but because in Eve there was already a certain sinfulness ready to come to fruition.

Cajetan finished his commentary on Genesis on 12 July 1530, when he was sixty-one years old,[2] having reached a fairly advanced age in relation to the average life expectancy in the sixteenth century.[3] *Ego iam senex*, he says in his preface, to justify his claim that he is interested only in the truth, that he has no time for mere novelty and no desire to engage in its pursuit. He presents himself in his subjectivity, disclosing the one principle that has sustained him in his project to gloss the Pentateuch, namely the quest for the naked truth itself, as found in Hebrew biblical texts rather than in the works of translators and glossators who have left us their understanding of it. Relevant to our reading of his entire commentary, his self-presentation has significant implications for our approach to his study of the narrative of the fall in Genesis 3, which might easily be dismissed by more traditional scholarship as a mere courting of novelty without regard for the exegetical tradition. Beyond being a poignant reflection on his age, suggesting that he has no patience for exegetical quibbles, Cajetan's words resonate with echoes of St Jerome. The translator of the Vulgate liked to refer to himself by a similar formula, especially when his interlocutor was Augustine, who, however, was only fifteen years younger.[4] But we may also hear echoes of Jerome in connection with Cajetan's determination to work only with the Hebrew text: *intendo autem iuxta hebraicam ueritatem textum exponere* ('I intend to gloss the text according to the Hebrew verity') (p. 2r). In the exegetical tradition, this expression was commonly understood as a label for St Jerome's translation of the Old Testament and for his attempt to uncover its true meaning, using as base text, against St Augustine's advice, the Hebrew version rather than the Septuagint.[5]

Appearing as it does in the general preface to the commentary, Cajetan's profession of commitment to the Hebrew text rather than the Vulgate is intended to inform the reader of the character of the commentary itself. But it has also the important semiotic function of letting the reader know what place in the history of biblical criticism Cajetan claims for himself. For the informed reader, it is a sign that, in every gloss that he writes, Cajetan aims to be compared with Jerome, whom he approaches with the humility of a student who has learnt much from him and the unyielding competitiveness of an adversary who may have something to teach him. Cajetan must have seen himself and wanted to be acknowledged as the Jerome of his own age. But there is more. As he returned to the text of the Sacred Scriptures after suffering opprobrium and imprisonment in the sack of Rome in 1527, Cajetan remembered, no doubt, Jerome's apocalyptic imagery and disconsolate tone in the passages, intruded by him into his *Commentary on Ezekiel*, in which Jerome spoke of the sack of Rome that took place in the year 410.[6] The uncanny parallelism suggests that the preface is informed by a psychology of admiration and confrontation leading the new writer to assume a revisionary stance with respect to the old. The phenomenon is familiar to modern literary critics as the anxiety of influence. This is the agonistic experience of a writer who, having taken cognizance of his own potential by reading and re-reading the inspiring work of a past writer of venerable memory, sees himself as his rightful successor but fears being crushed by his influence, which he struggles to supersede by raising his sights higher or by orienting them in a different direction than his predecessor's legacy would allow.[7]

A metaphorical serpent

Cajetan's first point in his agonistic programme is clear: avoid dialoguing with earlier commentators and focus on the text itself, reading it closely, with philological rigour and theological openness of mind. This is the opposite of Jerome's commentarial practice, which was to rehearse the entire exegetical tradition on a given point, ultimately leaving the reader with the task of choosing the best interpretation.[8] When he faces the first verse of Genesis 3, in which Moses, the human author of Genesis, said that the serpent was craftier than all other animals created by God, Cajetan observes that it is entirely appropriate to view the serpent as a sign for the devil:

> Tum communibus sacrae scripturae tum propriis textus huius quadrat / serpentis nomine non proprie intelligere animal illud brutum sed metaphorice diabolum. (p. 14v)
>
> (In both what is common to Sacred Scripture and what is proper to this text, it is fitting to understand the name serpent not as designating properly a brute animal but metaphorically the devil.)

This is how the sentence reads in the princeps of 1531, but not in the more popular 1639 edition, in which the initial phrase was altered by the Alcalá editors to read *tum communibus locutionibus*, interpolating a term that limits the ground of Cajetan's reflection to questions of grammar and style. There is no doubt, of course, that grammar and style are part of Cajetan's approach to the passage, and we cannot determine whether the 1639 editors moved, as they normally did, of their own accord or had access to archival authorial corrections, but there is obvious value in maintaining the greater semiotic amplitude allowed by the original text without their interpolation. By itself *communibus* refers to what is common to the conception of the work in its entirety, without specification of the categories in which it may be contemplated, including logic, philosophy and theology, or the codes in which it may be conveyed, including material, visual and linguistic codes. Biblical exegesis is a locus where the major disciplines of the time intersect and where different categories of semiotics are involved in the articulation and communication of sense.[9] Whether it is initially conceived as a word, as an image or as an animal, or, indeed, as all three things at the same time, the 'serpent' of Eden is a symbolic predication of the nature of the devil. In the passage at hand, the predication is in the form of an analogical transfer of sense, the linguistic correlative of which is a metaphor. Cajetan's exegetical approach to the serpent of Eden is framed in a statement of the logical procedure for the establishment and validation of truth. For Cajetan the task at hand is to show that *serpen*t is but one of the names or material images that can be used as signs for the devil.

St Thomas said that words are sometimes used obscurely in one part of the Bible and more openly in other parts (ST 1a.1.9). On this premise, we can use the contexts in which the meaning is clear in order to uncover the mystery of the obscure occurrence. The word 'serpent' occurs for the first time in Genesis, and we do not know whether its meaning is figurative or not, so we must invoke other occurrences of the same term in later books to establish its true signification. In Genesis the serpent is therefore a cataphoric sign, a sign that relies on a later occurrence of itself to clarify its earlier meaning. Modern linguistics understands this as a question of co-signification, in which meaning results from the collaborative relationship established in the mind of the reader among different occurrences of the same term. Since he suspects that, with respect to the serpent, that relationship may be figurative, Cajetan begins his hermeneutical project by directing our gaze towards the figurative uses of animals in other contexts and, in particular, metaphorical designations of the devil as a snake of some sort where the sense of the metaphor is crystal clear.

In his *De Nominum Analogia*, Cajetan observes that the reader cannot grasp the sense of metaphor unless he first comes to know to what that metaphor is applied in the text, *niso cognito illo ad cuius metaphoram dicitur*.[10] In the process of constructing a metaphor, we begin with a word that, within a specific semiotic domain, designates something that we can grasp without difficulty, as its proper name. We then transfer the word to another semiotic domain, transferring into it the referential value that it has in its original setting. As soon as it enters the new context, the term acquires a new referential value, becoming a metaphor in virtue of the new semantic field. Cajetan would agree with Lotman's observation that metaphors are born at the point of contact between semiotic domains, where they generate new meanings with which to engage the reader.[11] However, to grasp the sense of the metaphor, we must first ascertain what new semiotic field the original reference has entered. We need to know that the author has indeed shifted the reader's focus from one realm to another. Cajetan's general premise in this regard is that the Bible frequently uses the names of brute animals as signs for rational creatures, essentially transferring onto them the attributes of rational creature through the mediation of metaphorical reasoning. Thus we have the lamb of God as a metaphor of Jesus and the lion of Judah as a metaphor for the Hebrew tribe. A significantly relevant instance of this principle of metaphorical predication is found in Apoc. 12.9, a verse in which the devil is called both a dragon and a serpent, and in which the metaphorical predication is made plain in the text itself, *qui vocatur Diabolus et Satanas*. Once the principle of metaphorical predication is thus established as one of the modes of signification in the Bible, Cajetan returns to the book of Genesis to show that a metaphorical interpretation of the serpent of Eden is indeed a logical possibility.

To persuade the reader of this possibility, Cajetan makes use of a type of argument that was highly familiar to students of theology, an argument from fittingness. Though they do not come with the logical certainty of a deductive demonstration, arguments from fittingness have the power to persuade by showing that the ideas in question are entirely plausible and appropriate. Cajetan makes large use of this type of argument in his commentaries, frequently marking it with the verbs *quadrare* and, less commonly, *conuenire*, both of which signify the consistency of the conclusion proposed with the factual information provided. Such arguments, according to St Thomas, are very useful for the theological instruction and consolation of the faithful, *ad fidelium quidem exercitium et solatium*, precisely the objectives that we should ultimately expect from a commentary on the Bible.[12] On the strength of such an argument, Cajetan declares that the metaphorical interpretation of the serpent of Eden as the devil *quadrat* with the two sets of textual facts involved: those gathered from a reading of the Bible as a whole and those pertaining to the specific passage of Genesis 3 on the temptation of Eve.

The textual basis for an argument of fittingness includes two facts that Moses wove into the narrative in the form of paradoxes, contradicting reason as well as science. Natural philosophers were not agreed on whether animals were endowed with some form of intelligence, but no one would have ever suggested that the serpent was the cleverest of all the animals.[13] Therefore when Moses made such a blatantly 'antiscientific' statement about the serpent of Eden, he must have done so, Cajetan argues, in order to make it clear to the reader that the text was not really about a serpent at all but about the devil:

> immo ad hoc Moses serpentem descripsit prudentiorem caeteris / ut intelligeremus quod non de serpente quod est animal irrationale loquitur, sed de diabolo officium serpentis exercente serpendo ad uenenandum. (p. 14v)
>
> (Indeed Moses described the serpent as cleverer than the others so that we might understand that he was not speaking about a serpent, which is an unreasoning animal, but of the Devil carrying out the office of a serpent, creeping up to attack with his poison.)

Ut intelligeremus is an interpretative clause meant to render explicit Moses's authorial intention when he makes the absurd statement that the serpent was cleverer than all the other animals. It answers the question why Moses, as the human author responsible for the linguistic text, chose the specific words and images that he did in Genesis 3. Cajetan discerns in Moses's presentation of the serpent a performance of his authorship, a display of his creativity in constructing vivid imagery and in choosing one expression rather than another. Throughout his commentary, Cajetan frequently refers to details that reveal Moses's strategic use of language to convey his real intention. At the beginning of Genesis 3, Moses displays his literary ingenuity to generate doubt in the mind of the reader concerning the reality or fictionality of the serpent.

In this formulation of authorial intent, we find the philological base for Cajetan's view of the text as a narrative whose literal sense is constructed metaphorically. There are two components in that relationship, the serpent and the poison. Though as a noun *serpens* is the designation of the animal, the same term is also the present participle of *serpere*, a verb which means to creep up and carries the additional suggestion of treacherous and unobserved movement towards its victim. Frequently occurring in combination with *malum*, serpere was used in medical and political discourse to indicate the hidden progression of evil.[14] As a noun *serpens* carries all the semiotic associations of the verb. Cajetan could have found in Zeno of Verona from the fourth century that a serpent is so called because it creeps (*serpat*), and he surely knew that Christian Latin coined the adjective *serpentinus* as a genitive of *serpens* carrying the meaning of 'treacherous', as in the expression *tentatio serpentina*, used by Christian writers.[15] This philological base justifies the analogy between the serpent and the devil, which have in common the relationship between their nature and their progression: the snake is related to its advancement towards its victim the way the devil is related to his mode of progression to his own. As the designation of both forms of progression, *serpere* is the basis of an improper analogy, since its meaning cannot be predicated in the same way of both the serpent and the devil.

On this account *serpere* makes possible a powerful metaphor: the devil is a being who advances stealthily towards the control of his victim, carrying out his evil act in an invisible manner. The second component concerns the purpose of that act, *ad uenenandum*, said of both agents. The devil achieves his goal by behaving like a serpent, creeping up towards his victims to attack them with his poison. The metaphorical correspondence therefore includes the acts of undetected advancement and poisoning, both of a physical nature in the case of the serpent and of a spiritual nature in that of the devil. The above quoted sentence from Cajetan's commentary on Genesis 3 is an extraordinary expression of this correspondence. Strategically organized to be more highly significant than the sum of its words, the sentence shows that the ageing cardinal was a remarkable stylist, skilled in using the mimetic suggestiveness of language, especially its iconicity, to intensify the expressive power of his arguments. Iconicity refers to the power of language to mimic the objects that it describes. Semiotically it postulates that the relationship between signifier and signified is cast in the mode of resemblance, with the result that what is signified looks somewhat like its signifier, the way a picture (signifier) looks like the person (signified) that it represents. When the code of representation is language rather than painting, iconicity can be achieved in a variety of ways, including onomatopoeic phonology and suggestive word arrangement. In Latin, a language that allows writers much greater freedom in the determination of word arrangement than languages based on positional syntax, the word placement chosen by the author adds, intentionally, a significant layer of meaning to the sentence.

Cajetan was a master in the use of this technique. A striking iconic feature of the sentence just quoted is that the word order mimics graphically the action that the sentence describes. *Ad uenenandum* marks both the end of the sentence and the end of the action that the sentence describes, suggesting that the string of words that make up the sentence should be looked at as if they represent graphically the trajectory of the serpent's movement towards its prey. In the sentence itself, the appearance and re-appearance of the verb *serpere*, with the morphologically modified endings required by grammar (*serpente, serpentis, serpendo*), suggest serpentine motion between and around obstacles, themselves mimicked by the other words. These words, pronounced between occurrences of *serpere*, also contribute to the reader's visualization of a serpent with the conspicuous sibilance of their fricative (*s, f*) and affricate (*c*) consonants. Such sibilance, combined with that of the image-carrying derivatives of serpent, conveys by phonetic iconicity the hissing that we should expect to hear from a snake, in great contrast to the human speech with which the Edenic serpent appears to be endowed.

The power of speech is a contrary-to-fact ability attributed to the serpent. To resolve the absurdity of the attribution, Cajetan refers the reader to common sense backed by experience and scientific authority. But instead of resolving the absurdity by invoking the idea of a miraculous intervention by God, or by proposing the myth that, in Edenic and pre-historical times, snakes could speak by the will of God, Cajetan stresses the magnitude of the absurdity and interprets it as an intended semiotic feature of the text, alerting the reader to the fact that a real snake could not possibly have been involved. Real snakes can neither reason nor speak. Therefore Moses attributes such faculties to the serpent to show that in the narrative of the fall the term 'serpent' does not designate a real snake, as we might expect in an ordinary use of language, but the devil. The faculty of speech is a sign that the snake was present only in the mind of the woman and not anywhere in the external space surrounding her. Moses made the serpent speak *ut ... intelligeremus quod de serpente intellectuali loquitur*, so that we might grasp that the noun *serpens* here does not designate a material but an intellectual serpent – that is, a serpent of and in the mind: in the mind, in so far as the devil has insinuated himself into the woman's mind where, through her own thoughts, he continues to address and guide her in a dialogical development of the first thought; of the mind, in that the source of the devil's figuration as a serpent is a linguistic trope in which the signifier points the reader to a signified that is other than the one that it designates literally. In Cajetan's hermeneutics, the text itself orients the reader towards its own correct interpretation.

The devil within

Uere serpsit diabolus in mulieris animum (p.15r), truly the devil crawled into the woman's soul, and from that location he prepared her to surrender to his temptation. This use of the verb *serpsit* is one of several occurrences of *serpere* and its lexical derivatives in which Cajetan reminds his prudent reader of Moses's intention to dramatize an encounter with the devil entirely within the woman's soul, and at the same time to foreground the crucial role of the metaphor of the serpent in his commentary. Here the verb reveals how, in Cajetan's reading, Moses uses the physical movement of a serpent advancing furtively to its prey as a metaphor for the devil's argumentative stealthiness, advancing astutely and undetected to the point where it can pounce on the woman's soul.

He opens the scene with a question: Did God really forbid Adam and Eve from eating fruit from all the trees in the garden? Prior to the devil's opening question, the woman was untroubled by questions of freedom, but with his first words, he raises for her the question of liberty in a decisive way. He awakens her to the idea of freedom, generating at the same time a sense of displeasure at God's mysterious curtailment of it, and the urgency to assert, in order to counter the devil's assumption, the extent of the freedom that they do enjoy in the garden. The devil's question is cunningly framed to elicit the response that God's prohibition concerns only the Tree of Knowledge, a response that conveys her awareness of the restriction that would have to be overcome for her freedom to be complete. From that point on, says Cajetan, the woman's soul is impelled (*pulsatus*) to assert that her freedom allows to pluck and eat a fruit from any tree in the garden except one. Moreover, in giving her version of the precept, she uses the verbs in the future tense (*comedemus*) in order to signify her determination to continue exercising her freedom to eat from any other tree in the garden. With a few well-chosen words, Moses depicts the devil as a character able to bring invisibly into the woman's consciousness a full awareness of the limits of her freedom. Simultaneously he plants in her the seeds of imminent transgression by giving her reason to dream of a bigger freedom and to defend the freedom that she does have. Since the devil's provocation comes to the woman through an inner voice from somewhere inside her soul and not from a real serpent outside, Moses depicts the woman as gradually but quickly opening herself to the devil's venomous attack of her own volition.

The devil's strategy is to generate in the woman's soul an unsatisfied appetite for complete freedom and a doubt concerning God's determination to punish disobedience with mortality.

> Serpsit ergo diabolicum uenenum in affectum & intellectum mulieris. in affectum quidem per displicentiam praecepti, unde statim prodiit exaggeratio uinculi: in intellectum vero per haesitationem futurae poenae, unde prodiit haec relatio. (p. 15r)

(Thus the devil's venom crept into the affective and intellectual faculties of the woman: it entered the affective faculty, through her displeasure at the commandment, whence suddenly appeared the exaggeration of the restriction; it entered the intellectual faculty, through her uncertainty concerning the future penalty, whence came this report.)

With respect to the devil's affective strategy, the woman reports her version of God's prohibition to the devil by saying that the human beings in the garden were not only prohibited from eating a fruit from the tree of knowledge but also precluded from touching it. In the devil's question there was no mention of touching, so we can be sure, Cajetan suggests, that the additional detail is a result of the woman's desire to overstate the limitations imposed by God on the human inhabitants of the garden. The woman thus augments the restrictiveness of the divine precept, and, with this new detail, Moses intends to convey her increasing resentment. Cajetan says that in adding the prohibition of touching the fruit, the woman was acting rather like a wife who decides to obey her husband's order that she should not go out of the house by not even stepping out of her bedroom. This analogy, in which Cajetan lapses from his usual austerity and cites a comedic aspect of the contemporary culture of patriarchy, makes the point that the haptic part of the prohibition was skilfully woven by Moses into the woman's speech as a sign of great displeasure, to convey to the reader her growing disposition to violate God's debarment. The devil delivers his poison first to the woman's affective faculty, understood in this context as the appetitive part of the soul, which is what motivates us to action.

With respect to the devil's intellective strategy, Cajetan points out that the woman uses an unexpected adverb, *forte* (perhaps), to convey the way she was starting to understand God's threat: *ne forte moriamur* (lest perhaps we die). Moses has the woman use this adverb as a sign of her consideration of the potential risks involved in violating God's commandment. When he first addressed the two human beings to inform them of the prohibition, God certainly did not say that he would possibly, rather than certainly, punish the transgressors by making them mortal. The adverb was clearly added by the woman. On the face of it, it may appear that with the adverb the woman is softening God's commandment, making it more forgiving, but that impression is only an apparent and superficial sign of divine compassion. In reality things stand otherwise:

> Et quanuis in his mulieris uerbis appareat prima fronte manifesta diminutio diuini praecepti: (nam Deus asseruerat moriendo morieris, mulier uero refert quod dixit sub dubio ne forte moriamini) si tamen perspicacius consideratus

fuerit sensus intentus, apparebit quod propriam interpretationem mulier inseruit referendo diuinum praeceptum secundum sensum quo ipsa intelligit illud: huiusmodi enim relatio suapte natura pullulat ex displicentia praecepti. (p. 15r)

(And although at first glance these words by the woman appear to manifest a lessening of the divine precept – for God had said: *dying thou shalt die*, but the woman reports that he said this under doubt: *lest perhaps you die* – nevertheless if the intended sense is considered more attentively, it will be clear that the woman insinuates her own interpretation, reporting the divine precept according to the sense in which she understood it. Considered in its own nature, her report therefore comes from her displeasure at the precept.)

Strongly motivated by the resentment built up in her affective faculty, the woman reports the text of God's precept in a manner that makes it appear somewhat less formidable. She has dissolved away the certainty of the punishment by raising the possibility that, in the end, God may not do exactly what is declared in the devil's report of his words, that the transgressors will surely die. Suddenly the prospect of complete freedom appears within potential reach. When the devil first awakened her to the fact that the possibility of complete freedom lay at hand and awaited her decision, the woman responded by subjecting God's words, as reported to her by the devil, to a careful hermeneutical review. The result of her consideration was that *forte* mortality might follow. Having thus persuaded herself, she interpolates the adverb into the original precept and represents it to herself and to the devil so revised. She has already started to collaborate significantly with the devil in preparing her lapse.

The devil's final strategy consists in bringing together the woman's affective and intellective readiness in a final push towards transgression. He accomplishes this by means of an ocular metaphor designed to transform the woman's desire for freedom, including the freedom to know and to understand, into an existential urgency to be free. *Aperientur oculi uestri* (your eyes will be opened), he promises the woman, astutely arguing that God has forbidden them from eating the fruit of the tree in the centre of the garden because it is the taste of that fruit that can open their eyes. Although he is tempting her alone and not in Adam's presence, the devil addresses her in the plural (*uestri*), thus making sure that the possibility that Adam might follow suit remains prominent in her field of awareness. This grammatical detail seems to Cajetan an example of Moses's skill as a writer. Moses has the devil speak in the plural number in order to reveal how he uses language to manipulate the woman's psychology. But it is with his metaphor of vision that the devil causes the woman to yield to his power. He uses the metaphor with the hidden purpose of raising in the woman a profound sense of injustice by leading her to believe that she is being deliberately prevented from seeing. The serpent is speaking of the eyes of the mind and of vision as enlightenment, but the natural desire that living beings have to open their eyes in order to see is easily transferred to intellectual vision. The analogy casts the desire to know as a metaphor for the need to see, and uses the natural right to vision without impediments to enhance the intensity of the desire to know, transforming it into an urgent need. Moses's familiarity with the persuasive power of tropes equips him with the stylistic tools that he needs to articulate the devil's insidiousness, giving his serpentine voice power over the woman's other inner voice. Having already excited in her a passion for freedom in an indefinite sense, he now casts that passion as a need for freedom to see, *libertas ad uidendum* (p. 15v). Moses thus depicts the devil as a master of logic and language.

Renaissance readers find themselves in front of a narrative situation they know by heart, but the fact that it is so familiar to them does not make it any less extraordinary. In the earthly paradise the woman is apparently accosted by a serpent, standing erect, who engages her in a conversation. She appears to be in a cognitive environment in which she does not have to question herself about the sense of things. Except for the tree in the middle of the garden, which is a sign for the boundary of her freedom, all things are for her just what they appear to be. They are not mysterious signs of other things and do not require any special act of interpretation. Language, of course, consists only of signs, but the language of familiar situations and conversations does not normally generate problems of interpretation, not even when it is silently used as an instrument of thought rather than vocally as an instrument of communication. The devil is part of that cognitive environment in her mind and speaks to her using her own language without crossing the boundaries of ordinariness. That is why the woman has no reason to suspect anything. Suspicion would imply awareness that things may not be what they appear to be, and that the language of familiarity may conceal secret meanings or undisclosed intentions.

Viewed from Eve's perspective, says Cajetan, the serpent in the story appears to behave like a familiar conversation partner, *tanquam domestico interlocutori*, whose appearance, actions and speech are not in the least mysterious or foreign. She is not afraid to be in the serpent's proximity, and she is not surprised to hear him address her in perfectly intelligible language. But the atmosphere of domesticity, says Cajetan, is totally incongruous with what the reader might expect from the literal sense of a narrative, where a serpent's ability to speak like a human being should be perceived by Eve as a terrifying absurdity. The incongruity, Cajetan argues, is intentional. It is a sign designed to point out to the reader that the words used to construct the narrative do not mean what they say. By the incongruity, Moses is letting the reader know that his account of the fall is articulated as a narrative of a different kind. There are at least two ways of telling the story of the fall. In one of them, the words are taken to mean exactly what they say (*ut litera sonat*) and the narrative structures require no special interpretation. Narration of this kind makes use of a code in which the word 'serpent' designates an unreasoning reptile, while a scripted dialogue designates a conversation between two different speakers. Narration of the other kind uses a figurative code of words and colloquies in which 'serpent' designates the devil, while a scripted dialogue represents a silent thought process occurring in the mind of a person debating two ideas. In the first type of narrative, a crafty and speaking serpent would be an absurdity; in the second type, the presence of such a serpent would be perfectly logical. Moses cast his story as a narrative of the first kind but provides his readers with clues that they should read it as a narrative of the second kind.

In Moses's narrative of the fall, there is no serpent at all and hence no conversation. The serpent is just a metaphor for the devil who has insinuated himself into Eve's mind in the guise of a friendly thought, while the dialogue is a literary form that enables the author to give discursive shape to a character's interior monologue, or the process of thinking in which an idea develops from another that has mysteriously come into being from some secret internal source as a mere suggestion. Hence Cajetan's interpretation of the text:

> Non fuit igitur sermo uocalis sed sermo internae suggestionis quo diabolus serpere uenenosa cogitatione incoepit. Et eodem sermonis genere uniuersus iste dialogus inter serpentem et mulierem intelligendus est. (p. 14v)
>
> (Therefore, it was not by vocal speech but by the speech of internal suggestion that the devil began to creep in with poisonous thoughts. The entire dialogue between the serpent and the woman is to be understood as the same type of speech.)

With respect to visualization of a thought process as a dialogue, Cajetan's interpretation is rooted in the classical tradition which, since Plato, frequently regarded thinking as a dialogical operation. In the *Thaetetus*, for example, Socrates explains that, in the process of thinking, the mind enters into a dialogue with itself, asking questions and giving answers as if it consisted of two voices speaking to each other, not aloud but silently (189e). When the process reaches a point at which the mind's two voices say the same thing, then we say that the mind has formed its judgement. In Genesis 3, the two voices are Eve's and the devil's, and the judgement that is reached at the end is Eve's decision to eat a fruit from the tree of knowledge. With respect to the literary representation of thought as a dialogue rather than a treatise, Cajetan's reading of Moses is through the lens of one accustomed to dialogue as a literary genre, a genre that had regained much of its ancient vitality in the culture of Renaissance humanism. In writing the book of Genesis, Moses inserted a mental dialogue, all taking place in Eve's mind, between two voices – her own and another taken as a sign of the devil – at the very beginning of the narrative of the fall.

Moses, however, visualizes the devil's voice as a sign-image suggested by the figurative name of the devil, namely a serpent. In representing her thus, he was making use of an ancient narrative technique familiar to Cajetan from the medieval tradition of visualized words, *verba imaginata*. From Avicenna, who defined thought as an inner dialogue aided by concrete images, to Aquinas, for whom the images of words, when united with their meanings, are the origin of blasphemy (ST 2.3.ad3), Cajetan would know that the visualization of the literal meaning of words was an important way in which the imagination could participate in the cognitive process of the intellect, at all levels.[16] The second voice in Eve's mind was understood by Moses as a sign of the devil and pictured by him as issuing forth from the image of a serpent, itself pictured standing externally to Eve and speaking cleverly to her. The dialogue that ensues belongs to the genre in which a vocalized external scene represents the process of thinking in which the intellect is aided by the imagination.

Moses could use the image of a serpent for the devil because, as Cajetan points out, elsewhere in the Bible the devil was designated figuratively by that word. This suggests that the devil operates in Eve's mind analogously to a snake in the grass, both moving stealthily, as we have seen in Cajetan's discussion of the noun *serpens* as a derivative of *serpere*. The devil starts to creep (*serpere*) through Eve's mind, relentlessly pursuing it until she takes the decisive step of her fall, just as a poisonous serpent in a field appears to creep up to its prey, pursuing it until it can strike a fatal blow. The semiotic parallelism is sustained by an analogy in which there is a one-to-one correspondence between the signs that reveal what takes place in Eve's mind and those that describe an attack by a real serpent. The key to the analogy is the relationship between the serpent's poison that causes the death of its prey and the thought insinuated by the devil into Eve's mind, or the suggestion that new and better possibilities of being are within her reach.

All sins, says St Thomas, originate *ex suggestione diaboli* (ST Ia.114.3), a well-known phrase in medieval and Renaissance theology. Cajetan echoes this phrase when he observes that the dialogue of Genesis 3 should not be understood as having taken place externally and vocally but internally and silently, as a *sermo internae suggestionis*. Cajetan stays very much within the tradition of the theology of sin. But in what concerns the imaginative mechanics of sinning – the notion that a spirit can appear in the subject's field of awareness, speaking in a familiar inner voice, insinuating defiant ideas – Cajetan draws on other traditions. The image of a familiar spirit in Eve's mind may have been suggested to Cajetan by Plato. In the *Phaedrus* (242b-c), Socrates confesses that a daemon, long familiar to him, enters his mind and, by means of an inner voice, persuasively counsels him not to undertake the course of action that he had set for himself. The Greek δαίμων originally meant a godlike spirit, frequently a spirit with a tutelary function, but when it entered the vocabulary of Christianity with the New Testament and early theology, it acquired the familiar association with an evil spirit. In Ficino's Latin translation of Plato, which was available to Cajetan in several editions, the crucial passage from the *Phaedrus* was rendered as *daemonium et solitum mihi fieri signum factum est*, in which we have the key concepts that Cajetan needed to internalize the devil's temptation of Eve: the devil (*daemonium*), familiarity (*solitum*) and a sign (*signum*).[17] For the behaviour of the devil in Eve's mind, Cajetan had no doubt recourse to the Hebrew understanding of the devil as the adversary. In his own commentary on Job, Cajetan glosses the name Satan as 'latine adversarius'.[18] As an adversary, the serpent proceeds by means of suggestive interrogation, asking Eve leading questions.

The serpent's purpose in this mode of interrogation is to place in Eve's mind a thought which she previously did not have, causing it to grow to the point of making her vulnerable to doubt. This way the serpent gives rise in Eve's mind to an ambivalent memory of God's commandment, plants suspicions about the extent of his prohibition and excites in her the desire to transgress it.

Enmity against women

In his gloss on the first half of the verse, *Inimicitias ponam inter te et mulierem*, on which the Vulgate is consistent with the Hebrew version, Cajetan dramatizes the reading process by expanding God's simple words into a powerful trope, combining the idea of an authorial apostrophe, spoken against one character in the persona of the other, and a rhetorical prolongation of the narrative motif. This has the effect of giving both the devil and God a vivid dramatic presence in the reader's receptive experience of the text and of simultaneously catapulting the reader into the text, wherein he can directly witness God's performance as he delivers his invective against the devil:

> Noli putare ex eo quod superasti mulierem te habiturum dominium super *uniuersas* mulieres. nam quanuis mulier ipsa imbecillis sit, ego tamen ponam inter mulierem & inter te odium inimicitiae: ut habeat te non in dominum sed in inimicum, ut non pareat tibi sed hostem te sentiat, ut hostem caueat, ut odio te prosequatur. (p. 17r)

> (Do not think from the fact that you prevailed over the woman that you will have dominion over all women. For although woman is in herself feeble, I will nonetheless put the hatred of enmity between you and the woman, so that she may regard you not as her lord but as her enemy, and so that she may not surrender to you but as her enemy she might avoid you, and with hatred she might persecute you.)

Written at a time when much theology of patriarchy could be cited to authorize the suspicion that all women could be under the devil's dominion, this is an extraordinary gloss. In Cajetan's restatement of the words that Moses had written for God, the devil will never have control of all women. The words *noli putare* (do not think) foreground Cajetan's awareness that some members of his society thought indeed that all women were in some measure subject to the influence of the devil. In Cajetan's trope, God concedes that women represent the weaker sex (*imbecillis*), speaking like a sixteenth-century champion of a theology that is not immune to the influence of the social hierarchy of the genders. In reaching out beyond the text, Cajetan depicts God in a manner showing that he inherited the bias of the philosophy of gender and its correlative social practice, despite the fact that he cannot admit that the weakness of women is sufficient to warrant the devil's victory over all members of their sex. God promises to strengthen women's defences, enabling them to avoid the devil's attack on them, and to turn them into aggressive foes of the devil, capable of pursuing him relentlessly.

On account of their inherent weakness, however, women cannot exercise their militancy against the devil on their own, and so God pledges to help them with the gift of just hatred. According to Cajetan, strengthened by that divine gift, countless women are capable of resisting the devil's temptation:

> Et hoc impletum uidemus in innumeris mulieribus fanctae uitae: non ex mulierum uiribus sed ex diuino dono quo posuit in animis earum odium non

qualecunque sed omnis generis inimicitiae propter hoc enim dicit inimicitias in numero plurali inter ipsa et serpentem diabolum. Non sufficit inimicum esse diabolo quoad ea quae sunt fidei aut spei sed oportet inimicum esse secundum omnes partes: secundum ea quae sunt castitatis, abstinentiae, liberalitatis, misericordiae et reliquorum sanctorum officiorum. (p. 17r)

(And we see this fulfilled by innumerable women who live a holy life, not on account of their strength as women but by the divine gift with which he placed hatred in their souls – and not just any kind of hatred, but hatred from all kinds of enmity – for which reason he said enmities, in the plural – between them and the diabolical serpent. It does not suffice to be an enemy of the devil concerning things which belong to faith or hope, but it is opportune to show enmity in all of its parts, including the things that pertain to chastity, abstinence, generosity, compassion and all other virtues of the saints.)

Here Cajetan leaves the apostrophe and speaks *in propria persona*, glossing the words that he has just attributed to God. He confirms that countless women fight the serpent every day with the arms of their virtue. The purpose of his annotation is to show that Scripture is right, that it is being fulfilled by society, and hence that a general observation about society can function as a reliable orientative principle of interpretation.[19] Cajetan uses the social hierarchy of the sexes as a base for reading, not the text, but his own paraphrase of it in God's apostrophe to the devil. In his view of virtuous womanhood, the moral virtues which good women are expected to embody are reinforced by hatred of evil, without which they would not be effective combatants against the devil. In this gloss Cajetan leaves the text and reverses the order of reasoning that led him to choose the Hebrew version and to correct St Jerome's Vulgate. By negative implication, this reading of the passage calls attention to the women who, though virtuous, are insufficiently so and, unassisted by divine hatred of evil, fall prey to the devil's wiles. Here instead of glossing the text for the literal meaning of the words in their context, as he promised to do in the preface, Cajetan uses his theology as a base for his interpretation of the text.

In glossing the second half of the verse, in which God, continuing with the serpent metaphor, rebukes the devil, saying that his head will be crushed, Cajetan again moves from theology to exegesis rather than the other way around. The Vulgate and the Hebrew text report God's promise using subject pronouns of different gender. The Vulgate has *ipsa conteret caput tuum*, whereas the Hebrew text reads *ipsum conteret tibi caput*, assigning the role of serpent destroyer respectively to a woman or to her descendants. In the exegetical tradition, the feminine pronoun of the Vulgate, *ipsa*, offered an early scriptural base for the typological interpretation of Mary as the new Eve, the one who will make possible the reversal of the effects of the fall, while the neuter pronoun of the Hebrew text, *ipsum*, referred to the seed or the offspring of Eve in post-lapserian history. Cajetan does not spend any time on *ipsa* but gives a detailed gloss of *ipsum* in the Hebrew text. It may refer, first of all, to the good descendants of Eve, those who are successful in combating the devil with their exemplary lives. *Ipsa* is easily dismissed:

> Non de muliere sed de semine eius dicitur quod conteret caput diaboli. Et potest sententia haec referri tum ad genus electorum: quia electus quisque conterit caput (hoc est supremam partem) diaboli: hoc est officium diaboli prouocatiuum ad malum culpae. (p. 17r)
>
> (It is not said of the woman but of her seed that it will crush the devil's head. And this pronouncement may be referred to the race of the elect, because each of the elect shall crush the devil's head – that is, the devil's highest part or office, provocative of culpable evil.)

Having decided that the agent of God's defeat of the devil is *ipsum*, Cajetan tries to find the referent signified by the seed of the woman. He is unsure and therefore chooses his language carefully: the pronoun *ipsum* can (*potest*) point us to those elected by God to eternal life. Though the textual base is not certain, the sense is at least theologically possible. Since no one is predestined to evil, each of the elect will naturally express hostility towards the devil, for they are all enemies of evil. Anything else would be to accept evil, and that would contradict the reason for predestination. The main task that the devil has chosen for himself is to provoke human beings to commit acts of culpable evil, a task figuratively represented by Cajetan as the head of the serpent, to be crushed by the enemies of evil. But *ipsum* can (*potest*) also refer to Christ, who was most exceptionally *semen solius mulieris* (the seed of only a woman). If *ipsum* is indeed taken as a sign for Christ, then it can be understood in two ways: as a reference to the man Jesus Christ, who could crush the serpent's head with his inherent goodness, and to Jesus Christ as a corporate metaphor for the church, his mystical body, in which case the serpent's head, identified with sinners, is crushed by the church on a daily basis (*quotidie*) in its defeat of sin.

Having thus interpreted the text of the protoevangelium of Gen. 3.15, where we encounter Moses's first mention of the defeat of the devil and of salvation to come, Cajetan reminds the reader that none of it would make sense if the serpent of the temptation had been conceived by Moses as an external corporeal being rather than as a metaphorical sign of evil thoughts within the soul. *Perspicaciter contemplare prudens lector has poenas* (contemplate this punishment carefully, wise reader), Cajetan says, exhorting his reader to see that figurative language is the only thing that makes the text intelligible where it mentions the punishments that will be inflicted on the serpent. If the serpent is taken to be a real physical animal, here as well as in the passage in which it appears as a speaking and crafty reptile, the narrative makes only childish sense (*puerile esse*), for such things can take place only in fables.[20] The contradictions in the text are such that it not only invites but actually compels the reader to accept the fact that there was no serpent: *textus ipse ad metaphoricum sensum non solum inuitat sed cogit* (p. 17r).

In the history of biblical exegesis, Cajetan's conclusion was both original and highly controversial, but beyond the circle of biblical commentators the idea that the fall took place without a serpent, or at least without a visible serpent, was by no means exceptional. The iconographic database of the Warburg Institute includes numerous manuscript images from the fourteenth and fifteenth centuries in which Adam and Eve are alone under a fruit-laden tree at the time of the fall.[21] In most of them, Adam and Eve stand on either side of the tree trunk and eat or reach for a fruit, but there is no trace of a serpent anywhere in the picture. Clearly the moving force behind these visualizations of the fall was an internal suggestion of the sort described by Cajetan. We cannot know what the source of that suggestion may have been for the artists, but we can surmise that their visualization of the literal aspect of the narrative told in Genesis must have somehow been metaphorical, in Cajetan's sense of the term: a metaphorical serpent is invisible and inaudible, and has no physical presence that can serve as an anchor for the artist's imagination as he composes the rest of the picture.

Cajetan had the same response to the literal meaning of the text, except that he, being an exegete, also provided the reader with a rigorous explanation. In his view, Moses is a great writer: he first invented the metaphor of the devil as a serpent and devised a dialogue as a two-voiced representation of Eve's thinking, and he then filled out Eve's double thought forms with suggestions and leading questions in the imagined voice of the serpent and responses in the voice of her conscience, showing her increasing vulnerability to the temptation of freedom. Moses managed the two voices with consummate skill, weighing the implications of every word, and thus saying much in a few captivating lines of dramatic poetry. The semiotic idea underpinning this process is that the account of the fall in Genesis is the word of God as structured, managed and articulated by Moses, a writer endowed with great skill in exploiting the pragmatic potential of literary forms and the suggestive power of word arrangement. Most of all, he was a master of the persuasive force of imagery. His style is so vivid, Cajetan suggests, that the majority of readers literalize his key metaphor, taking the devil as a real serpent, and reading the devil's subtle prodding of Eve's mind as an external dialogue under the tree of knowledge. Theologically, Moses leads his readers to the conclusion that the fall did not result from an external temptation but from an internal disposition of the soul, made increasingly vulnerable by the subtle enticement of the devil, who did not operate externally in the form of a speaking serpent but internally, inside the woman, cajoling her to transgress the boundaries that God had drawn around her.

4

Workers of evil

When Dante and Vergil cross the ring of the soothsayers and sorcerers, Vergil points out to the poet the shades of women who had abandoned their feminine occupations in the home and in society to become fortune tellers and to practice harmful magic: *fecer malie con erbe e con imago* (*Inf.* 20.23). Like all the other souls in this ring, they suffer the pain of having had their necks so distorted as to force them always to face backwards, as a reminder that they misused their intelligence in attempting to predict and change the course of human affairs with the art of black magic. The fourteenth-century commentators tend to gloss this verse very briefly, explaining that the women were guilty of causing harm to others by casting spells (*malie*) with the aid of herbal charms (*erbe*) and effigies (*imago*), and relating Dante's view of them to antecedents in classical literature. But in the mid-fifteenth century, about 120 years after the death of Dante (1321), we begin to notice a major hermeneutical shift in the interpretation of this verse, as occasionally scholars started to read the culture of their own times back into Dante. Thus, writing around 1440, the humanist Guinoforto delli Bargigi – born in Pavia, educated at Padua and active mostly in and around Milan – interprets Dante's female soothsayers as witches in league with the devil and expands *malie* to include such evil activities as turning love into enmity, inciting the innocent to illicit lust, causing people to go mad, and countless other things accomplished with the aid of the devil. At the end of his gloss, Guinoforto adds the following note:

> Tali femmine . . . trovai che erano arse nuovamente in gran copia in diversi luoghi tra le montagne del Delfinato, quand'io passai per indi, ove ancora pareva il carbone e quasi la cenere fresca.[1]
>
> (Such women . . . I found were again being burned in large numbers in various locations among the mountains of the Dauphiné, through which I recently passed, where the charcoal and the ashes were still quite fresh.)

This is an extraordinary remark to find in a critical commentary on a work of poetry. Dante's powerful imagery could suddenly find a correlative in news on the prosecution of witchcraft in the contemporary world, about one and a half centuries after the composition of the *Inferno*. The Cottian Alps of the Dauphiné marked the border between southern France and northern Italy. The ecclesiastical oversight of the region was divided between two dioceses, one French (Embrun) and the other Italian (Turin), and news was easily carried back and forth by travellers. Guinoforto's annotation must be one of the earliest notices to the Italian literary public of the sudden rise in witchcraft trials and in the execution of witches in the Dauphiné in the 1430s. Guiniforto had probably visited the places of execution overseen by Claude Tholosan, chief secular magistrate of the Briançon and author of a treatise on the subject, who, since around 1425, had prosecuted and burned at the stake many women found guilty of witchcraft in league with the devil.[2] Writing in a simple and unassuming style, Guinoforto focuses immediately on what must have been horrifying details for a cultured reader of Dante in the age of humanism, namely the fact that the execution of witches was taking place not in one but in various communities, the large number of women being burned at the stake, and even the morbid interest in observing their ashen remains, still undisturbed by nature or society. Guinoforto happens upon these places as an outsider and, in his annotations to Dante, records his clear impression that in the Dauphiné witch-burning was a continuing and widespread phenomenon.

Guinoforto's hermeneutical shift suggests that literary themes of sorcery and enchantments could be viewed as signs with real referents in contemporary culture and in the reader's external reality. The shift is perhaps a residue of the tropological reading of the Bible, in which the question to be answered was always what does a particular episode in Scripture mean for the reader in the here and now of his personal life, or, which would amount to the same thing, in what way do signs in the text point to a referent in the reader's culture. Behind this shift is the idea of types: the expression of an idea in the text may be regarded as embodied by particular individuals or events in the present, which seem to have a similar form. A significant implication of this approach to textual meaning concerns the possibility of appropriating motifs of sorcery and enchantment from classical literature and using them as a paradigm of perception through which to discern analogous aspects of witchcraft in actual investigations or in theoretical discussions of the subject. Thus, the label *malefica* can cover Medea and Circe as well as a witch of the contemporary world, erasing the line of demarcation between fiction and reality, between literary sorceresses and real women convicted of committing abominable crimes as mistresses of the devil. By such osmosis, the domain of literature and anecdote continued to permeate into that of theology and law throughout the history of witchcraft trials.

After Tholosan's treatise there was a succession of theoretical, juridical and theological works on demonic sorcery, as theologians and canonists tried to keep pace with the growing affinity for witch-hunting throughout Europe, especially in the Alpine regions of Italy, France and Switzerland. One of the most tangible results of this interest was the publication of numerous learned works that, under the guise of factual narration and theological analysis, justified the detective work of barbaric inquisitors and encouraged zeal for inquisitions. Among the milestones of this developing area of scholarship are two works which, on account of their official character and of their connection with the semiotics and theology of the fall, are of special interest to the present study. The first of these is the bull *Summis desiderantes affectibus*, by which on 9 December 1484 Pope Innocent VIII authorized two Dominican professors of theology – Heinrich Kramer (occasionally Latinized as Henricus Institoris) and Jakob Sprenger – to serve as inquisitors over a large territory of Germany, with the authority to investigate, unhindered, all accusations of witchcraft and to punish with the appropriate severity those found guilty of the crime. The second is the infamous *Malleus maleficarum* (1487), frequently described as a witch hunter's reference work and credited jointly to Kramer and Sprenger, though Kramer was without doubt the primary, if not the only, author. The *Malleus maleficarum* played a dominant role in the demonological culture of the early modern period, in which it figures as an extremist work thematically linked to a large constellation of works of theology, including the brief and much more rational *De Maleficiis* (1500) and other treatises by Cardinal Cajetan, at least until the early seventeenth century, when other studies of the subject, such as Francesco Maria Guazzo's *Compendium maleficarum* (1608), moved into the limelight.

In the course of the fifteenth century, the practice of witchcraft was thought to consist of the use of harmful magic in combination with 'demonic conspiracy', a synthesis that gave rise to the classification of witches as heretics conspiring with the devil to overthrow Christianity. The *Malleus maleficarum* was an early embodiment of this tradition, compounded of medieval demonology and recent confessions extracted under judicial torture. The picture that emerged from this material was centred on the idea that witches were united to the devil by a pact and had sex with him, that they were capable of transvection to orgiastic meetings and were guilty of such abominable acts as infanticide and cannibalism. This composite idea of witchcraft, aptly called by modern scholars the 'elaborated theory', took some time to reach full development, but throughout its elaboration it served to confirm that the continued identification of witches as a special sect of heretics was entirely correct. The composite idea of witchcraft, with its clear parameters, both facilitated the arrest of new witches that fit the stereotype and justified the methodical effort to uncover and prosecute entire groups of suspects rather than only single individuals.[3]

Given this conception of witchcraft, it is not surprising that, in the Renaissance, religious academics, especially Dominicans, whose mission included the extirpation of heresy, had such keen interest in witches and their confessions. The narratives obtained by inquisition judges included first-person accounts of the way the devil operated in society to acquire ministers and to spread evil. The narrative structure of the confession is virtually formulaic and has almost the conventions of a genre. It begins with an account of the woman's seduction by the devil when she was a novice, proceeds to her renouncement of Christ and repudiation of baptism, and then moves on to a factual description of each crime committed since her apostasy. At the same time, the narrative puts all the evidence in a logical order, interpreting each item as a sign of the witch's total surrender to the devil and indirectly justifying the judicial torture used to extract her confession. This constituted evidence – usually given under torture, but confirmed later without physical coercion – not only of the existence of the devil but also of the role that he played in the life of mankind through the agency of human beings who had entered into a pact with him. As Walter Stephens has argued, witches are the best witnesses in debates on the existence of the devil and his involvement in human affairs, since 'a woman who confessed to having been ravished by a demon was testifying to the existence of a superhuman presence that left her no choice but to believe in its reality'.[4] Paradoxically, in the Renaissance, a period in which demonology was on the rise, witches were very useful to theologians because, through the narratives of their crimes, they provided them with an empirical base for the further development of an area of theology that was not well represented in Holy Scripture. Witches were the only deponents who had direct knowledge of the workings of the devil, because they were themselves workers of evil and willing ministers of his power. Their experience could thus be incorporated into the theology of evil and enlisted in the church's struggle to extirpate all diabolical heresy.

Leading the attack

To understand the witchcraft crusade, we must start with the official document that authorized the investigation and prosecution of suspected witches on mass, by declaring all convicted witches enemies of Christianity, intent on subverting the church's design for the salvation of mankind. When Pope Innocent VIII issued the bull *Summis desiderantes affectibus*, Kramer had already been serving as inquisitor for some time, but his methods had met with considerable resistance from local clergy, who thought that he went to excesses unwarranted by either the evidence or reason. Innocent's bull was meant to neutralize that resistance by giving Kramer and Sprenger the authority to overrule local objections. The bull was not the first document from the papacy on the crime of witchcraft, but it was without doubt the most significant one. In the church's hideous crusade against witches, it gave the prosecution hitherto unknown support and momentum. Innocent officially recognized the existence of large numbers of witches, both male and female, as enemies of God and mankind, persons in erotic league with the devil and devoted to acts of evil, and he left no doubt concerning the need to exterminate them. In the bull he gives a precise outline of the types of crimes committed by witches and provides the inquisitors with licence to proceed against them with due severity. The paragraph on crimes of witchcraft is of considerable interest:

> It has indeed lately come to Our ears, not without afflicting Us with bitter sorrow, that ... many persons of both sexes, have abandoned themselves to devils, incubi and succubi, and by their incantations, spells, conjurations, and other accursed charms and crafts, enormities of horrid offences, have slain infants yet in the mother's womb, as also the offspring of cattle, have blasted the produce of the earth, the grapes of the vine, the fruits of the trees, nay, men and women, beasts of burthen, herd-beasts, as well as animals of other kinds, vineyards, orchards, meadows, pasture-land, corn, wheat and all other cereals; these wretches furthermore afflict and torment men and women, beasts of burthen, herd-beasts, as well as animals of other kinds, with terrible and piteous pains and sore diseases, both internal and external; they hinder men from performing the sexual act and women from conceiving, whence husbands cannot know their wives nor wives receive their husbands; over and above this, they blasphemously renounce the Faith which is theirs by the Sacrament of Baptism, and, at the instigation of the Enemy of Mankind, they do not shrink from committing and perpetrating the foulest abominations and filthiest excesses to the deadly peril of their own souls, whereby they outrage the Divine Majesty and are a cause of scandal and danger to every man.[5]

Innocent notes first of all the erotic character of the allegiance with the devil involved in the practice of witchcraft. Whatever else they may be, the criminals against whom the pope unleashes the full power of his inquisitors are first all the devil's sex partners. The devil assumes a male form, an incubus, to have sex with women, and a female form, a succubus, to have sex with men. The crimes for which such men and women must be held accountable are all subsequent to their erotic union with the devil. The bull proceeds to describe the means that they use to commit their crimes, and these include verbal formulas (incantations, spells, conjurations) as well as objects (charms). Then comes a long list of the crimes that they are known to have committed, including causing impotence and sterility, harm to animals and humans, and destructive natural phenomena. These are all crimes that affect society and, in many cases, have witnesses that can help gather evidence on which to judge whether the accused is guilty or innocent. The most grievous crime, however, is their rejection of the faith, attempting to reverse the sacramental action of baptism, at the instigation of the devil.

Sex with incubi and succubi does not normally involve witnesses or material evidence to be used in laying charges, but all crimes against other persons, animals and fields normally involve witnesses or victims who can report what they see and hear to the inquisitors, who may then order an investigation. The repudiation of the faith, reversing the renunciation of the devil professed in the baptismal rite, is ultimately the crime that can warrant consigning someone to the flames. The renunciation of any article of the faith characterized the crime of witchcraft as a crime of heresy, the only one that an ecclesiastical court could punish by death – by burning in Europe and hanging in England. Theologically, through the renunciation of baptism, the sacrament that undoes the effect of original sin, witchcraft negates the course of redemption and returns the subject to union with the serpent. Semiotically, Innocent's bull suggests that the signs by which the inquisitors can disclose the operation of the devil in the crime of witchcraft are conceived as reversals of the sacraments. In their pursuit, the inquisitors must rely on the aid of witnesses and on the collaboration of local authorities. For that reason, anyone who hinders the work of the inquisitors in any way or form is subject to excommunication and to 'yet more terrible penalties . . . without right of appeal'.[6] This threat at the end of the bull is meant to give rise to a significant culture of informers and collaborators in which the inquisitors could hunt down alleged workers of evil.

Pope Innocent VIII speaks explicitly of perpetrators of both sexes, but, in reading the bull, Kramer was most probably thinking of women, since in his work as inquisitor he considered it a fundamental principle that women, on account of their lustful nature, were more strongly propelled then men towards connubium with the devil and to the subsequent rejection of their faith. In his prosecution of one Helena Scheuberin on 29 October 1485, a prosecution in which the local bishop and canonists thought indeed that Kramer was prone to excesses, he observed that 'it is a general rule that all witches have been slaves from a young age to carnal lust and various adulteries',[7] and by 'witches' here he meant to limit his remark to the female gender. Women were potentially culpable because they were inherently libidinous. Kramer carried this anti-feminist perspective into the *Malleus maleficarum*, feeling justified, no doubt, by his own misogyny and by the tradition that, by feminizing the serpent of Eden, had laid the ground for the demonization of women who did not fit the matrix of acceptable female conventions. Such women, estranged from the norm by some peculiarity or other, had the makings of witches and were to be observed with suspicion when they engaged in normal activities. The way they performed such activities could well be a sign of the identity of witches concealed under the cloak of normality.

One such activity was the taking of Holy Communion in church. In a remarkable passage of the *Malleus maleficarum* we read that when he serves communion to a female communicant, the priest should make sure that she opens her mouth widely, that she thrusts her tongue forward as far as possible and that her clothing is well clear of her face. Anything else would not offer a guarantee that she will not hide the Host under her tongue, retrieve it as soon as the priest turns the other way, hide it in her clothing and smuggle it out of the church for later abuse. By keeping an eye on women communicants, parish priests can collaborate with local inquisitors in identifying witches who may be hiding in their community of devout Christians. 'And the more care is taken in this respect,' say Kramer and Sprenger, 'the more witches become known by this means'.[8] For witches will not want to receive communion without the possibility of retrieving the Host, for fear that, if swallowed, the power of the Eucharist would nullify their renouncement of the faith, which is the condition sine qua non of their existence as witches. This passage is of considerable interest, not only because it represents a systematic attempt to magnify the theological significance of witchcraft investigations but also because, in a blatant effort to instrumentalize the liturgy in promoting misogyny, it visibly circumscribes women as potential witches and demon worshippers, justifying a close observation of their physical disposition not only by the priest but possibly also by other communicants, motivated by the need to demonstrate their own innocence by the gestural iconization of one in their midst as deserving investigation by the local inquisitor.

Gestural iconization is understood here as a semiotic version of the linguistic concept of iconization, which refers to the circumscription of a group of people that share the same linguistic features because they share the same origin, character or essence. In more general terms, as Bouissac notes, 'it is a cultural process through which stereotypes are sustained and, at times, renewed or modified.'[9] In the gestural equivalent proposed here, iconization is nothing other than the circumscription of suspicious forms of conduct for the purpose of distancing certain types of individuals from the community. Such individuals are perceived to act and move differently because they are essentially different, their movements being only a physical sign of their nature. Motivated by the need or the desire to otherize certain members of the community, iconization frequently signifies by negative implication: a woman who does not fully open her mouth, who does not protrude her tongue or who does not pull back her veil or head scarf far enough from her face while receiving Holy Communion exhibits signs that warrant suspicion of being a witch, caught in an attempt to snatch a Host for the symbolic denigration of Christ in service to the devil. One witch, according to Kramer and Sprenger, had gone as far as to bury the Host with a toad near a house (p. 116). But a witch's denigration of Christ, we learn from other examples in the *Malleus maleficarum*, can take many forms, including spitting on the ground during the Elevation of the Host or uttering abominations 'verbally or otherwise', *per verba aut sine verbis* (p. 114) – that is to say, by making gestural signs that, despite the witch's effort to conceal her thoughts, reveal her identity as a witch and manifest her culpability. The same signs of culpability become conspicuous and ominous if the social context is enlarged, which occurs whenever someone testifies to the fact that the suspect associates with other suspects and generally behaves like them, in conformity with the expected stereotypical manner of a woman who has deviated from the faith and has somehow gravitated towards heresy.

The denouncement of suspects to the authorities on the basis of verbal, gestural and behavioural iconization can automatically enable a frightened or an aggrieved neighbour to seek the safe role of a witness moved by righteousness to give a deposition. The social status and moral worthiness of the witness and the seriousness of the sworn evidence brought forth were taken into account in assessing the magnitude of the suspicion, but they need not always be very high on the scale of gravity to warrant further investigation, in the course of which the exact degree of suspicion would be established before the trial and sentencing. In investigations of heresy, there were three degrees of suspicion. The first is slight suspicion, which arises from conjectures lacking definitive proof or confession. It may involve such things as forms of behaviour different from those expected of the faithful, particularly if the suspect meets with others in barns or remote fields, while the true faithful attend Mass. The second is strong or vehement suspicion, and it is incurred by people who cannot clear their name other than by a strong defence, capable of dissuading the judge from accepting as valid the conjectures, arguments and evidence linking a suspect to known heretics. Such people are guilty at least of 'heretical sympathy' even though they may not have caused harm to animals or human beings. The third is grave or violent suspicion, and it is incurred by people who consort with heretics, receive aid from them, take part in their rites and ceremonies and behave accordingly. The evidence against them is such as to convince the judge that they are guilty of 'some belief in heresy' (p. 238).

Persons brought to the inquisitor under grave suspicion of the heresy of witchcraft include women who are known to bewitch men and animals, utter threatening prognostications about members of the community, and who are seen taking part in witches' ceremonies. By such actions, they openly display their fellowship with the group iconized by society as stereotypical witches and are hence justifiably brought under grave suspicion of heresy. Within that group, the worst witches are those who, in addition to professing loyalty to the devil, cause all manner of harm to human beings and animals and devastate agriculture with hail and tempests, cause sterility and impotence in otherwise happy couples, engage in the abominable practice of pre-baptismal infant cannibalism and offer the remains of murdered children to the devil. During the investigation, they can remain silent under judicial torture and can cause others, who could potentially speak of their guilt, to withstand the pain and say nothing.

Appearance and everyday behaviour

In the absence of self-incrimination, inquisitors must learn to read a suspect's body as if it were a text. Over the sixteenth century the most reliable sign that a suspect had entered into a pact with the devil was believed to be an indelible mark that the devil left on her body, in a place where it was easy to conceal, to seal her promise of fidelity. Known as the devil's mark, such a sign could be a blemish of some form or other, or even a scar insensitive to piercing. It was usually found concealed by hair or folds of skin, under an eyelid, on the back of the neck, under the arms and in the pubic region. The presence of such a sign turned an individual witch into a member of 'a broader conspiracy'.[10] In the *Compendium maleficarum*, Guazzo describes such marks by the analogy of branding, impressed on runaway slaves so that henceforth they may be readily identified as belonging to their rightful owner.[11] The devil's mark was a sign that the suspect was a loyal subject of the devil. In the course of an investigation, many inquisitors ordered the shaving of all hair on the suspect's body, so that the skin might be closely examined for the presence of a revealing mark. When evidence of this sort was confirmed, the blemish was interpreted as an indexical sign of the devil's covenant with the suspect, an evil equivalent of the divine *vestigium* that we encountered as sign of divine grace in the theory of the sacraments.

Though with time it was generally regarded as a reliable part of the investigative procedure, the physical examination of the suspect was not conducted in the same way everywhere throughout the history of witchcraft trials. In the *Malleus maleficarum*, for example, we read that in northern Italy, forty-eight women were recently (just before 1485) burned at the stake after they had been shaved all over, since the removal of all body hair revealed the presence of hidden signs of loyalty to the devil, possibly in the form of blemishes. But in Germany judiciary shaving was limited to cutting off all the hair on the suspect's head for signs on the scalp, since shaving other areas of the body that are normally covered by clothing was considered an indelicate activity (p. 230). If there were signs in the private areas of the body, they would have to be discovered through confession. Sensitive inquisitors therefore made other attempts to induce the suspect to confess. The authors of the *Malleus maleficarum* report that German inquisitors relied on a physiological test which included asking the suspect to drink three times on an empty stomach from a cup containing holy water and a piece of blessed wax. This was believed to be a potent drug against taciturnity. Breaking the silence under the influence of this drink was understood as a sign of potential innocence, since the suspect could either proclaim her innocence or confess her guilt, whereas persisting silence was a definite sign of guilt.

Physical signs of diabolical presence, however, need not be hidden. Virtually any anatomical feature perceived as anomalous with respect to community standards of normality could be interpreted as the sign of a malevolent nature. In the anonymous tractate compiled from the notes of many inquisitors, and published after the notorious trial at Arras, the *Recollectio casus, status et condicionis Valdensium ydolatrarum* (1460), it is reported that the signs exhibited by the body include such evidence of demonic presence as large fiery eyes and a terrifying gaze, a hoarse unclear voice and infrequency of speech, soft flesh and frigid skin, or, respectively, visual, vocal and haptic signs of deviation from the prevailing norm. Charges of demonic witchcraft based on the separate senses have considerable weight, but it is when they are considered in contemporaneous (or near contemporaneous) perception that their impact on the investigation is decisive, because multisensory semiosis can enable the judge to use the signs perceived through two senses to confirm the value of those perceived through the third. 'Therefore', according to the author of the tractate, 'accusations based on sight are reliable, and those based on hearing and sight are even more so, and those based on touch, especially in carnal embraces, including sight and sound, are the most certain and the most forceful, and have the greatest weight'.[12]

Inquisitors must thus learn to read the bodies and behaviour of the accused as assemblages of signs encoding ideas and messages from the devil. They required systematic scrutiny and careful interpretation. Physical features and peculiarities of behaviour are signs that must be approached with the suspicion that the code of which they are a function may have a concealed ironic structure. The accused are always presumed to be under the influence of the devil and hence to express themselves, physically as well as verbally, in an equally duplicitous manner, *signis . . . mendacibus* or by means of lying signs, as St Paul teaches (2 Thess. 2.9) concerning demonic signs. On the surface, the signifier appears to indicate a particular referent, but in reality it may actually signify something altogether different and quite possibly the opposite of what it signifies in appearance. The interrogation process conducted by an inquisitor is largely a dialectic between two different hermeneutical codes: one manifest to all and used by the accused to proclaim her innocence; the other concealed but discernible to the inquisitor to demonstrate her guilt. Here we use the feminine gender advisedly, since virtually every page of the *Malleus maleficarum* oozes contempt for women and fear of their sexuality. Drawing on the powerful misogyny of Ecclesiasticus 25 and on the lamentable teaching of the theological tradition, the authors present women as little more than an incarnations of wickedness and insatiable lust, easily subdued by the devil, whom many of them invoke and are glad to serve.

Said in semiotic terms, the visual appeal of alluring demonic women may signify innocent beauty in one code but moral and spiritual ugliness in the other, which the authors take as the real code. Similarly the sensual delight of their touch, the sweetness of their voice and the charm of the gait and posture may all be signifiers of deception and erotic entrapment. For inquisitors like Kramer and Sprenger, women have a feeble intellect but an inordinate lust, leading them to express themselves in a manner that can bring others to perdition. Just as Eve caused the fall of Adam and, by implication, that of mankind, so contemporary women, who are well disposed to evil acts, may be deliberately drawing others into their circle of wickedness, tempting them with the signs of erotic fulfilment considered typical of their gender.

Because they are more carnal then men, women can offer little resistance to the devil, who approaches them through their sensuality and takes advantage of their weak intellects to persuade them to renounce their faith. In the demonological tradition, coupling up with the devil was either an intellectual activity of learned scholars, such as Doctor Faustus, or a sexual activity of women, mostly unlettered and universally trained to be passive, a feature that made them easily dominated by demons.[13] The authors of the *Malleus maleficarum* argue that the proclivity of women towards abjuration is reflected even in the Latin word for the female sex, namely *femina*, which according to the folk etymology that they cite means *fe minus*, that is, faith diminished. Abjuration is ultimately what the devil wants of them, so that they may renounce God as they renounced Satan in their baptism. Reversing the baptismal repudiation of the devil would be undoing the first sacrament of salvation, casting out God and replacing him with Satan. It is an ideal of attainment for the devil, who subordinates all of his other ambitions to it. Though charges of formal apostasy were rarely brought against witches and wizards, the charge of witchcraft clearly included apostasy,[14] in some form or other and to some degree, since to become a witch the subject had to renounce the Christian faith and profess loyalty to the devil. Witches renounce God and enter into a covenant with the devil and serve him as his lovers, disciples and allies. Thus they collaborate with him in his effort to re-establish the spiritual conditions of the fall, which brought sin into the world.

Inquisitors were asked to believe that, in that role, witches aid the devil by stirring up images found in men's phantasy, where they lie in storage as visual residues of sense impressions. The devil can influence what goes on in a person's phantasy also by affecting his or her perception of external reality. That is how he can reach into a wife's imagination and 'darken her understanding' (p. 55). Once images become the focus of consciousness, they grow in significance and in men may generate inordinate passions for strange women, thereby preventing the consummation of new marriages and breaking up the bond of love in established ones. Working for the devil, witches can cause wives to become sterile and husbands to become impotent, effectively undoing the sacrament of matrimony (p. 48). The joint operations of witches and devils in the project to overturn the faith includes the attempted nullification of two sacraments: the sacrament of baptism, by which the pact undertaken by Eve with the serpent of Eden is nullified, making redemption possible, and the sacrament that legitimates the sexual act and exculpates concupiscence by giving it the sacred objective of procreation. There was a real fear that the theology of the sacrament of marriage was being undermined by the experience of couples who, for unknown natural causes, could not have any children, which would indicate that the purpose of marriage had been wrongly framed by theologians. But the *Malleus maleficarum* makes the argument that such undermining was not due to natural causes but to the work of witches acting as demonic agents. Baptism and matrimony are related in that, in the interpretation of the *Malleus maleficarum*, sin first entered the world of humanity through a forbidden sexual act. These two sacraments are, respectively, the sign of faith and incorporation into a community of believers and the sign of a covenant between husband and wife to act jointly for the continuation of the same community, namely the church. By threatening them, witches imperil sacramental theology and undermine the foundations of the church.

The gravity of these two offences against the faith could be compounded by any of various actions commonly attributed to witches, including various acts of desecration and violence, as illustrated authoritatively with examples by Innocent VIII in *Summis desiderantes affectibus*. At a deep structural level, these acts are related to the renouncement of faith and the pursuit of inordinate passions. The visible consequences of many acts of demonic witchcraft amount to natural phenomena or unexplainable biological accidents, such as natural abortions, premature death, the blighting of animals and humans and destructive weather. In accusations of witchcraft, these phenomena were regarded as signs of demonic intent on the part of the accused. The presumed manner of signification is a form of reverse causality in which the effect is regarded as a signifier of the cause. The order of the semiotic analysis retraces backwards the order in which the phenomena occurred, starting as it does with the consequences and arguing back to the identification of their causes. It is analogous to the medical analysis of symptoms, regarded as visible signs of the frequently invisible causes that precede them. There is an important difference, however, for, in crimes of witchcraft, the symptoms of disease in a sick patient are considered signs of a cause that resides in another person in the form of an evil intent. The link between cause and effect might be a verbal utterance, a gesture, an effigy, an animal, particularly a serpent, or a material object, physical contact, an unexpected appearance, a suspicious glance and the like, all part of a witch's arsenal of weapons and of the inquisitor's repertoire of interpretative signs

In this repertoire, no sign of a witch's supposed allegiance with the devil is more eloquent than a serpent. The term occurs several times in the *Malleus maleficarum* with echoes of the enmity between the serpent and mankind resulting from the temptation in Eden. To illustrate the enmity, the authors of the *Malleus maleficarum* relate the story of how a mage and a serpent killed each other. Standing on the edge of a pit in a public place, a man started to summon all the snakes within a mile and to charm them with his incantations, leading them all to their death in the pit. But a huge serpent came as far as the edge of the pit on the other side of the man and refused to descend, communicating its refusal by means of various signs. Since the man did not consent to free him from the power of his charm, the serpent leapt across the pit onto him, coiled itself around his body and dragged him into the pit, where they both died. From this dramatic story, say the authors of the *Malleus maleficarum*, we learn that incantations of this nature, reminiscent of rituals of exorcism, are not generally allowed, being permitted only when there is a useful goal to reach, such as freeing a house from the threat of a serpent, or preventing a serpent from being used by a witch in her spells (p. 181). In such cases it would only be right to destroy the serpent, because that would be tantamount to destroying a sign of demonic witchcraft. Snakes, in fact, are among the animals that served witches as their familiars, small demonic creatures that helped the witch attain her goal, because of their association with the ancestral temptation of the first woman in Eden. 'The power of witches', we read in the *Malleus maleficarum*, 'is more apparent in serpents . . . than in other animals, because through the means of a serpent the devil tempted woman' (p. 48).

In their diabolical work, witches may be said to operate under the sign of the serpent, or as metaphorical serpents themselves, though they make use of real serpents and even of the head of a dead serpent in their evil operations. Thus we learn that witches hide the skin or the head of a serpent under the threshold of the home or bedroom of a couple whose spousal harmony they wish to destroy. The head and the skin were signs that cause what they signify, namely diabolical discord. They are among a witch's weapons of aggression, instruments of evil with which she may bewitch a husband, driving him to hate his wife and pursue inordinate passions for other women, thereby undermining the institution that is the fountainhead of society. It is only to be expected that the serpent could be used by a witch to cast spells of disharmony and lust, since it was 'the first instrument of the devil, and by reason of its curse inherits a hatred of women' (p. 172). The curse refers to the hostility that God put between the serpent and the offspring of the woman (Gen. 3.15). Witches are also among the offspring of Eve, but because they have already surrendered their body and soul to the devil, working as his instruments, they make use of the serpent as a material sign that has the ability to bring into effect what it signifies, operating like a negative sacrament. Competent inquisitors know that when a witch is arrested in connection with a crime of adultery, they need to search the house very carefully to ascertain whether there are any material traces of a serpent, as a sign of her covenant with the devil, as evidence of her intent to undermine spousal love and as proof of the route by which her evil design reached its victim.

Once they are discovered, such malefic signs can be destroyed, thereby neutralizing their evil effect. One must not fall prey to the temptation of calling on another witch or on the devil himself for aid in neutralizing evil, for that would simply compound the problem. Cajetan calls such a restorative action a *dissolutio signi*, or the dissolvement of a sign, and says that it is perfectly legitimate:

> Quoniam hic nulla euenit daemonum inuocatio, sed sola dissolutio signi, quo durante, Diabolus statuerat malum conseruare alterius.[15]
>
> (Because here no invocation of devils takes place, but only a dissolvement of the sign with which, while it existed, the devil had ensured that evil would be preserved in the other.)

This usage of the term is common to indicate a seal of a pact with the devil and a sensible channel through which his power enters the human subject, through whom it can operate through the collaboration of both. If the sign is destroyed, the covenant is broken, the conduit is dissolved away and the restoration of the victim's innocence begins. Such signs both communicate the idea of joint commitment to acts of evil and make those acts possible. In a way, they are a perversion of sacramental signs, which are both communicative and efficacious. Like sacramental signs, they are indexical, appearing as a *vestigium* of the devil rather than God. There is no surprise in this mimicking of sacramental signs, since the fundamental characteristic of the devil is that he wants to be worshipped like God. Unlike the sacraments, however, the devil's signs are reversible and can be undone.

The discernment of the intent and the identification of the trajectory by which it was brought to bear on the victim constitute a narrative of how and by whom the crime was committed. In all cases, once the charge has been laid, the inquisitor has the task of demonstrating the truthfulness of the narrative. The procedure involves two types of analysis. By treating the observed occurrences as effects of causes to be identified, the inquisitor reconstructs the story by means of a cognitive process that moves backwards in time, composing retrospectively the full sequence of events that culminated in the crime, telling the story of how the crime was committed. However, the inquisitor conducts a semiotic analysis of the same material by viewing the same traces of evidence as signs of referents in the past, reconstructing the sign-referent chain until he reaches the referent that set everything in motion. In this sense the inquisitor's work is analogous to that of a detective who reconstructs the crime by treating all traces of evidence as signs. In such cases, as Marcel Danesi has argued, no ontological difference can be discerned between the detective's reconstruction of the crime and his semiotic analysis of the evidence, as we can see, for example, in Umberto Eco's *The Name of the Rose*.[16] Danesi's theory of forensic semiotics constitutes an excellent set of working premises for a rigorous consideration of the inquisitor's activity, since crime detection and witchcraft inquisition both need to generate a logical narrative of the crime before the accused can be brought to justice, and both do so by analysing traces of evidence as signs through which the accused unintentionally communicates his or her culpability. But the criminal nature of witchcraft, the semiotic aspects of the evidence and the methods available to the inquisitor for the reconstruction of the causal chain and the chronology of the deed itself – these are all profoundly different from those that the modern detective has to contend with and require special consideration.

The proof that the suspect committed a crime, and can hence be tried for that particular crime, is the normal goal of the detective. The inquisitor is also interested in the crime, though primarily because it is a point of access to the identity of the suspect as a witch. The detective, says Danesi, is a semiotician, 'someone who reads signs and then reasons backwards to figure out what they mean', employing a process of provisional guessing known in semiotics as abduction.[17] The inquisitor is also a semiotician in that he makes use of graphic signs on the body (blemishes and warts), gestural signs (spitting at the Host, stepping on a cross, peculiar glancing), verbal signs (blasphemy) material signs (snake's head, bones) and so on. With the aid of witnesses, he collects signs of criminal engagement and interprets them in an interrogation process. The interrogation normally begins with the presumption that the signs have been deciphered and that the arrested person is guilty, and it proceeds with a series of questions designed to extort a confession, or the suspect's confirmation that the inquisitor's suspicion was correct. Since the suspect's interrogation was largely conducted under torture, the confession was only a first-person narration of the reported facts in a way that made them conform to the inquisitor's preconceived plot. Among the highlights of that plot, a highly significant one was the witch's confession that, in joining the dark fellowship of the devil and other witches, she explicitly rejected the sacraments and the Anomalous Woman, the name by which witches and devils designate the Blessed Virgin Mary (p. 99), signifying her rejection of redemption.

Upon interrogation various women confirmed that they were lured to the devil's fellowship by one of three methods. Some women, mostly respectful matrons, having suffered 'grievous losses in their temporal possessions' (p. 96) as a result of misfortunes caused by the devil and other witches, found the promise of satisfaction and vindication in witchcraft too appealing to resist. A second group consists of young girls who, being 'more given to bodily lusts and pleasures', were seduced through erotic temptations, when the devil appeared to them as an attractive incubus with great promises of erotic delight. A third group includes women tempted 'through the way of sadness and poverty' (p. 97). These are women who, having been repudiated by lovers who had promised to marry them, are scorned by the community as wicked women and have nowhere to turn to other than witchcraft. In all cases, the underlying cause is great suffering and despair of finding help anywhere else. It is truly remarkable that the authors of the *Malleus maleficarum* recognize the social injustice that drove women to the fellowship of other witches without seeing any injustice in the charge of witchcraft and in the interrogation process through which the confession of guilt was extorted.

A basic principle of witchcraft justice is that a witch cannot be condemned to death 'unless she is convicted by her own confession' (p. 223). The interrogation process, before, during and after torture, is designed to lead, step by step, to the production of such a confession. It is not difficult to see how, under those conditions, a confession was usually forthcoming. We are reminded of the statement by the eighteenth-century jurist Cesare Beccaria who, in his argument against judicial torture in *On Crimes and Punishments* (1764), observed that in such settings the truth is only a mathematical function of the physical strength and power of endurance of the accused:

> The effect of torture, therefore, is a matter of temperament and calculation that varies with each man according to his strength and sensibility, so that, with this method, a mathematician could more readily than a judge resolve this problem: given the muscular force and nervous sensibility of an innocent person, find the degree of pain that will make him confess himself guilty of a given crime.[18]

But if a confession is the final guarantee of truthfulness, then all the ways of getting one are legitimate. The contradiction inherent in the use of torture, which is a form of punishment inflicted before the determination of guilt by means of the very method employed to determine it, is an indication, as Foucault has shown for the secular courtroom, that guilt and innocence were then conceived as graduated concepts: 'The suspect, as such, always deserved a certain punishment; one could not be the object of suspicion and be completely innocent.'[19] The charge of witchcraft, based on indirect evidence and reports by witnesses, is already evidence of partial guilt, meriting the punishment of torture through which the judge extirpates evidence of a further degree of guilt. If definitive proof of total guilt cannot be obtained, the victim will have been punished for partial guilt. The signs that indicate guilt of witchcraft must be confirmed, one by one, by confession.

The suspect's resistance to pain and refusal to confess under torture was itself, paradoxically, regarded as a powerful sign of guilt, the sign of taciturnity. It was argued that only an inner demonic power could enable a witch to raise such an obstacle to the manifestation of the truth. Witches were enabled by the devil to withstand pain to a very high degree, and it took a discerning and ruthless inquisitor to recognize taciturnity as a sign of guilt, since it could also, at least in some cases, be interpreted as a sign of partial innocence, of resistance to self-incrimination because the charges were not warranted by the facts. When a confession could not be obtained and yet the suspicion of guilt was strong, the accused was subjected to a canonical purgation, a legal process in which the accused cleared her name of any crime by taking an oath of innocence in front of a select group of respected citizens, on the understanding that if she failed in her purgation, she would be given a sentence as if convicted of the crime. In some cases, when the suspicion warranted it, a secular judge might grant an accused the possibility of a common purgation, in which she could clear her reputation by carrying red hot irons for a certain distance, although ecclesiastical judges generally frowned on such methods suspecting that the devil could somehow protect the witch from the pain. In such cases, resistance to pain could be easily interpreted as a sign of innocence, with protection from God, or as a sign of guilt, with protection from the devil.

In most cases, however, the court had at least one way of corroborating the charge that a suspect's denial of collaboration through taciturnity was a criminal sign of witchcraft, and that was the shedding of tears under torture. Tears were regarded as a sign of potential innocence, whereas the inability to weep was considered 'a most certain sign' (p. 227) of diabolical infection. A guilty subject may assume a tearful countenance and may even try to put drops of saliva on her cheeks in order to give the impression that she is crying, but a discerning judge would be able to see immediately through such tricks, and to add false weeping to the list of signs pointing him to the suspect's guilt. Because 'the grace of tears is one of the chief gifts allowed to the penitent' (p. 227), witches are not allowed by the devil to cry any such tears. The judge could obtain satisfactory evidence of guilt or innocence by placing his hand on the head of the accused and ordering her to start weeping, as he, in the name of the Holy Trinity, invoked the burning tears shed by the Virgin Mary and all the saints over the wounds of Jesus. If the grace of tears was not granted to her, and it was never granted to a witch, she would be unable to cry, and the absence of tears would be considered a sign of guilt. In medieval and Renaissance culture, tears had acquired a central position in the discourse on piety as signs of empathy and of such feelings of kindness as always spring from a compassionate disposition. Witches had surrendered that ability when they rejected Christ and willingly turned themselves over to the devil. At that point, the dryness of their eyes became the final sign of a guilt that merited death by burning.

Not everyone endorsed the witchcraft semiotic developed in the elaborated theory, though they shared some common ground. Among those who agreed fully with it and helped spread it to the area of literary criticism is Giovan Battista Gelli, a literary scholar with enough interest in witchcraft and commitment to its extermination to assist at many trials. He applauded the authors of the *Malleus maleficarum*, and stressed the fact that, in the mid-sixteenth century when he was writing, demonic witchcraft was already over 100 years old, having first flourished in the pontificate of Innocent VIII. Gelli makes this observation in his commentary on the same passage of *Inferno* 20 annotated by Guinoforto delli Bargigi with a reference to witch-burning in the Dauphinate. In his judgement, classical mythology and literature are full of nefarious events and metamorphoses that cannot be explained other than as actions of the devil, controlling the minds of men and women and enabling the use malefic magic. This was an easy task for the devil to accomplish, because pagans 'were not armed with the sacraments' ('non erono armati de' sacramenti'). In order to achieve comparable results in the modern period, the devil must persuade his new recruits – and he begins with 'foolish little men and women' ('omiciatti e donnicciuole deboli'), though he too believes that women, on account of their lustful nature, yield readily their body and soul to the devil[20] – to repudiate the Christian faith and defile the sacraments. Specifically, the devil requires them to take part in a ritual of denial that includes denying the faith, uttering blasphemies during the Elevation, walking over a cross, stealing a Host, baptismal water, chrism, sacred oil, trampling them and discarding them in a latrine. Having defiled the sacramental signs the witches are asked to kill unbaptized babies and use the fat of their bodies to make an ointment, which they should apply to their private parts. After such a ceremony, the new witches become ministers of the devil, and he organizes them into a satanic church, an assembly of witches loyal to the devil, ready to work together, teaching novices their malefic arts and helping each other accomplish evil deeds. The reason for this organization is that, only by coming together into an anti-church could they truly abjure the Christian faith and disavow the benefits of all the sacraments that Christ had entrusted to His church for the redemption of mankind.

Among those who did not agree was Cajetan. In this cacophony of witchcraft talk among the Dominicans, his was the voice of reason. In his commentary on the *Summa Theologica*, Cajetan relates the stories of women who confessed that, after smearing themselves all over with a diabolical flying lotion, they were transported every Thursday night to feasts in honour of Diana, worshipped by Italian Renaissance witches as their leader from the underworld. He also provides examples of others who claimed they flew naked to various places of diabolical pleasure. Cajetan is careful, however, to say that these are not truthful accounts of what actually happened, though the women themselves believed them to be true. For Cajetan, such activities were no more than fantasies, workings of the imagination (*sunt enim haec in imaginatione*), which they believed to have occurred in external reality. Cajetan is certain that the vast majority of stories about what witches do are totally imaginary, though he concedes that such scepticism cannot be extended to all cases, for demonic influence of the kind related by witches can and does take place:

> Per haec tamen non negamus quin Diabolus, Deo permittende, quandoque aliquam voluntariam etiam corporaliter ducat de loco ad locum. Sed hoc rarissime videtur accidere.[21]
>
> (Nevertheless, by this we do not deny that the Devil, if God allows it, at times can bodily transport a willing person from place to place. This, however, appears to take place very rarely.)

It happens very rarely, but it does happen. Loyal as he was to the intellectual tradition of his order, Cajetan believed in the ability of the devil to bewitch people, turning them into agents of evil and enabling them to perform acts that violate the laws of nature and reason. Given the stance of his order on demonology and witchcraft investigations, his concession that acts of demonic magic do take place is neither surprising nor interesting: if the three necessary factors are all present – a willing person, the devil and God's permission – witchcraft is indeed possible, though it is rare.

More significant seems his discussion of the fact that, in the majority of cases, demonic actions take place in the imagination and have no material correlative in external reality. As in the temptation of Eve in the Garden of Eden, the devil instils a suggestion in the mind of a woman predisposed to his influence and then lets it do its work, inwardly transforming her while he situates himself in her mind. This part of his discussion, which seems to soften his stance on demonic power over witches, in reality strengthens his view that there is predisposition to evil within the individual. Just as in the fall it was an inner metamorphosis that caused Eve to surrender to the fascination of sinful suggestions, so here, we can argue, a succession of activities immanent to the imagination causes the women to yield their minds to the power of darkness.

The psychology of Dominican Scholasticism distinguished four inner faculties of perception: reason, memory, imagination and common sense, all related to the external senses, through which they receive impressions and information.[22] In malevolent magic, the devil uses the external senses to influence the imagination and cloud the understanding, leading his subjects to yield to his power and begin performing acts of iniquity on his behalf. The suffering inflicted by witches on innocent victims naturally caused some to look for corrective measures that could undo demonic magic and prevent further suffering. In his short treatise *De Maleficiis*, Cajetan considers demonic magic in various contexts, including situations in which a worker of such magic may be naively summoned to undo the effects of an act of demonic iniquity. The question for Cajetan is whether two wrongs can make a right, and the answer is that an act of evil cannot be corrected by another act performed with evil intent and demonic help, and it would be a grave sin to attempt it, for both the performer and the one seeking his assistance. In carrying out such a restorative act, the helper must not let the devil gain control of his will. He must practise his art without the assistance of demons and with a genuine intent to help. Such a restorative use of magic is an act of charity towards the individual who has been stricken by the effects of evil, a form of exorcism which liberates a victim from unjust suffering.

But in the witchcraft madness that seized Europe in the Renaissance, others were much less sceptical than Cajetan concerning the pervasiveness of demonic evil in society and much more sceptical concerning the value of corrective magic. For them the gravity of the situation warranted the development of a code of signs and a body of knowledge that could enable officials with experience in the ways of evil to read a person's appearance, speech and behaviour as a text with a secret layer of meaning, a deep structure of strategies of wickedness governed by the devil. To uncover this layer of meaning, the experts paid meticulous attention to the juridical value of signs, including signs of evidence that warrant indictment, signs of veracity and deception under interrogation and torture and signs of demonstrated guilt legitimizing punishment. Such experts in procedures against the forces of evil were recruited chiefly among the Dominican professoriate, whose most fanatical members led the attack on witches with the backing of doctrine and the rigour of the law since the nefarious Bull of Innocent VIII. In combination with a misogynistic theology of gender, authenticated by the visualization of the serpent of Eden as a woman, their learning justified the prosecution of countless women as aberrant members of society engaged in perpetrating evil in the Christian community. Ultimately it gave the appearance of rationality to wild accusations of evil and the monstrous investigative procedures that they entailed.

5

The fall from harmony

In the *City of God* Augustine superimposes the image of the enclosed garden of the Canticle of Canticles (*hortus conclusus*), generally interpreted as the church, onto the Garden of Eden and thus interprets the earthly paradise as a figure for the church. In doing so, Augustine establishes a relationship in which the major constituents of the church are mapped onto the earthly paradise, suggesting that the four gospels are represented by the four rivers of Eden, the saints by the trees, their good works by the fruit, Christ by the tree of life and the free will (by which we freely choose the ways of God) by the tree of knowledge of good and evil.[1] The Garden of Eden thus becomes a semiotic domain that represents the church in its entirety, in so far as it is both the community of the elect in heaven and the community of believers on earth. This interpretation of the earthly paradise, which Augustine believes is not likely to offend anybody, can generate a multitude of other correspondences in which the idea of a part, an aspect or an activity of the church is associated with a part or an aspect of the garden as a referent is with its sign.

In the ecclesial and musical imagination of the faithful, a significant development was the enrichment of the picture, on both sides of the relationship, with a chapel for the purpose of performing sacred music. The development illustrates an interesting fact of semiotics, which is that signs are used not only to signify and communicate existing ideas but also to produce new ones. If the Garden of Eden is interpreted as an allegorical sign for such a chapel, the semiotic picture lends itself to interesting ramifications, one of which is that the figure of God in the earthly paradise may be represented by the signs of a Maestro di Cappella, overseeing the music in paradise the way his modern human counterpart would oversee it in a chapel on earth. Their goal and their instructions to the musicians are analogous, though they have an allegorical meaning with respect to God and a literal one with respect to a human Maestro di Cappella: make only good music that celebrates the ideal of innocence, sing to the beat and re-establish harmony when it is lost. The purpose of this chapter is to explore some aspects of both sides of the analogy, focusing first on the presentation of the fall as a fall from harmony in the universe and in the chapel of Eden, and then on the use of music as an aid to celebration and conversion in the chapels of Rome, the heart of the Catholic Church. In both cases we shall explore how the Christian imagination makes use of the destabilizing function of signs of alien origin in the semiotic domain of the musical and theological code, whose logical harmony they undermine by generating parodic inversions of meaning.

The chapel of Eden

There is a story from baroque culture in which theology, justice and music coexist immanently in each other, by virtue of their shared dependence on the idea of harmony, understood at its primordial level of conception, before the term acquired specific meanings in the different areas of human activity with which it came to be associated. It was common among theologians, preachers and composers of the baroque period, and it is constructed as two intertwined narratives, the story of the fall and the story of a divine composer whose beautiful music was disharmonized into a cacophony by its performers. The two narratives function as hermeneutical allegories of each other, like mirrors positioned to reciprocate reflections, in accordance with a distinctly baroque taste for such examples of cleverness.

The most complex and baroque version of the musical story of the fall from harmony was told by Antonio Glielmo, a theologian and priest of the Oratorians in Naples, a congregation especially devoted to the popularization of sacred music.[2] He tells his story in the second person, addressing God directly, as in a prayer, reviewing for him (and for the reader) the relationship between music and the fall. Starting with the eight tonalities (*tuoni*) that were used by contemporary composers to set the psalms for liturgical and paraliturgical performance, Glielmo gives us an overview of God's work as a composer.[3] God used the first tonality to write a motet for two voices on the theme of original innocence and justice, a simple song (*sí facile*) to be performed by Adam and Eve. He used the next six tonalities in as many compositions celebrating the six ages of the world, each reflecting one of the six days of Creation, in accordance with St Augustine's periodization of universal history.[4] And he reserved the last tonality for a large choral work with full instrumental accompaniment to be performed in heaven by the angels and the saints, singing music that can never sink down to disharmony or generate tedium ('soggiacere a discordia o generar tedio', p. 681). As a performer in his own compositions, when he is perceived as the Father, God sings with a soprano voice, raising the quality of that sound, as the etymology of the term 'soprano' implies, to a place high above that of the human rabblement and known only to the angels. As the Holy Spirit he is a tenor, for he always holds a steady course in the dispensation of grace, but as the Son he has bass singing voice, descending to the level of the flesh that he shares even with prisoners on death row.[5]

Before the onset of human history, when there were no saints in heaven, the grand celestial work was performed by angels, who were endowed with an alto voice, and by God, who sang the soprano part. The choir included the figure of Lucifer, who was so proud of his ability that he presumed to sing the part of the soprano, asserting that he had the voice for it. But as he started to sing, he introduced such disharmony that God expelled him from the heavenly choir and cast him into hell, understood musically as a domain of meaningless noise, from which he comes out to inject dissonance into the music of mankind, both literally and metaphorically.

Glielmo obviously regarded music as a code that could effectively express the narrative of creation in its entirety and complexity. He has rewritten sacred history up to the fall, like a running commentary on the implications of the Bible for the theory of music. The key to it is the interpretation of the fall of Lucifer as a fall from harmony. In a context in which all explanations and all answers to difficult questions can be given in narrative form, the musical commentary by Glielmo may be regarded as a story with the function of an argument for a theology of harmony and disharmony. The starting premise in both the biblical narrative and the musical commentary is that God is harmony, which is the musical equivalent of beauty, whereas disharmony, which is the musical equivalent of ugliness, is the result of disregard for the logic of musical beauty. Such indifference may be understood in two ways. It occurs in the first way when the attempt is made by the wrong voice to sing a part written for a higher pitch, which is what Lucifer did, presuming to be able to sing like God but ending up as a parody of God – that is, of harmony – in the process. It occurs in the second way when the interference involves the intrusion of an element from a foreign code – Lucifer's code for the deliberate production of cacophonous sounds.

The production of cacophony by intrusion is what we witness in the part of Glielmo's story that takes place in the Garden of Eden. As soon as Adam and Eve started to sing God's song of innocence and justice in the appropriate tonality, a third musician, Lucifer, moved by envy, entered the chapel of Eden and immediately started to chant a song of hell, uniting the melodious sound of their motet with the harsh and toneless sound of his own voice, as he sang the words *eritis sicut dei* (you shall be as gods). In this manner, he seized control of their melodiousness, using sin to throw their concert into such dissonance (*col peccato gli sconcertò*, p. 681) that they were not able to regain the harmony of their lost state of innocence. Wherefore God, angered by the musical coarseness to which his performers had yielded, tore to shreds the score of this, his first and most beautiful composition, and cast the musicians out of his chapel of paradise, so that in their peregrinations they might henceforth sing lugubrious songs of penance and funereal chants of death. Wherefore God, like a good Maestro di Cappella, let them know that they had wondered from the music on the score and tried to bring them back into the tune.[6]

Whereas in the narrative of the fall, by asking the question *ubi es?* God tells Adam to come out from his hiding place, in the musical narrative, says Glielmo, by the same question God asks Adam and Eve to return to the notes of his composition from wherever they have wandered with their voices. In this rewriting of the account of the fall, there is no question of gender, no innate concupiscence and no yielding to erotic temptation. There is only the intrusion of a malevolent musician, who comes into the chapel from somewhere beyond the earthly paradise to disrupt their singing. By allowing their voices to be joined to his, Adam and Eve went off tune, wandering into a domain of the acoustic imagination were the only sound possible consists of disharmony and noise. God sternly calls them back, yelling (*gridando*) at them to sing the notes that he had written for them in his score. Adam and Eve turned red with shame, recognizing that the music which they were no longer able to sing was actually quite simple, a very easy motet. God was angered by the way in which they had collaborated with Lucifer in the corruption of his music, undermining the harmony that he had created.[7] He therefore tore up the score and expelled them from the chapel in the earthly paradise, so that they might sing elsewhere their dark new songs of penance and death, until – the story leads us to conclude – with His grace, His teaching and their own efforts, they learn to appreciate again the just and the sacred, discovering in the process that they could sing heavenly songs of both.[8]

Glielmo's account of the birth of cacophony includes a narrative of the fall of Lucifer, rewritten as a fall from cosmic harmony, and of the fall of Adam and Eve, rewritten as a fall from harmony in the performance of a work in the genre of sacred music, the motet, well known to contemporary readers. His allegorical rewriting of two key episodes in the Bible explains why noise exists in the first place and illustrates how the relationship between beauty and ugliness in music can be analysed in terms of theology. In such an exercise, the events in the biblical narrative constitute a series of signs that send the music-minded reader to the theory and practice of music, in order to see its foundational ideas associated with the Bible. The net results of Glielmo's effort are the divine origin of harmony, as one of the attributes of creation, and the analogy between sin and noise: what sin is to innocence, noise is to harmony. The theoretical presumption behind this analogy is the principle that it is possible to consider the ideas of God and creation from an aesthetic point of view, looking at him principally under his aspect of beauty, understood as an aspect of divine perfection.

Having thus reviewed the music of the fall, Glielmo turns to other areas of theology and considers another form of imaginary music, written for and embodied by the Blessed Virgin Mary. Among your musical compositions, Glielmo tells the Lord, Mary is by far the most artistic and beautiful (la piú artificiosa & bella).

Glielmo expresses his praise of Mary by citing the words that God said to Ezekiel about his voice, adapting them, however, to read *Ipsa est quasi carmen musicum, quod suavi dulcique sono canitur* (she is like a beautiful song sung with a sweet and delightful voice), rather than *et es eis* (and thou (prophet) art for them). His admiration is such that he waxes baroque with enthusiasm. As a musical score, Mary is a harmonic symphony, written on a staff of virtues, in the key of grace, with white notes of joy and black ones of sorrow, with the lower pitches of her sweetness and the higher ones of her endurance at the foot of the cross, with transitions of vocal register that were her journeys to Bethlehem and Egypt and so on. Who sings this 'song' that is Mary and how is it performed? The Almighty Father sings the soprano part, the Holy Ghost sings tenor, the Son sings bass, the choir of all mankind sings contralto and all are accompanied by an orchestra with a multitude of instruments, including psalters played by the patriarchs, flutes by the prophets, trumpets by the apostles, timpani by the martyrs, lyres by virgins, organs by doctors of the church and harpsichords by the clergy, both secular and monastic, including, we can add to the list, Father Antonio Glielmo of the Oratorians of Naples.

The glorious opulence of Glielmo's vision of Mary as a musical score, whose imaginary performance is comparable in many ways to the triumphs of saints depicted in flight to heaven on the ceilings of contemporary baroque churches, includes, at least by implication, the entire history of salvation, the church triumphant in heaven and its ministers on earth. The vision is majestic and the luxuriance can be tiresome, but we must not let the heavy baroque style of

Glielmo's vision conceal from us the fact that his transformation of Mary into a musical opus consisting of a score in performance involves a sophisticated semiotic operation. That Mary is such an opus means that all pictorial images and visualizations of her are for Glielmo signifiers of a musical score. In the imaginary domain of its performance, Glielmo invokes the Trinity, the history of Christianity, the church triumphant, the saints, the martyrs and the clergy, all as signs that, in addition to signifying what they normally represent when they stand alone, signify the musical corpus of Mary as a score when they are combined in accordance with the logic of the theology of salvation.

The elements of Christian spirituality, it seems, normally considered signifieds – saints and virtues represented by words or images – are here considered signifiers, each with a double semantic edge: individually they refer the reader to their original referents, like words in a dictionary, while together they form the complex assemblage of signs that symbolizes the musical score of Mary in performance. This occurs because the events of sacred history have been flattened into synchronicity, joined to ideas and virtues of moral theology, and transformed into verbal discourse. The signs of Christian spirituality are now all part of the same code, whether they were originally characters of sacred history or moral virtues, and they become available on an equal footing for other groupings. As such, they are floating signifiers, which can be separated from their meanings to be used as elements of another message, in a discourse for the glorification of Mary as music.

The Roman oratorio

When we move from the imaginary settings and harmony of paradise to real chapels and music on earth, the edifying power of performances and the proclamation of theological principles must be understood differently, to account, among other things, for the political and ideological dissension that distinguished the Catholic Church from other Christian denominations. In considering the issues involved in the formative use of music by the church, we focus on the church's approach to the genres of vocal music, especially the oratorio, which was invented for that very purpose. If there is no salvation outside the church, then everything that the church does to strengthen its position and to proclaim its message contributes to the history of salvation. In the last decades of the seventeenth and the early ones of the eighteenth centuries, the oratorio played a highly significant role in the church's pedagogy of salvation, as it consistently provided the faithful with messages of conversion, reminding them, through the exemplary lives of the martyrs and through carefully selected passages from Scripture, that their salvation depended not only on the grace of God but also on their own efforts to overcome their fallen state under the tutelage of the church. Our consideration of the oratorio libretto will take us to the end of the historical period covered in this study, namely the first decade of the eighteenth century at the height of the Jansenist controversy. Clement XI issued a bull in 1705, *Vineam Domini*, in which he rejected the Jansenist view that the operation of divine grace and predestination were totally independent of the human will, ideas that had brought the Jansenists very close to Calvinism. And he vigorously reaffirmed his condemnation of Jansenism in 1713, in the bull *Unigenitus*, issued under the influence of the Jesuits, fierce adversaries of Jansenism who had risen to great prominence in Rome. Moreover, in 1707 Clement XI declared the feast of the Immaculate conception of Mary a universal feast of obligation, very much to the chagrin of the Jansenists, who had adopted a strong anti-Marian stance in their theological anthropology.

Working in this climate, Arcangelo Spagna wrote the first poetics of the oratorio libretto as the genre in which dramatic poets could most usefully serve the church. This was a small treatise called *Discorso intorno a gl'oratori* (*Discourse on Oratorios*), which Spagna wrote as an old man, after his long career as a librettist and playwright in Rome. The *Discourse*, first issued in 1706, is a theory of the oratorio libretto that reflects a number of theological and dramaturgical ideas that enjoyed great currency in contemporary Roman culture. Spagna regards the oratorio as a dramatic form in which music and poetic language are designed to penetrate, with aesthetic delight – something that, at that time, was usually called *dolcezza* – and spiritual guidance in equal measure, deeply into the soul of the listener. Though a little later they could be performed in private and secular settings, at that time oratorios were still meant to be performed in oratories, the chapels attached to the main churches under the influence of St Phillip Neri, who had proposed their use as venues for edifying spiritual entertainment. There St Phillip had envisaged performances designed to strengthen with aesthetic delight the faith of the young, offering them as an alternative to profane forms of entertainment:

> Li introdusse quel sapientissimo Padre, per allettare e trattenere con profitto spirituale i fedeli in quelle hore della notte che ne' tempi dell'autunno e del verno sogliono essere piú pericolose delle altre, e massime alla gioventú.[9]
>
> (That wisest of fathers introduced the practice of these exercises in order to attract and entertain with spiritual profit the faithful in those hours of the

evening which in the fall and in the winter are usually more dangerous than others, especially to our youth.)

From the perspective of the church, especially in Rome, no spiritual entertainment could be considered edifying if it did not interpret Christian spirituality from a strictly Catholic and Vatican-centred perspective. The formative power of culture depends very much on the material signs by means of which it is articulated, signs that permeate the people's consciousness and condition their thinking as well as their behaviour. Such gatherings as those envisaged by St Phillip were a golden opportunity for the church to promote the development of a repertoire of vocal music that could be employed to tell the narratives of the faith and to impart the principles of doctrine outside religious services, in a non-liturgical context. The oratories were places of fellowship and reflection in which visitors could immerse themselves in a domain of sacred signs with clear referents in the Catechism of their upbringing. Vocal music is the sonic analogy of paintings on the same sacred themes. Its development was actively promoted by the church for many reasons, not the least of which was the fact that it invited transformative reflection – on the self and on the faith – in the aesthetic experience that it provided.

Working in such a context, Spagna places the oratorio squarely in the domain of dogmatic theology, as he says on the title page of his treatise, where he calls his work a *Discorso dogmatico sugli oratori*, a phrase meant to be seen by his readers before they came into contact with the text itself and to remind them of the appropriate parameters for its interpretation before they began to read it.[10] In Catholic countries, the field of theology was then divided into four disciplines: scholastic, polemical, moral and dogmatic. Dogmatic theology was concerned with the interpretation of Scripture and doctrinal decisions of the church, including pronouncements by popes, councils, the saints and the doctors of the church, all grouped together under the label of 'Tradition'. A sharp distinction here needs to be made between Catholicism and Protestantism: whereas in Catholicism the Bible and Tradition serve jointly as sources of doctrine, in Protestantism Tradition has no role to play in the articulation of the faith, which was based on 'sola scriptura', or on Scripture alone. As a work of dogmatic theology, the oratorio libretto becomes an aesthetic expression of the Magisterium of the Catholic Church, an instrument for the proclamation of its teaching and for the assertion of its leadership and authority.

Spagna dedicates his discourse to the current pope, Clement XI, a patron of music and poetry, and he derives his theory from the librettos, then unpublished, of another pope, the late Giulio Rospigliosi, or Pope Clement IX, who had himself been an active librettist before being elevated to the throne of St Peter in 1667. In the last decades of the seventeenth and the early ones of the eighteenth century, the patronage of music and poetry by the distinguished Cardinals Pietro Ottoboni, Benedetto Pamphili and Carlo Colonna was truly exceptional, but it did not suddenly appear like an oasis in a desert, nor was it as liberal in matters of dogma and authority as their love of the arts might lead some to assume. These men were indeed enlightened patrons of the arts, but they were also conservative representatives of the church, all appointed to their offices by popes who had themselves a special attachment to the arts, but who also had an agenda to promote. The odd disagreement notwithstanding, the agendas of cardinals and the pope included the advancement of the arts primarily as instruments for the social and cultural progress of Catholic theology, at a time when composers, performers, artists and men of letters came into easy contact with their counterparts in Protestant countries and with patrons less loyal to the doctrines of the Catholic Church.

By grounding the oratorio libretto in dogmatic theology, Spagna was openly placing the genre in the service of the Catholic Church and its performance under the patronage of its cardinals, but in doing so, he was merely making explicit that he fully endorsed what must have been the general practice in Rome. Nor could the situation have been otherwise. In Rome, writing the libretto or the music of an oratorio, or any other sacred work – or, for that matter, taking part in its performance – meant precisely serving Catholic dogmatic theology, endorsing the Catholic faith in opposition to that of other Christian churches, and contributing to its proclamation as understood by its popes, its college of cardinals and its bishops. In the early eighteenth century, the Catholic Church was occasionally challenged by a few of its own more liberal or more conservative members to amend some of its articles of faith – in its moral and scholastic theology usually, but in general not in its dogmatic theology, which to most Catholic intellectuals seemed to be beyond reproach. That is why, the liberal-minded Ludovico Antonio Muratori once observed, the church can continue to use with confidence its dogmatic theology to settle doctrinal disputes in councils or to bring back into the fold children who may have strayed from the faith.[11]

Whether oratorio composers and librettists adhered to this version of the Christian faith with sincere devotion or simply as a career strategy was another matter, and it was ultimately irrelevant. The two significant things to remember are, first, that in Rome the oratorio *always* advanced the cause of Catholic theology, and, second, that through its patronage of composers and librettists, the church *always* exercised its leadership and affirmed its authority, with both firmness and design, especially when it was most generous in its support of the arts. That generosity was at the same time an investment in the production of signs and symbols of the faith, which could signify the doctrine with their themes and cause its internalization by means of a carefully constructed aesthetic experience. When the verbal text of a cantata or an oratorio is taken directly from the Bible, its performance and reception – that is, the aesthetic experience that it generates and the spiritual impact that it has on those in attendance – are more a function of the skill of the performer and the setting of the performance than they are of the faith or the intention of the librettist and composer.

We can see how this works by analysing a performance of Handel's setting of Psalm 109, *Dixit Dominus*. It was composed by a distinguished Lutheran composer, but it was performed in Rome, under the patronage of Cardinal Colonna, just one year after the latter's elevation to the purple, for the faithful of Santa Maria in Montesano (April 1707). The performance text was a powerful celebration of some aspects of Catholic dogmatic theology that had fuelled much controversy during the Reformation and Counter-Reformation. For our purposes, there are three relevant ways of looking at *Dixit Dominus*: from the perspective of the composer–text relationship, from that of the text–audience relationship, and from that of the performance–context relationship. Clearly the last two perspectives, both didactic and aesthetic, rather than the first, which is concerned with the author's motivation and compositional practice, are of primary interest to the patron supporting the event. For the setting of the performance and the audience's predisposition towards it are central to the conception of the event itself, if it is to have cultural and spiritual significance for papal Rome.

Consider the second part of the fourth verse on the eternal priesthood in the order of Melchizedek, *Tu es sacerdos in aeternum secundum ordinem Melchisedech* (Thou art the eternal priest in the order of Melchizedek). In the tradition of the church, the name Melchizedek was a sign for the ordained priesthood and the Eucharist, on account of his description in Psalm 109 and his offering of bread and wine described in Genesis 14. This is how the name was interpreted in contemporary Catholic dogmatic theology. The Mass or the celebration of the Eucharist was itself understood not only as a commemorative celebration but also as an act of worship and as a propitiatory offering of crucial value in the economy of redemption. As a sacred and musical sign, Melchizedek would not carry this message if *Dixit Dominus* were performed in a Protestant celebration or in a secular setting, but there can be no question about its meaning when it was performed in the church of Santa Maria in Montesano in Rome.

In public performances, the meaning of signs is largely determined by the ecclesial setting in which they are performed, where they are subject to the semantic pull of other signs with a stable meaning. When the name Melchizedek is mentally coupled with the term 'priesthood', an isotopy of meaning is created in the text – that is, the text can suddenly have two objectively valid meanings, depending on the context in which it is seen to operate. Since in the Christian countries of concern to Handel, the concept of priesthood is theologically equivocal, the isotopy will point in radically different directions for Catholic and Lutheran audiences. In each case, the performance setting transforms Melchizedek into a sign of the Catholic or the Protestant conception of the priesthood, as the case may be, and engages the listener differently, both intellectually and emotionally. The Lutheran isotopy, in which every believer is a type of Melchizedek who can speak to God without a mediator, leads to a culture of spiritual solipsism in the communication between man and God; the Catholic isotopy leads instead to a culture of communal loyalty to the ordained priesthood.

This raises a very interesting question of theory and method. Unless in vocal performance we are prepared to separate tones from sense, as if the verbal and the musical dimensions of a sung biblical word were endowed with independent phenomenal existence and could be received in two different acts of perception, we must treat the theological and the aesthetic aspects of the performance text as indivisible, like the two sides of the same coin. In the act of performance, the ecclesial setting and the theological tradition become material constituents of the text, by virtue of the fact that they inform its language with meaning – the meaning in which they are themselves steeped – and provide the audience with the hermeneutical paradigm for its interpretation, of which they are an institutional embodiment. Cardinals Ottoboni, Pamphili and Colonna understood this principle very well, and that is why they could extend their patronage to non-Catholic composers. In works marked by semiotic isotopy, the personal beliefs and intention of the composers are largely irrelevant. The message embodied by the vocal music would advance the theological cause of the Catholic Church anyhow because it would be subject to the transformative and interpretative filter of the performance setting.

The same principle applies to librettos based on the Bible but scripted by poets. To be sure, the poets' individual words do not have the same valence as the words of a cantata whose verses do not alter the text of the Bible, but the stories they tell cannot be at variance with church doctrine. In Rome, oratorios based on the book of Judith, for example, became vehicles for theologically binding articles of faith. As with the name of Melchizedek, the expectations raised among Catholics by the name of Judith alone were strikingly different from those raised among Protestants. The reason for this is that, whereas for Catholics the book of Judith is a fully canonical book of the Bible, confirmed as such by the Council of Trent (1546), it is not found in Protestant Bibles. For non-Catholics the book of Judith is an apocryphal story without any theological implications for the faith. In Catholic theology, on the other hand, Judith is presented as a type of Mary, who is interpreted as a type of the church, crushing the head of the Antichrist just as Judith beheaded Holofernes. Both figures, Judith and Mary, together with the church, were seen by Tradition as a promise of redemption made by God himself in the book of Genesis (3.15), when he said to the serpent that *she*, a future female figure, shall crush his head. The pronoun *she* occurred in the text of contemporary Catholic Bibles, but in non-Catholic versions, the pronoun remained masculine: *he*, not *she*, shall crush the serpent's head. Anglican and Protestant Bibles do not allow the typological presentation of Judith as the adversary of Lucifer promised by God in Genesis, nor do they allow the interpretation of Judith's act as a prefiguration of Mary and of the church as types of the serpent-trampler with a crucial role in the economy of salvation – an interpretation that would sound pretty close to idolatry to Lutheran ears. But the Catholic version authorized precisely such an interpretation, and the Catholic educational ethos automatically raised the expectation of that message from any oratorio dramatizing Judith's beheading of Holofernes.

That educational ethos was necessarily informed by the Magisterium of the church. This is a term with which the church refers to the teaching office and authority of the pope and bishops, believed to have been transmitted by Jesus to the apostles, and by them to all the pontiffs and bishops, in uninterrupted succession to the present: 'He who hears you, hears me,' said Jesus in the Gospel of St Luke (10–16), and 'he who rejects you rejects me'. Clement XI and his cardinals and bishops were the direct descendants of the apostles addressed by Jesus, and, by uninterrupted continuity, they had the authority to speak on his behalf. The Magisterium was something to be taken seriously, and Spagna took it seriously without hesitation. Wherever he may live and work in the Christian world, the librettist must select his subject matter with great care, to make sure that it reflects the teaching of the church. 'This consideration', Spagna specifies, 'is especially important for us, who live in this holy city, which is the head of Christendom, the city to which the rest of the world should look for good examples, and from which it should take all instruction.' Uttered in a book dedicated to Clement XI and based on the librettos of Clement IX, Spagna's words are not a vacuous rhetorical gesture but a strong affirmation of Rome as the rightful centre from which authentic Christian doctrine is disseminated to all poets, who are bound to accept it with devout obedience – there being no Catholic theology that is not at the same time a theology of obedience.

The oratorio is one of the artistic channels through which that instruction flows out to the faithful who have an interest in vocal music, and, in that sense, it may be considered a formal structure for imparting doctrine and influencing belief. It is an artistic channel available to the church in carrying out its ministry of proclamation. It serves the function of imparting dogmatic principles of spiritual fulfilment together with the aesthetic pleasure of music and poetry. It also strengthens the relevance that Scripture narratives and the lives of the saints have for contemporary society as signs of ideals that offer common mortals much needed guidance and inspiration.

By supporting the oratorio financially and by making possible its success as an art form, the church makes use of the genre the way the state, for example, makes use of such institutions as schools, the law and the press: to impart values, to instil a sense of identity within the world community, to generate a universe of shared signs and symbols and to create a culture of loyalty for the officers who govern it. The church, however, does so more directly, because, whereas the institutions that serve society are meant to be relatively free of government interference, the oratories in which the performances of oratorios took place were under the direct control of the diocese, as venues for exercises that had always been meant to draw music lovers into its spiritual culture. Attracting and entertaining are operations whose success depends largely on the poet's knowledge of the aesthetic sensibilities of his intended audience. Spagna's contemporaries were a highly sophisticated audience whose oratorio needs could be met only by an equally sophisticated form, which in Spagna's view was the form of an unstaged spiritual opera, complete with recitatives and arias. In such a structure, the recitative passages have the function of making the theological message explicit and hence represent a part whose centrality in the work must be appreciated by poet and composer alike.

In the libretto form of the earlier generation, the theological voice was assigned to a narrator, usually called Historia or Textus, though there is no reason why the same voice could not be the collective one of a chorus. The role of the narrator was akin to that of the storyteller of epic poetry, namely to provide the context – the narrative, thematic and interpretative context – for the scenes of dramatic action and dialogue that followed it. In Spagna's view, this type of mixed structure owed its existence as a vernacular oratorio form to the influence of the Passion texts of Holy Week, in which the epic voice of the evangelist dominates the entire episode and offers the listener guidance on how to interpret the details of the event. Appropriate enough to Passion celebrations, in which the script cannot alter the sense of the biblical text, such a form is no longer suitable for an oratorio libretto, which is entirely written in the words of the poet. The trick, of course, is to accomplish the same didactic task by maintaining a continuous and clear theological subtext in the dialogical texture of the recitatives and arias. This subtext is a distinguishing feature of the oratorio as such and could not possibly be removed from it without dissolving away the walls of the genre itself. Like Aristotle, Spagna believed that dramatic forms undergo an evolution similar to that of organic substances, which continue to grow under the direction of an internal sense of finality until they achieve the fullness of their being. It is essentially because of this that he is insensitive to the aesthetic subtleties of the epic form, which he rejects as a primitive dramaturgical structure. He compares oratorios with an epic character to medieval paintings in which, below or near the human figures, the artist includes banderoles or scrolls inscribed with words that identify the figures depicted and verbalize the sentiments they, as pictorial signs, were meant to express.

In Rome one could see one of the oldest theological examples of this iconographic style in the church of Santa Maria Antiqua, in which inscripted scrolls make sure that the artist's depiction of the four church fathers – Gregory, Ambrose, Augustine and Jerome – is clearly understood as an institutional anti-Byzantine gesture, which is to say as a form of Western theological propaganda.[12] For Spagna the painted words of medieval murals and the sung narratives of early baroque librettos belong to the reality outside the picture and outside the drama. They belong to the world of the frame that encloses them, and the frame in turn belongs to a different order of reality. Spagna objects to such epic elements as relics from the past, when, in his judgement, the art of the librettist and the art of the painter were still at an early stage of development. In the early eighteenth century, they would be foreign to mainstream culture. In the figurative arts, they would be products of artistic mediocrity, signs of the painter's inability to make his figures represent their identity and express their sentiments without the use of words from the world outside the painting. Likewise in the non-dialogic libretto, whose epic elements would be considered evidence of the poet's inability to make the narrative context and the theological principles understood by the audience from the dialogue alone. Dialogic drama is for Spagna a more highly evolved form of the genre than epic drama. Spagna's theological position is conservative, yet in Rome the type of oratorio that he is describing is on the forefront of the art. In Rome the two things go hand in hand: to think in solidarity with the church and in service to it does not mean to be backward artists.

Behind this rejection of the sense of foreignness that he found in the epic forms of earlier librettos is the conviction that all art forms – especially, we may think, those that were designed to bring sacredness within the reach of everyday life – should strive towards a poetics of imitation and an aesthetics of verisimilitude. Characters, dramatic actions and poetic language can be derived from Scripture or from the lives of the saints, but the dramatic form must be modelled as an imitation of reality – that is, of human interactions and conversations – if it is to represent for the audience an alternative way of living. For the librettist, that means first of all restricting the dramatic form to dialogue and limiting the range of themes and character types to those sanctioned by the church as integral to the faith. The audience could then consider different possibilities of being by learning to think in solidarity with the church, opening themselves to its teaching while savouring the aesthetic *dolcezza* of its poetry and music.

6

Passiontide drama

In a moving passage of the *Divine Comedy*, Vergil takes Dante by his hand and leads him to a bush whose leaves have been scattered by savage hounds. Pouring out at once words and blood from its injuries, the bush cries out its pain, asks that its mutilated leaves be brought back to it as an act of pity and describes itself as the transformed soul of a suicide from the city of Florence. He must have been one of those who, in a mysterious impulse to commit suicide that threw the city into mourning at the end of the thirteenth century, succumbed to unknown despair and took their own lives in the secrecy of their homes. His anonymity protects the good name of his family, suggests Boccaccio lecturing on Dante in the Florentine church of St Stephen, and leaves the readers free to imagine that the tormented soul imprisoned in the branches and leaves of the bush is that of a suicide they may have personally known in their community. The number of those who hanged themselves in Florence at this dark hour of its history seemed to Boccaccio to be large enough to be unintelligible other than as evidence of the wrath of God, delivering terrible punishment upon the city for some unconscionable and unredeemed sin. The wayfarer is so moved to pity that he gathers the scattered leaves and gently places them at the foot of the bush inhabited by the soul of his unhappy compatriot.[1]

The moral culture of the transitional period between the Middle Ages and the Renaissance was a profoundly troubled culture, in a manner and to a degree that may at times be obscured in our historical consciousness by the magnitude of its aesthetic expression in art and literature. Paul Tillich described the condition as a contagious moral disease, a general anxiety of guilt, experienced as an existential urgency to ward off the prospect of despair before death and the risk of eternal damnation in the afterlife.[2] That was certainly a reason why many joined religious orders, practised conspicuous penance, participated actively in sacred rituals, made pilgrimages to holy places, became self-torturing mystics, and purchased indulgences, surrounding themselves with signs of the Passion and redemption from all the arts. It seems that, at the hour of their death, they all wanted to be in the odour of sanctity, or, failing that, in a state of moral purity sufficient for them to enter purgatory. Some, however, were unable to overcome their despair and, their religious education notwithstanding, committed the terrible sin of taking their own lives.

Narrating the story of the anonymous suicide as a stern theologian, Dante is careful to say that, as the wayfarer, who experienced the narrated action as its protagonist, he was impelled by love of country ('carità del natio loco' *Inf.* XIV, 1), and not by charity for an unrepented sinner, to perform his moving gesture of piety. The theologian is quick to provide us with proper hermeneutical coordinates at every step of the journey through hell, lest we be fooled by the damned into commiserating them for their tragic fate, blinding ourselves to the justness of their suffering and falling prey to a process of reverse catharsis that would cause us to sin under the cloak of mercy. The medieval theologian knows nothing of the Willy Lomans of the modern world and would not be moved by their plight. Desperation, for whatever reason, is a sin, the result of a disordered mind and a fallen soul. However tragic the fate that led them to hell may still appear to them, the damned are all unrepented and are fixed for ever in their will-to-sin. The souls of the damned are generally aware of the fact that human beings, prone as they are to commiserate the tragic fate of others, can be swayed to feel pity for them without realizing that such pity is actually tantamount to contempt for divine justice. When it is considered in isolation from its embedding presentational narrative, the represented action of the *Divine Comedy* is structured as the dialogue of an episodic play, to be performed on an imaginary stage with many mansions, while the narrative assumes the role of the stage directions needed to govern its proper enactment and its correct interpretation by the reader. As he advances in his journey through hell in the Paschal Triduum of the year 1300, the wayfarer can be seen occasionally yielding to human passions, in ways that the theologian, who knows better because he has completed his journey, would not. The fullness of our visualization of the action depends to a very large extent on our ability to hear both voices simultaneously, while our emotional and our intellectual response to it depends on our willingness to let our interpretative consciousness slide without interruption back and forth along the dialectic by which presentational and representational signs are linked in the poem.

The episode of the anonymous Florentine suicide – a small detail, to be sure, on the large and complex canvas of the *Inferno* – is a convenient point of departure for the question that I intend to examine in this chapter, which is how, in the transitional period between the Middle Ages and the Renaissance, Christian culture understood the issue of spiritual catharsis before dramatic re-enactments of the supreme spectacle of Christ's suffering. This is not the suffering of a great hero, morally or intellectually responsible for his own downfall, but the suffering of the Lamb of God for the redemption of mankind. To enter this arena is to raise once again the question of the possibility of a Christian tragedy that is grounded in, or analogous to, classical tragedy. The issues to be considered are basically three: whether there can be a tragic hero without *hamartia*, a tragic action without a downfall and a tragic plot that does not cause the catharsis of compassion, since Christ and his martyrs are flawless heroes and, in the transcendent order, always triumph over the immanence of reality, and since compassion remains a supreme Christian virtue. These questions, however, are here, and generally elsewhere, posed from the perspective of Athenian tragedy and Aristotle's *Poetics*, on the principle that they represent with sufficient clarity the distinctive features of the genre as a whole. For modern criticism, with its grasp of the Western dramatic tradition in its full historical development, it makes good sense to begin with questions such as these, since it is on the ideas that they presuppose that the conventional theory of tragedy is generally based. Scholars are nonetheless divided on the issue because they are not all equally willing to regard the defining traits of Athenian tragedy as the informing principles of tragedy as such. A larger textual base and a wider purview could lead us to a variety of definitions and relativize the Athenian concept of tragedy. The same approach would certainly make less sense in a period of Western history in which the classics were less perfectly known, and in which the Greek origins of the genre were still a matter of contention. In high Renaissance Italy, as late as 1556, the Jewish scholar Leone De' Sommi could surmise with confidence that the cultural origins of Western drama were Hebrew rather than Greek, the first great tragedy being the book of Job, 'la elegantissima et filosofica tragedia di Iobbe'.[3]

If the defining features of tragedy as such were derived from the story of Job, we would have, of course, a different concept of tragedy, the large Greek corpus of the genre notwithstanding. Among modern scholars, Sidney Lamb would surely agree, since for him the book of Job, which he classifies as a proto-tragedy, dramatizes the principle of the incompatibility of suffering and justice, which is 'at the basis of all tragic situations'.[4] The tradition of considering the book of Job a tragedy is at least as ancient as Theodore of Mopsusestia, who suggested that it was an imitation of classical Greek tragedy, but it was only after Theodore Beza divided the book into acts and scenes in 1587 that a succession of scholars pointed out similarities, until the early twentieth century, when Horace

Meyer Kallen argued the unlikely thesis that the book of Job was consciously written in the manner of Euripides.[5] More to our point, however, is the earlier observation by George Goodspeed that the story of the Hebrew sufferer, though not consciously patterned on any dramatic work, was nonetheless a prototype of both that of Prometheus, 'the Greek Job', and that of Hamlet, 'Shakespeare's Job'.[6] The conception of the book of Job as a tragedy that is typologically comparable to *Prometheus Bound* has weighty implications for a theory of Christian tragedy in the late Middle Ages. For, in the first place, the interpretation of Prometheus by early Christian apologetics and iconography as a classical type of the biblical creator – the 'verus Prometheus', in the words of Tertullian – eventually led to his allegorical identification with Christ.[7] A fourteenth-century preacher could speak the name of Prometheus with confidence in a sermon because it was a sign for Christ 'Dei sapienciam signat, qui Christus est',[8] while his torment on the Caucasus came to be viewed as a classical adumbration or a proleptic sign of Christian martyrdom.[9] In the second place, Job was typologically regarded by the religious culture of the Middle Ages, principally on the authority of St Jerome and Gregory the Great, as a prefiguration of the *Christus patiens*, an anticipative sign of the suffering Christ of the Passion and, by extension, as a symbol of suffering Christians everywhere, all part of the mystical body of Christ, which is his church: 'beatus Job passiones Redemptoris nostri, ejusque corporis, id est Sanctae Ecclesiae, et passione sua significavit et nomine.'[10] (Blessed Job has signified the sufferings of our Redeemer, and of his body, that is the Holy Church, with his suffering and name.)

Redemption in Christian tragedy

The question of the possibility of Christian tragedy in the late Middle Ages is historically prompted by the hermeneutical discovery that the sufferings of Prometheus and Job are proleptic signs of the Passion of Christ. It now remains to be seen whether the same question can be ontologically grounded in the theology of the Passion, for without such grounding the question can have little interest for Christian thought. If such a thing as Christian tragedy exists, its principle of being and its principle of explanation must be sought in the foundation of Christian thought itself. We must therefore inquire under what semiotic aspect medieval theology might lend itself to such a possibility. In this context Honorius of Autun, whose *Gemma animae* was probably one of Dante's sources for the theatrical pageant he witnesses in Eden, offers us a reliable theoretical orientation: 'Tragicus noster pugnam Christi populo Christiano in theatro Ecclesiae gestibus suis repraesentat eique victoriam redemptionis suae inculcat.'[11] (Our tragic actor portrays the struggle of Christ to the Christian people in the theatre of the Church with his gestures and teaches it the victory of his redemption.)

Honorius is not speaking of a dramatic work in the ordinary sense of the word, but of the originary Christian tragedy, in relation to which origin is not a chronological beginning but the ontological foundation of the genre. It is the tragedy in which the meaning of all ordinary Christian tragedies must be ultimately rooted. From the perspective of a developing theory of Christian tragedy, the orientation offered by this definition could not be clearer: the foundations of Christian tragedy are located entirely in the Mass, which is the sole source of its ontological clarity. This term does not mean logical or linguistic clarity but clarity of substantiation, whether or not that is understood by observers. This is the sense in which the late medieval Schoolmen used it. For Scholasticism ontological clarity represents a principle of substantiation that includes intelligibility and mystery simultaneously, since there is always mystery where the mind is invited to reach out to something beyond what is apparent to it in contact, especially when that beyond is deep within the observer's conscience.[12] The Mass is the source of ontological substantiation of Christian tragedy also with respect to its semiotics of performance, by which it must signify in the rememorative and transformative manner of the liturgy. The place of performance is the church, a material area of focus for the ubiquity of God, a place visible to us either as a real church or as an architectural sign of one. The audience are the faithful, that is, members of the mystical body of Christ, impelled to take part in the celebration by their need for redemption. The achievement of consciousness of redemption, in the here and now of the communal experience, is the intended cathartic effect of the performance.

We are here at the very heart of the question of Christian tragedy, for in the hermeneutics of Honorius the theory of Greek classical tragedy and the theology of the Eucharist are made explicitly to intersect. Hardison has observed that, throughout his interpretation of the Mass as a dramatic form in performance, Honorius uses the vocabulary of the classical theory of drama 'with considerable sophistication'.[13] Ultimately the contact between the classics and Christianity in his analysis of the Mass is philological, in that it presupposes a concatenation of texts, echoes and citations from the dramatic theory of antiquity to the allegorization of the liturgy in the late Middle Ages. It is not possible to know with precision just how far the surviving classical tradition had permeated medieval consciousness, inducing it to think of the Mass in terms of Greek tragedy, but we can determine the dimensions and character of the contextual classicism that made such an association meaningful. In the pursuit of this determination Dante is a good reference point. His knowledge of the classics is unmatched by anyone in Europe prior to the Renaissance, as is the degree to which he manages to weave classical allusions and citations directly into his own language in relation to analogous borrowings from the Bible. A quantitative analysis of relevant textual citations in Dante's works and a simple census of the characters assigned to the three spiritual realms of the *Divine Comedy* may be regarded as good indicators of the extent of his contact with the classics, direct or indirect though that contact may have been, and may safely be considered the upper limit of the classicism of his age. Against the 500 or so citations of the Vulgate, there are more than 300 textual references to Aristotle, around 200 to Vergil, approximately 100 to Ovid, about 50 each to Cicero and Lucan, somewhere between 30 and 40 to each of Statius and Boethius, and between 10 and 20 to Horace, Livy and Orosius, plus a few each to Plato, Homer, Juvenal, Seneca, Ptolemy, Aesop, Lucretius, Galen, Svetonius, Vegetius, Euclid and Valerius Maximus. As for the census of the characters in the netherworld of the *Divine Comedy*, we know that of the 332 mentioned, a total of 89 are classical, almost twice as many as the 48 of biblical origin.[14] Among the characters of classical origin, we find the most famous protagonists of classical tragedy, whose stories had reached the late Middle Ages through non-dramatic sources, though it is safe to assume that Dante had direct knowledge of the tragedies of Seneca, which had started to circulate in the eleventh century.[15]

Something of the overall perception that the late Middle Ages had of the classical world may be surmised from the fact that Dante placed most of the great spirits of antiquity in a special part of limbo, a castle bathed in light where the only punishment suffered by the pagan souls is privation of the sight of the true God. As the wayfarer and his guide approach the castle, which Vergil had temporarily left in order to succour Dante, they are met by Homer, Horace, Ovid and Lucan who come to welcome Vergil back among them, and, after their reunion, they all invite Dante to become the sixth member of their company. By joining their *bella scola*, Dante shows that he understood the imaginative universe of his poetry to stand in a direct line of continuity with the classics, almost as the Christian *eschaton* to which the enlightened minds of pagan antiquity were unknowingly reaching out. Such vision of continuity was a direct function of the power of assimilation that informed medieval hermeneutics, in which historical exegesis and allegorical eisegesis flowed freely into one another. Among the classical authors, Vergil became early an unknowing prophet of Christ in his fourth eclogue. Seneca found his way into St Jerome's list of Christian saints chiefly on the strength of his presumed friendship and correspondence with St Paul, while in Dante's vision Statius converted secretly to Christianity, largely under the salvific influence of Vergil's poetry, and was secretly baptized during a persecution ordered by Domitian. Moreover, Cato Uticensis is the guardian of Dante's purgatory and is idealized to such an extent that, in the *Convivio*, he alone among all men is said to be worthy of being used as a sign for God by his very existence, his suicide being allegorically sublimated into an act of martyrdom in the name of freedom.[16]

Beyond the world of literature the disposition of medieval culture to Christianize the classical tradition may be observed in the Mass, the very heart of Christian worship, where it is expressed forcefully in two brief texts of the period: the *Dies irae*, the famous sequence of funeral services, in a line of which the Hebrew David and the pagan Sybil join voices ('teste David cum Sybilla') to prophesy the Christian day of judgement, and the *Ad Maronis Mausoleum*, a hymn chanted in the service for the feast of St Paul in Mantua, which describes the Apostle weeping with grief over the tomb of Vergil for having lived too late to bring the noble pagan to the Christian fulfilment of his calling.[17] The Mass at the time was the Franciscan Mass, and in that context it may be worth recalling that, according to a contemporary hagiographic legend, St Francis of Assisi would lovingly pick up all discarded pieces of written parchment that he might find on the ground, indiscriminately, showing as much care for relics of classical works as for those of Christian works, because all good things eventually lead the mind back to their origin, which is God. 'Litterae sunt', he apparently explained to a disciple who was puzzled by his care for written fragments of a pagan culture, 'ex quibus componitur gloriosissimus Dei nomen'.[18]

It is within such a semiotic reconfiguration and transfiguration of classicism that the Mass can be considered functionally equivalent to the religious sources of classical tragedy. In contemporary theology there was a general agreement that the Mass was an allegorical ritual of the Passion in dramatic form, but there was some variance of opinion concerning the nature of the relationship between the enacted representation and the historical event at its origin. The majority view was the one upheld by St Thomas Aquinas, who argued that, in so far as the reality of the death of Jesus is concerned, the relation between the Mass and the event is one of simple signification. The celebrant (the *tragicus noster* of Honorius) signifies by his words and actions the essential aspects of the Passion but does not himself suffer it in the process – he embodies the signs but not the referents of the Passion. However, in so far as the salvific effect of the celebration is concerned – its sacramental value – the Mass and the event are for St Thomas functionally equivalent.[19] To attend Mass with the right disposition is to benefit spiritually from the celebration, anywhere and at any time. Viewed against the background of Honorius' superimposition of the theory of classical tragedy, the argument advanced by St Thomas brings into great prominence the notion of the spiritual impact of the Mass as a form of sacramental catharsis. The suffering and death of Jesus are present only symbolically, but the spiritual effect of their enactment is as real as the original event, and is equally real each time that it occurs before a congregation of believers. The analogy with classical tragedy is clear and does not call for detailed commentary: for each person in attendance, the catharsis is real in both cases, the only difference being that at Mass the experience is spiritual rather than merely psychological, since the Mass is a sacred liturgy of salvation and not a secular play with a paraliturgical function in festivities.

As a sacramental ritual, the Mass is both timeless and unlocalized. At the signifying level, the struggle of Christ is enacted in the here and now of any particular celebration, but at the signified level it takes place in the minds and hearts of the people present, individually incorporated into the mystical body of Christ by virtue of their spiritual disposition to be thus united. But when the boundary between ritual and representation is crossed, the signifying elements of the Passion move into the imaginative world of localized space, linear time, sequential narrative and structural particularity. It is at this point that Christian drama emerges as an art form in its own right, and that the analogy with classical tragedy can be on the same plane of meaning.[20] In the composition of such works, the selection of a particular gospel as the controlling narrative is significant. For although in the collective religious imagination the four canonical accounts of the Passion are generally fused into a single narrative, in a dramatic perspective it is useful to keep them apart as much as possible and to read one without being influenced by the others. If the story of the Passion is taken from Mark or Matthew, the tragic dimension of the suffering and death of Jesus emerges with overpowering force. In these two gospels – especially in Matthew, in whom the tragic end is prepared with a greater abundance of *hybris*[21] – Jesus dies in utter desolation, abandoned by his disciples and forsaken by God. There is no attenuating acceptance of the divine plan that calls for his death on the cross, such as we find in Luke when he commends his spirit to God, and no tenderness of human concerns, such as we see in John, when he commends his youngest disciple to his mother. In John and Luke, Jesus dies at peace, 'a fellow to

Socrates'.[22] In Mark and Matthew he dies a tragic hero of the greatest magnitude, titanic in his solitude and in his suffering. Here he is a fellow to Prometheus.

The cry of forsakenness issued by Jesus from the cross in Aramaic (*Eli, Eli, lamma sabacthani*) is the ultimate argument against all theories of the presumed incompatibility of tragedy and Christianity. Hans Urs von Balthasar reminds us that in proclaiming the death of tragedy at the beginning of the Christian era, scholars such as George Steiner and philosophers such as Karl Jaspers failed to take into account that Jesus does not die in the knowledge that with his death he was fulfilling the divine economy of salvation, but really forsaken, his final question remaining unanswered.[23] The fact that the crucifixion of Jesus is followed by his resurrection, that Good Friday is followed by Easter Sunday, does not attenuate the tragedy of his death as a man but only invests it with the meaning of the divine plan for the reconciliation of all to God. The tragedy is fully contained in the Passion; the Resurrection is the hermeneutical ground on which Christians are asked to stand in order to interpret it correctly. In the Scholastic culture of the late Middle Ages, the form of any object, including sacred narratives, was understood as an internal principle of clarity, a metaphysical source deep within that warranted the object's intelligibility. The form of Christian tragedy, the retelling of the story of the crucifixion or of another modelled on it, is distinguished by the fact that at every point of its unfolding two distinct principles of intelligibility are simultaneously operative, warranting what Maritain calls its intelligibility *in itself* and its intelligibility *for us*.[24] Though they work in unison, these are radically different principles. The first principle is grounded in the mystery of the forsakenness of Jesus and is perceived as an invitation, issued silently from within the story, to listen more attentively and to look more carefully, for there is always more to know at every stage of reflection. Why does God abandon Jesus at the point of his death? What implication does this have for the meaning of other details of the Passion? Questions such as these are generated by what we might call the Promethean principle of the Christian idea of tragic form, according to which the metaphysical clarity of the narrative is warranted by the darkness of God's silence. On the other hand, the principle that generates the narrative's clarity for us is grounded in the light of the Resurrection. This principle of Christian tragic form has a Socratic character, in that it throws the light of understanding onto the Promethean tragedy on the cross, and it makes every detail of the Passion available to us as something revelatory of meaning in our own lives.

Equipped with these two principles of form, we can see, among other things, that no despair can be attached to the humanity of Jesus on the cross, not even when he emits his final cry. Unlike the classical and the modern worlds, in which the psychology of despair may easily figure as a legitimate part of the aesthetic substance of tragedy – at least in the sense that, though it does not lend particular grandeur to the hero that yields to his despair, it can generate in the commiserative experience of the audience a definite sense of ethical nobility – medieval culture had no positive use for it. Despair was a terrible sin against the goodness of God and an outright rejection of the economy of salvation. As an expression of the psychology of discouragement and anxiety, despair elicits compassion and solidarity in all periods of history. But as a voluntarily accepted metaphysical perspective that sees the finitude of contingency as absolute, despair denies the very foundations of Christian thought, namely the transcendence and love of God. Its gravest consequence is suicide, from which it is virtually inseparable. In the Scrovegni Chapel, Dante's contemporary Giotto painted the allegory of despair as a woman in the act of hanging herself from a beam in the ceiling, much like the Florentine suicides recalled by Boccaccio in his gloss on the lines of the anonymous suicide in the *Divine Comedy*. Medieval theology is not moved by either despair or suicide and sees no artistic potential in them, other than in an aesthetics designed to condemn them both. The rhetoric of desperation, which plays so memorable a role in Sophocles (e.g. *Ajax*, 430–80) and Euripides (e.g. *Alcestis*, 935–61), appears only as a distorted logic of self-delusion in Pier delle Vigne's account of the apparently rational argument that led him to commit suicide at *Inferno* XIII, 72: *ingiusto fece me contra me giusto*.[25] Despair and suicide transform innocence into guilt.

Medieval Christianity took much from the moral philosophy of antiquity and prefigured much of the moral philosophy of the post-medieval world, but not the philosophical justification of suicide by Roman Stoicism nor the moral acceptance of it by the returned Stoicism of the Renaissance. The only form of voluntary death acceptable to it was martyrdom. Soon after the fall of Edessa, St Bernard sent a fiery letter to Pope Eugenius III, urging him to raise another crusade against the enemies of Christ, who was once again suffering crucifixion in the place where he was first put to death.[26] The warriors who have died – and, by implication, those who will die in the crusade – defending and proclaiming his Word participate fully in his Passion by way of their martyrdom. Their death is a typological recurrence of the crucifixion. St Bernard begins his exhortation of the pope by quoting to him from Seneca's letter to Lucilius on the futility of halfway measures in the face of difficulty, arguing that the spirit should rise heroically to the occasion. In this letter, Seneca also tells his disciple that if he cannot do anything to come out of his predicament, suicide remains the logical option. By quoting Seneca's words on the need to respond with courage to the adversities of life, St Bernard is not advocating Stoic suicide, of course, but the urgency to rise in one's spirit high above one's attachment to earthly life. Yet there is a level on which the martyrdom of warriors, in so far as it consists of walking into the spears of the enemy, may appear as a form of heroic suicide grounded in faith. However, because it is not a seeking of death in order to prevent a humiliation of life but the free relinquishing of life in order to prevent a violation of the spirit, martyrdom is not reducible to Stoic suicide in any perspective that values the sanctity of the spirit.

The reverse is also true. Suicide can be raised to the order of martyrdom only if, through subtle hermeneutical manoeuvres, its immediate cause is given a theological dimension, analogically or figuratively. In such cases, the sin of suicide vanishes, and what remains is the allegorical value produced by the interpretative act. This is how Cato becomes the guardian of purgatory: his suicide is viewed as an act of martyrdom suffered for the sake of freedom, and the spiritual nobility of his sacrifice is such as to elevate him to the role of guardian of purgatory, the realm through which all souls of the saved must pass in order to achieve their ultimate freedom. This is the result of the principle of anagogic interpretation applied to the exodus motif from within the heart of Christian thought, which is the theology of the death and resurrection of Jesus, ritualized in the feasts of Good Friday and Easter. Cato's suicide, in other words, is ontologically grounded in the story of the Passion, and by this fact achieves the status of a potentially tragic act, analogous to the martyrdom suffered by many heroic individuals who confessed their faith by their acceptance of suffering and violent death. Cato's salvation is figured as a product of Christian typology, and that is why he can represent God himself.

The typological linkage of events in salvation history is the result of a hermeneutical operation conventionally called rememorative allegory, one of the chief tools used in the Middle Ages to describe the ritual of the Mass as sacred drama. From Amalarius of Metz, who wrote in the ninth century, to William Durand of Mende, who wrote in the thirteenth, the Mass was allegorically interpreted by means of rememorative techniques in order to show that the nature and placement of most of its components actually brought the historical elements of the Passion to renewed presence in the mind of the faithful.[27] Educated to this method by rote in their observance of the liturgy itself and, no doubt, made familiar with the doctrine of the mystical body by the homiletic tradition, the faithful would naturally allow the rememorative dimension of the Mass to recast as Christological signs all the martyrs whose story they had cause to recollect. As a ritual form of drama, the Mass is not restricted to the temporal linearity of secular dramatic actions but is endowed with a dimension of timelessness that enables both the priest and the congregation to move back and forth in the history of salvation, understanding the significance of distant events as typological functions of each other and anchoring them all to the significance that the actual celebration of the Mass has for the individual in attendance *hic et nunc*.

That significance is not, and cannot be, tragic in its entirety. It is tragic, in the classical sense of the term, in so far as the Passion and its typological associations are recalled for the suffering that they entail; but it is positive, and therefore comic, in the Dantean sense of the term comedy, in so far as the Passion is regarded as the necessary condition for the salvation of all mankind, pagans and other enemies of Christianity included. The overall dramatic form of Christianity must embrace the Resurrection, and in that sense cannot be other than comic, just as surely as it is tragic in dramatizing the cry of forsakenness from the cross.[28] The liturgy of Maundy Thursday in particular shows that the Promethean element in the tragedy of the Passion is attenuated by the overall Socratic hermeneutics that is grounded in the doctrine of salvation. Couched between Wednesday and Friday, the days in which the church, among other things, utters prayers for the salvation of her enemies, and including as it did a Mass for the penitents, Maundy Thursday stood in medieval faith as a reminder that the ritualistic enactment of grief must also ring with the note of prayer for the forgiveness of all, the emotional and intellectual basis of which is the cathartic purport of the ritual.

Passion plays and tragedy

In fourteenth-century Italy this message was made especially clear with enacted scenes from the first stages of the Passion embedded in a homiletic frame that could guarantee their correct interpretation. This type of Christian drama is a hybrid genre in which scenes of performed action are summoned forth, one at the time, by a preacher from the pulpit and are incorporated, in the manner of illustrative quotations, in an expository homily that controlled both the signs of performance and their interpretation. The thematic material of the plays in the genre, which are generally known as *devozioni* or devout representations, comes from the historical account of the Passion in the gospels and from a variety of other works of popular piety that reinforced basic theological principles. It is in this genre that the suffering of Jesus, from just before his arrest to the moment of his execution, is dramatized at the end of the Middle Ages in Italy. The cathartic objective of passion plays must consequently be viewed against the background of the relationship between history and faith, and must be interpreted in relation to the function of the liturgy in the salvation of mankind. My method will be to identify the principal signs involved in the cathartic aspect of the spectacle of suffering and to sort them out for dramaturgical interpretation. I therefore propose to consider them chiefly in relation to the idea of a production script, in which the representation of a given action is governed by the presentational narrative given in the form of stage directions, in much the same way the poet controls the reader's understanding of the actions performed by the protagonist as he moves about the imaginary set of the *Divine Comedy*.

The relative newness of dramaturgy as an instrumental science of theatre history calls for a word or two of commentary. Dramaturgy is not a self-contained area of study, endowed with a sophisticated technical tradition and susceptible of positive definition without reference to adjacent fields of inquiry. On the contrary, it is a relational discipline, concerned, in the first place, with the possibilities of emplotment and characterization available to the playwright in the writing process, as he transforms an action and a theory of drama into a production script. In the second place, it is concerned with the possibilities of enactment available to the director in the staging process, as he or she transforms the production script into a performance text. And in the third place, it is concerned with possibilities of interpretation and emotional response available to the audience in the reception process, as they transform the performance text into an experience both aesthetic and intellectual. Though it is frequently convenient to separate these components of dramaturgy, almost as if they represented three autonomous and sequential moments of operation, in fact they are simultaneous and interdependent activities, governed by the same purpose, which is to consider the possibilities of development available at each stage of the process and to understand how and why only one possibility among them tends to become a necessity.

In a dramaturgical treatment of the spectacle of the Passion, the cathartic moment belongs to the last of the three sets of possibilities, those concerned with the ethical and emotional impact of reception. In this context we can speak of a theology of catharsis, that is to say a theory of the intended impact of the re-enactment of the suffering of Jesus derivable from the stage directions or the embedding narrative of the script. Borrowing the words of St Paul, who worked out the Christian theology of suffering, we can quickly summarize the impact of all passion plays: to suffer along with Jesus for the redemption of man and to triumph in the experience: *gaudeo in passionibus*.[29] This places the concept of catharsis in a non-Aristotelian dimension. For though the theology of the late Middle Ages was everywhere permeated by the teaching of *il maestro di color che sanno*, Aristotelian catharsis is not a technical term of the vocabulary of Christianity. To be sure, the root of the term occurs in various lexical forms in the New Testament and a few times even in the Patrologia Latina, but Christian theology paid little or no attention to the concept in Aristotle's *Poetics*. Moreover, 'catharsis' is not a significant term of the Aristotelianism of the late Middle Ages, which flourished despite its almost complete lack of interest in issues that, under this rubric, were to burden much Aristotelian research in later periods of history.

Two factors can be cited to account for this: (i) the so-called context editorial tradition of the works of Aristotle and (ii) the interpretation of the *Poetics* by Islamic scholars. The first factor refers to the hermeneutical impact of the editorial work of Simplicius, who, around 533, first grouped the *Poetics* and the *Rhetoric* with Aristotle's logical works, thereby casting them epistemologically as instruments for the attainment of knowledge, rather than primarily as constructive arts and objects of knowledge, and blurring out of focus concepts such as catharsis, which had little relevance for epistemology. The second factor refers instead to the Aristotelianism of Arabic scholars, which was itself conditioned by the 'context' theory of the editorial tradition. The fundamental assumptions of the Arabic interpretation of the *Poetics* are that drama is a type of lyric poetry, that tragedy is a species of lyric poetry devoted to the encomium of great heroes and that the *Rhetoric*, by virtue of its editorial association with the *Poetics*, represents a valid point of access to its central issues, on the principle that there is a substantive analogy of purpose and method between the poet and the orator.

One of the most significant consequences of this position is that the careful elucidation of catharsis is neither an interesting nor a necessary pursuit for medieval Aristotelianism. The term was variously glossed as a modification of emotional behaviour by means of pity and fear (Abu Ishr Matta), or as the healthy excitation and development of pity and reverential fear (Avicenna), and as the moderation of emotional excess by means of pity and fear (Averroes).[30] Some of the factors involved in this commentary tradition were of a philological order, since the transmission of the text in Arabic was sadly wanting. But other factors were of the more strictly hermeneutical type, concerning as they did the idea of poetry of encomium. Averroes, for example, made a concerted effort to adhere to the text more closely than his predecessors, but in doing so he ended up with an interpretation of catharsis that was more deeply rooted in his major assumption: 'poetry of praise moves people to noble emotions because it portrays people who themselves are normally pure and noble.'[31] The ideas of the Arabic commentators were assimilated by Christian Aristotelians of the late Middle Ages and echoed again and again until well into the Renaissance. In the end, the received wisdom was that tragedy achieved its effects by the excitation of pity and fear, understood as positive and edifying passions rather than negative dispositions to be purged away.

When the process of Christianization was over, pity had become commiseration (*misericordia*) or the impulse to alleviate the pain of others by suffering along with them, while the purpose of the dramatic action was to strengthen belief in Christian virtues, to encourage intelligent participation in the liturgy and to illuminate the principles of faith. Once the edifying function of the representation of suffering is firmly established, the other passion involved in catharsis (fear) is not especially problematic. It too is to be viewed positively, on the principle that if we were ourselves guilty of the same sin, we would naturally visualize the punishment of typical sinners as our own. Fear has an alienating dramaturgical function, in that it causes the members of the audience to resist the temptation to identify too closely with a particular character, while encouraging them to be prepared to sit in judgement of him.

Of course, no such consideration of fear needs to be made for re-enactments of the suffering of Jesus and the martyrs. They are neither morally nor intellectually guilty, since they are in possession of the truth, and their will is equal in all respects to the will of God. In an authentically Christian response to spectacles of their suffering, the audience is expected to experience sorrow, exaltation and enlightenment at the same time. 'The true martyr', says T. S. Eliot's archbishop in *Murder in the Cathedral*, 'is he who has become the instrument of God, who has lost his will in the will of God, and who no longer desires anything for himself, not even the glory of being a martyr.'[32] For that reason the church 'mourns and rejoices' at the same time. This double experience, coupled with a fuller understanding of faith, is the only catharsis possible for Christians at the performance of the supreme forms of Christian suffering.

In order to understand how this experience can be achieved, it is necessary to examine closely the dramaturgical governance of the theme of redemptive suffering in the construction and delivery of the performance text. To do this, we need first to look at the idea of performance style. Now the problem of how to study the performance style presupposed by religious medieval play texts has never found a satisfactory solution and probably never will. In the absence of technical manuals and production data, students of performance style are naturally compelled to resort to conjecture and analogy, rather more frequently than scholars working in later periods of theatre history. Religious iconography from the period is, of course, plentiful, but its relation to the drama of a particular time and place is at best oblique. Most attempts at shedding light tend to revolve around the degree of historical precision that is needed in the interpretation of the verbal text and the degree of verisimilitude that can be assumed in producing it – both ideas no doubt due to the fact that the modern rediscovery of medieval drama occurred in the age of naturalism, a time when it became fashionable for directors to control the meaning of the text while pretending to serve it. Since the nineteenth century the question has been studied in a variety of contexts, but on the whole, comparatively little has been done from a dramaturgical perspective, that is to say from a perspective consciously anchored to the principle that the play texts that have come down to us, whatever else they may be considered, are first of all production scripts, either real or only intended, and must be read as such. 'Scripts' are conceptually different from 'play texts' in that they automatically bring to the foreground of consciousness a sense of their built-in intentionality to be staged in a particular way and in that they invite reflection on other possible stagings. Scripts are performance texts in a state of semiotic latency and are therefore more easily envisioned as performances from within the text itself.

This apparently innocent principle has serious implications for the study of the drama of Christian suffering. The first and most important is that, in a play, stage directions have the same textual status as the dialogue, and that what we call the dramatic text is an indivisible whole of which dialogue and stage directions are equally essential parts, philologically as well as aesthetically. In a dramaturgical purview the meaning of the dramatic text is no more, but also no less, than the structured relationship of reciprocal dependency by which the stage directions and the dialogue are linked, as a combination of visual and vocal signs throughout the play during performance and in our recollection of the play when the performance is over. The theories of drama predicated on the ontological hierarchy of primary and secondary texts, with the stage directions, explicit or implied though they may be, relegated to a secondary semiotic level, are incompatible with the dramaturgical principle of the equivalence of their textual status.

Principles, however, are always easier to define than to observe, and this one is no exception. A company that proposes to retrieve onstage a play of Christian suffering, as a living work of art endowed with a message that needs to be reckoned with, must filter the dramatic text through the creative imagination of a director, and it is hardly necessary to recall that, for a director, preparing a production plan is largely a matter of writing new or additional stage directions that restrict the range of possibilities available to the actors and designers. Whether by the playwright or the director, stage directions are, among other things, textual devices by means of which plays protect themselves from spurious production concepts, chiefly by controlling the freedom of interpretation available to actors and designers in constructing the performance text. Such restrictions are especially significant when the intent is to protect not only the aesthetic integrity of the play but also the doctrine that it teaches and the effect that it is intended to have on the audience.

Two scenes of the passion

In the rest of this chapter, we shall examine how this dramaturgical control of the performance and audience response is exercised in two scenes of supreme Christian suffering, one with and one without externally inflicted violence: the agony of Jesus in the garden and his flagellation at the column. They are taken from two relatively unknown Passion plays known as *Devotione de Zobiadí sancto* and *Devotione de Venerdí sancto* – that is, *A Devout Representation of Holy Thursday* and *A Devout Representation of Good Friday* – plays which were designed to be structurally embedded into homilies on the Passion and obviously meant to be produced in church with conspicuous visual allusions to the liturgy.[33] Preserved in a manuscript dated 1375, but written probably fifty years earlier, within a few years of the *Divine Comedy*, these are the oldest Italian plays in the vernacular. Very briefly the first play dramatizes the return of Jesus to Jerusalem and his agony in the garden, both episodes in the vernacular of early fourteenth-century Umbria, and ends with his arrest, dramatized in Latin as a variation on the *Quem queritis* trope. The second play, entirely in the vernacular, begins with the flagellation, focuses on the principal stages of the Passion, includes a few extravagant theatricals complete with demons and resurrections of the dead, and ends with a truly powerful scene, in which Mary shows everyone the nails used to crucify her son.

The stage directions are long and detailed in some scenes and little more than generic indications in others. Yet if we were to separate them, artificially, from the dialogue and print them in a separate column, we would have no difficulty following the narrative that they tell gesturally and visually, alongside the one that is told verbally in the speeches of the characters. At times the two narratives overlap, while at other times they seem to go in opposite directions, like two melodic lines whose movement of convergence and divergence gives rise to a pattern aesthetically and semantically richer than either considered by itself. There is an important lesson in method for us here, and it is that, where the gestural narrative is thin or uncertain on account of the sketchiness of the stage directions, we cannot freely and reliably use the dialogue as a base from which to infer the nature of the presupposed gestures, following the faulty convention of attributing to the verbal text narrative dominance over the visual one, since we might be seeing convergence where in fact we should see divergence.

Having thus separated the stage directions from the dialogue, our first observation concerns the frequency with which expressions like *more consuetudinario*, in the usual manner, occur in the scripts, in various forms, such as 'come è consueto' (pp. 19, 25) and 'secondo che è consueto' (p. 25). These expressions refer to the fact that the script was written in the context of an uninterrupted performance tradition that was thoroughly familiar to the actors before rehearsal. The actors therefore did not require detailed stage directions on every point of the action. They already knew what costumes to use, what gestures were appropriate, and to what degree they could legitimately feel free to improvise. This accounts for the brevity of the stage directions in many scenes, scenes which in all likelihood recurred frequently in other dramatizations of the Passion. On the other hand, it seems safe to assume that long and detailed stage directions, specifying hand gestures, facial expressions, stage properties, blocking and exact movements, with a degree of precision not inferior to that of nineteenth-century texts – such stage directions are likely to signal an action so peculiar to the logic of the narrative and so crucial to the play that it had to be prescribed in detail in the script.

The relationship of these stage directions to the iconographic tradition is naturally quite different, as is the use that the theatre historian can make of it in studying the dramaturgical structure of the play. It is here useful to outline a working typology of the relevant visual culture, by which I mean images as well as descriptions of images. In the first place, we have a visual semiotic culture produced before the composition of the script and depicting a received tradition in the visualization of the Gospel narratives, a tradition familiar to actors and audiences alike. For the theatre historian this corpus of visuals constitutes an archaeological base from which to give fullness of stage direction to the script, integrating the stage directions that are too cryptic to stand on their own and generating new ones where stage directions are silently presupposed, in order to render the visualization of the action dramaturgically possible from within the script. In the second place we find a body of imagery painted or described after the performance by artists and writers intimately familiar with it or, more probably, by artists acquainted with productions of the same general type. These images can be further divided into two categories, depending on whether they are focused on the material surface of the production, regarded as opaque to viewer's gaze, or whether they are focused on the original narrative, as seen through the prism of the production itself, which is regarded as transparent and used as a semiotic matrix for the visual interpretation of the story. In the images produced before the performance, theatre history finds a useful philological base from which to elucidate the aesthetic materiality of the performance text, whereas in images produced after the performance it finds a convenient hermeneutical base from which to assess its reception history.

The scene of the agony in the garden depends heavily on the iconographic tradition for its role in the dramaturgical economy of the script. In contrast with the original account in the Gospel, in which Jesus speaks to God metaphorically of his imminent death when he asks him to take away the chalice of his passion, the script dramatizes both the metaphor and its message. The metaphor becomes a visible sign in the form of a stage property, a chalice to be discovered on location by the actor playing the role of Jesus, while the metaphorical words of the evangelist are rendered by simple non-metaphorical language. In the script Jesus, without the slightest recourse to figurative language, asks God to spare him his cruel death, if it be His will that this be done. He does not mention the chalice at all and does not allude to it verbally. But he speaks his prayer while holding a chalice in his hands, kneeling on the ground, and looking upward. The stage directions are very specific: 'e stando inzenochiato e' pilgia lo calice in mano cun li occhi levati su, e dice al suo padre' (p. 18). The episode narrated verbally is the historical event of the prayer in the garden, but the one symbolized gesturally is clearly the celebration of the Eucharist, in the context of which the play was meant to be performed. The dramatization of the historical event, in other words, is performed in a manner that alludes visually to the liturgy in which that event is celebrated *sub specie aeternitatis*. The result is that, in this dramatization of the passion narrative, the relationship between the liturgy and history is neatly reversed, the liturgy being here not the agent but the object of anamnesis.

In the theatre of verisimilitude stage properties and accessories handled by the actors are material signs, aids to performance that have normally a descriptive nature and a referential function, representing as they do the equally tangible objects of the characters in the text by a mechanical association of ideas, though, of course, the mechanism of association may vary considerably, from literal and metaphorical likeness to ironic difference. But this is clearly not the case of the chalice in our dramatization of the scene in the garden, which is not in the least based on the aesthetics of verisimilitude. Here the object held by the actor in his hands cannot be regarded as either descriptive or referential with respect to the story, since in the Gospel narrative Jesus spoke of a chalice but did not have one in his hands, whereas in the speech assigned to the actor impersonating him in the play no chalice is mentioned. But since its function is to bring silently to consciousness, on the one hand, the physical sign through which God the Father manifested his will to Jesus in the Gospel, and, on the other hand, the paradigm for its proper interpretation, both of which are outside the story told in the verbal text of the play, the chalice can be regarded as a performative and evocative sign, thematically with respect to Jesus in the play and theatrically with respect to the audience in the church.

Now Jesus and the audience are both confined to the finitude of humanity, a fact much exploited in the fourteenth century – though, to be sure, not nearly as much as in our own unhappy times – for the purpose of arousing empathy. In our story Jesus walks to his place of prayer, and there he finds a chalice waiting for him. In a dramaturgical context, the scene would have little sense if the audience did not know who put the chalice there for Jesus to find, to kneel before it, to take into his hands and to pray with it for possible deliverance. But the context leaves no doubt: the chalice has been left there by God himself as his sign, and the iconographic tradition allows us to conjecture comfortably that God accomplishes this through the agency of the angel mentioned by Luke. The richness and consistency of the visual tradition on this point enables the theatre historian to add a silent character to the cast, to put him on the platform depicting Gethsemane where he is to place the chalice for Jesus. Though in actuality a stage property for the actor, the chalice is thematically a stage property for God, used by him invisibly as a material sign from within the realm of eternity to make manifest his will in the realm of history, to which Jesus is still confined.

In the there and then of the story in the script, the chalice is for Jesus a material channel through which his human imagination may come into more intimate contact with God, from within the limits of his existence as a man – it is a material sign through which he, overcoming the greatest temptation of his humanity, accepts from his Father the mandate of his crucifixion. In the here and now of the implied performance text, described by the theological voice of the narrative and the theological echo of the iconographic tradition, the chalice found in the set of Gethsemane is for the audience a visual evocation of the one on the altar, while the actor playing Jesus is also an evocation of the priest celebrating the Eucharist. In this correlation of the liturgy with the story of the garden in the script, the play is on safe ground, since it offers us nothing more than a then very popular interpretation of the Mass, as described by William Durand in his *Rationale divinorum officiorum*: when the priest walks towards the centre of the altar, Durand says, he symbolizes Jesus going to his place of prayer in Gethsemane; when he bows his head, he symbolizes Jesus suffering before the prospect of his death; and when he looks up, he symbolizes Jesus uttering his prayer.[34] The dramatic form of the play simply reverses the order of signification: when the actor goes to the platform representing Gethsemane, he re-enacts the movement of Jesus but symbolizes the priest approaching the altar; when he picks up his stage property, he symbolizes the priest raising the chalice and so on with his other movements and gestures. The verbal text is the diachronic vehicle of signification; the liturgy, the synchronic sacramental reality signified. The mechanism of signification is visual allusion.

This correlation of the script with the liturgy has significant implications for the visual dimension of early passion plays, since the colours, blocking and gestures of the liturgy were codified in great detail and at times represented in diagrams and illustrations in perspective. If the chalice in the garden scene is an allusion to the chalice on the altar, it cannot be made of glass or wood, but must be gold plated – as it is, in fact, in the iconographic tradition. If the actor playing Jesus is also playing the celebrant, the hillock of Gethsemane must be the altar, and the actor's movement towards and about it must be studied in relation to what was prescribed for movement around the altar.

On the question of gestures and costumes, something dramaturgically analogous occurs in the scene of the flagellation, with which the Good Friday play opens. The script begins with a long stage direction on how to perform it:

> Quando lo predicatore ave predicato fin a quello loco quando Pilato comanda che Cristo sia posto a la colonna, lo Predicatore tase, e vene Cristo nudo con li Frustatori, e vano a lo loco deputato dove sta la colona, e portenlo per mezo de la zente tanto homini quanto femine, si se puo' fare; e Iohanne sta con Cristo, e posto che l'ano a la colona li Frustatori lo frustano un poco devotamente, e poi stano in pace, cioe' quando Cristo vole parlare a Iohanne, e Iohanne sta ante Cristo inzenochiato, e Cristo dice a Iohanne. (p. 19)

> (When he reaches in his sermon the point where Pilate orders that Christ be brought to the column, the preacher stops talking. Then Christ comes out, naked, with his scourgers, and together they go to the set where the column is located.

They bring him through the crowd, which should consist of men and women, if this can be done. John is with Christ. And having brought him to the column, the scourgers whip him a little, devoutly, and then, when Christ motions that he wants to speak to John, they remain there peacefully. John kneels before Christ, and Christ speaks thus to him.)

With respect to the number of soldiers whipping Jesus, the scene called for in this stage direction is essentially the same as the standard iconographic version of the time, which tends to limit it to two, a fact corroborated by the properties list of confraternities that staged passion plays routinely in the area of Perugia using only two whips. But the question of the nudity of Jesus and of the visible attitude of his tormentors is not easily disposed of. The verbal text of the script calls for a naked Jesus, but in the performance text this means only that the actor wore a costume for nudity, which was typically a body suit made of flesh-coloured leather with wounds and drops of blood painted upon it – hardly capable of arousing empathy with its presumed realism.[35] As far as the acting style of the intended performance text is concerned, the flagellation is strikingly different from the style called for by more famous passion plays, in which, it is generally assumed, the scourging needs to be carried out with a considerable degree of realism. In our play there is no doubt that the torturers whip Jesus devoutly and that, having whipped him, remain peacefully on the platform for the rest of the scene. These adverbial qualifiers, *devoutly* and *peacefully*, are laden with semiotic implications for our understanding of the gestural action carried out and of the theory of performance presupposed. The actors are expected to play and yet not to play the roles of the historical torturers. They must perform the action of scourging Jesus, while speaking words of savage cruelty to him, but they must appear to do so as an act of piety rather than as an act of cruelty. And when they have performed their action, they must appear on stage as men who are now at peace with themselves and with God.

The stage directions, in other words, call for a very complex and very demanding style of acting. In pretending to whip Jesus, the actors mime the flagellation as an event in history; in pretending to do so devoutly, they perform the scourging as a ritual of atonement; in pretending to be at peace with themselves and with God for having done so, they perform the efficacy of the ritual. The flagellation thus enacted is at the same time a visualized sign of sacred history, a lesson in moral theology, and an invitation to penitential practice. At no time must the actors pretend to transport the audience into the reality of the past, so that they might experience more intensely the horror of that moment of sacred history and be overcome by an upsurge of hatred for the scourgers.

This would be a spurious production concept decidedly excluded by the stage directions. On the contrary, their effort must be to transport the past into the present, wherein the same event, recognizable for its uniqueness, can occur rememoratively and efficaciously as a moment, both horrible and redemptive, in their own lives. Viewed from the perspective of Christian theology, the purpose of theatre is to enable man 'to recollect himself and to remember who he is'.[36] In a place of performance that is nothing more than an architectural signifier for the mystical body of Christ, tragic catharsis is an act of self-recognition and participation in the signified metaphysical substance of that body rather than in the material one that signifies it. The audience must not be made to feel that, in the actors performing the flagellation, they can imaginatively see the cruelty of the historical torturers. They must instead be enabled to see that these torturers are semiotic projections of contemporary Christians like themselves, in pursuit of atonement through a sacred ritual.

In order to transport the past into the present and yet to respect its historical distinction from the present, the actors must perform their roles from outside the imagined self-understanding of the characters, in the alienated mode of one who does not make his character's emotions his own. But in order to superimpose on the characters of the scourgers appropriate projections of typical spectators in the audience, they must perform their roles from inside the presumed self-understanding of typical members of the congregation in attendance. Their bodies and their voices must be protean enough, and their understanding of their roles must be clear enough to them, for them to fuse the two levels of reality and to produce them as indivisible signs in a single act of performance, like the vowels of a diphthong pronounced with a single issue of breath. We may recall that the iconographic tradition of the flagellation is divided on this point: in some cases, the soldiers are caught in a posture of savagery, while in other cases they are shown more or less at peace – an indication, perhaps, that passion plays with intended performance texts in the liturgical mode were not as rare as the surviving scripts would lead us to believe.

Some final reflections

As we make our final approach, it may be instructive for us to reflect for a moment on these issues from the perspective of the concept of time involved in them. It may seem from the verbal text that passion plays, being intentional recollections of historical events, are concerned chiefly with ways of turning our gaze to the past, by way of the spectacle of suffering. But recollection is an activity of the mind in the present, and to remember is simply to live the present moment performing that activity, as a species of meditation, on the assumption that it may fulfil our present yearning for meaning. From an Augustinian perspective, we can observe that recollection is but the present time of things past, just as hope is a present time of things future, and perception the present time of things present. The chief concern of the plays and, we may add, of the liturgy in which the same events are celebrated is not with the magnitude of the suffering of Jesus as a man in history but with the here and now of the community in attendance. The dramaturgical task of ensuring that the audience retain throughout full consciousness of their location in the present does not fall to the speeches in the text but to the stage directions that support them. By prescribing the right properties, costumes and gestures, they ensure that the community does not get catapulted by the language into the reconstructed spectacle of violence and is not confused by the desire to pursue a more intimate knowledge of the Passion as an end in itself – propelled, perhaps, by that unhealthy spiritual disposition that medieval theology called *mala curiositas*. Sacred history, the visual text of the stage directions tells the members of the audience, is not meaningful in itself if it is not meaningful for each of them at that particular moment of their lives.

The conception of dramaturgy to which my argument reaches out is of considerable sophistication in the history of the theatre: the dramatic form with which the plays are invested is at once bifocal with respect to the representation of history, and ambivalent with respect to intended response. The complexity of this idea of drama may not be immediately clear to scholars easily persuaded that popular art forms are of necessity technically crude and intellectually shallow, even at their most majestic. Such an attitude – which Vico might call the conceit of scholars – is ultimately the result of an unwitting infantilization of the unschooled, thought to lack all tools of sophistication because of insufficient access to intellectual apprenticeship. Yet I would submit that the uneducated congregations of the time, accustomed by preachers to reflection on a Bible that they could not read, deriving their education from the walls of a church that imparted moral theology by means of architecture and imagery, were likely to be in more intimate contact with the theological principles underlying the art of Passiontide drama, and with the way in which script and performance text were related to their Scriptural and liturgical referents, than modern audiences are with the ideological principles that inform the popular art forms of our times.

To be sure, we may never find out what sort of preparatory exercises the medieval player had to go through in order to make himself ready to become a stage sign for a soldier whipping Jesus and a member of his own community performing an act of devotion and redemption at the same time. We can, however, say with some confidence that the theoretical basis for such a conception of spiritual dramaturgy was an aspect of contemporary culture familiar not only to the preacher, who probably made routine use of it in his sermons, but also to the congregation listening to him. The double historical focus and the intended ambivalence of response are ultimately rooted in the contemporary apparatus for the conceptual interpretation of the Bible and the liturgy. In the account of William Durand each component of a liturgical act is subject to a fourfold interpretation: historical, allegorical, tropological and anagogic.[37] For the art of preaching and for the dramaturgy of sacred catharsis the central moment of this hermeneutic is the tropological one, when each member of the congregation – which is to say, each member of the audience – seeks to discover the meaning that the scriptural event has for him or her, at that particular moment, his or her life as a private individual and as a member of his or her community. The call of tropology is a call to theological introspection and redemptive practice, and it is issued to the individual as well as the community. In a tropologically clear dramaturgy of the Passion, Jesus cannot be naked other than through a body suit, he cannot be whipped other than devoutly and he cannot hold a chalice that is not also a sign for the one on the altar.

These considerations enable us to draw at least two inferences, both significant for the study of passion drama: one concerning the structure of the play text and the other the structure of its perception as a sacred tragedy, in so far as the structure of perception can be governed from within the text. The first inference is that the direction of narrative dependency normally assumed to exist between the dialogue and the stage directions should be reversed, the higher degree of semiotic autonomy belonging to the stage directions and not to the verbal speeches of the characters. The play's primary narrative voice is the visual one of the stage directions, and the story that it tells, with the help of the surrounding visual culture, is the host narrative into which the other is inserted in the manner of a corroborating quotation. The primary narrative is a story of sacramental spirituality, and it is necessarily conceived in the present tense. It uses the visual rhetoric of the liturgy, it is focused on the theology of the Eucharist and it carries a message of reconciliation with God. The dialogue, on the other hand, consists of supporting scriptural material, enriched with details from pious apocryphal sources, transformed into rhythmical verse and offered in the manner of a rhapsodic quotation in the present tense, though it is semiotically confined to the preterit. The primary narrative voice is presentational, and therefore speaks from the present to the present. The quoted narrative voice is representational and speaks from the reconstructed past for the benefit of the present. The material of the presentational narrative is neither historical nor emotional but openly theological and sacramental. In this sense it is analogous to the theological vision of the authors of the Gospels, the vision within which they redacted the parables and episodes of the life of Jesus, boldly adapting them to the different theological goals by which they knew to be governed.

The second inference is that the audience's perception of the play is structured as an oscillation of consciousness between the presentational and the representational objects of the performance text. This mode of experience is necessarily dialectical, since the mind, other than by abstraction, cannot move towards one of the semiotic dimensions of the play without responding to the magnetism of the other, both being present at every moment of the action. Were this not the case, the representational story would have no necessary relation to the liturgy and would be formally indistinguishable from any other historical drama of suffering. By the same token, the presentational dimension would be no more than a dramatization of a sermon on the Eucharist.

These two dimensions of the text give rise between them to a structured semantic space, an intertext flanked by the spoken narrative of the Passion and the visual discourse on the Eucharist, within which the audience can experience the performance both aesthetically and hermeneutically. On the aesthetic side, the dialectic governs our experience of the play by showing that the place in which it operates is the ultimate origin of its form, the source of both its conceptual organization and its ontological clarity. On the hermeneutical side, the same dialectic governs our understanding of the play, by showing that neither dimension of the text is self-contained and by directing us to the inference that history and faith are thereby related by continuity and reciprocal implication.

7

Signs of the Passion and signs of compassion

In his *Disputed Questions on Truth*, St Thomas Aquinas famously observes that the sacraments *significando causant*, a formula by which he means that sacraments are efficacious signs that vehicle into human reality the divine grace that they designate.¹ This formula is also a good point of departure for the analytical consideration of non-sacramental signs that have a causative function of some sort. It can be easily adapted to cover signs that, in addition to providing information, also cause the perceiver to act in a particular way towards that which they signify. Figurative signs in the sacred art that decorates churches, prayer books and private places of devotions are meant not only to teach the viewers a sacred narrative but also to initiate in them a transformative psychological action. While signifying, such signs provoke the viewer to action. They combine two of the basic functions of language – a term that in this context is understood to cover verbal as well as non-verbal modes of communication – namely, the referential function, by which they designate spiritual truths, and the conative function, by which they invite the viewer to assume a spiritual attitude and to engage in a particular course of action. All signs that seek to enlighten and to convert the viewer – or the hearer and reader, as the case may be – could be grouped under this rubric. Such signs are used to tell a story (*significando*) and to influence spiritual attitude (*causant*) towards what they signify, which is usually an episode from Scripture or other spiritually edifying narrative inspired by a sacred text and validated by the church.

Narratives that do not have an authoritative textual source behind them present special challenges, since their constituent signs must be so chosen and combined to tell an intelligible and plausible story and to influence the viewer's spiritual approach to it. Among these, a highly problematic narrative is the story of the Passion, since, despite the centrality of its message in Christianity, the Gospels give almost no details about those who witnessed it and about the way the crucifixion was carried out. Writers and artists were thus required to visualize the response of those who accompanied Jesus to his death and the mode of crucifixion to which he was subjected, as the paradigm or template of their own interpretation of the narrative of the Passion. In doing so they followed, and contributed to the further development of, devotional practices and theology. The purpose of this chapter is to consider the semiotic process involved in making such artistic choices, starting with Cajetan's analysis of the proper way of representing the suffering of Mary as a witness of the Passion of her son, and following it with various depictions of the crucifixion in a manner that does not elicit a strong emotional response.

Cajetan on the swoon of Mary

By the time that in 1506 Thomas De Vio, then professor of theology at the University of Rome, wrote his tract *De Spasmo Beatae Virginis Mariae* (*On the Swoon of the Blessed Virgin Mary*), the swoon of the Virgin was a popular motif in Marian devotion and religious art, wherein it figured as a visible sign of the unspeakable pain by which she was seized when she first saw her tortured son dragging his cross to his place of execution.[2] The swoon was part of a semiotic code used by artists, writers and preachers to create an emotionally charged image of the *mater dolorosa* and to promote devout exercises in the empathic exploration of her sorrow. As a theme, the practice of its commemoration and its artistic representation was rooted in a long tradition of Marian piety that had gained much momentum in the late Middle Ages and early Renaissance, reaching a high point towards the end of the fifteenth century.[3] By that time, belief in the historical reality of the swoon of Mary and in the penitential significance of its recollection in affective meditations had gained such acceptance that in Flanders a group of devotees constituted themselves as a fraternity devoted solely to the practice of Marian compassion, while the local clergy petitioned Pope Julius II to authorize a feast on the Friday before Palm Sunday for the celebration of the Mary's sorrow focused on her swoon, and to promote attendance at its liturgical commemoration with the reward of indulgences. Once authorized, the feast formally marked the beginning of the popular worship of Mary as Our Lady of Sorrows.

The whirlwind of piety around the sorrows of Mary and the increasing enthusiasm for the commemoration of her swoon were a cause of concern for some theologians and custodians of doctrine, and the Marian momentum soon ran into some opposition. As a sign for the grief of the Mother of God, the swoon had significant theological implications. In addition to emphasizing the human dimension of the Passion to pathological proportions at the expense of its spiritual message, it showcased Mary sharing the Passion of Christ almost to the same degree, and it invited belief in the salvific value of penitential meditation on her pain, thereby profiling for her a crucial role in the economy of redemption. In recent decades, Mariology had been growing at a rapid pace, re-elaborating images and sentiments that had been previously part only of meditative exercises on the Passion of Christ. As an expression of the sharing of Christ's pain to the point of virtual death, the swoon had great appeal for artists concerned with showing Mary's role in the Passion, so much so that around one half of the crucifixion paintings from the fourteenth and fifteenth centuries show the Virgin swooning. Erasmus found the whole thing offensive, there being no scriptural basis for such an exaltation. It pointed to a theology of active collaboration in the attainment of grace. Such an anthropology was difficult to justify, and there was need for clarity.[4] Nobody questioned the reality of Mary's pain, but whether a swoon was a correct sign for it was not at all clear. Therefore when the petition for the approval of a general *Festum Spasmi Beatae Mariae* or *Notre Dame de la Pâmoison* ('Feast of the Swoon of the Blessed Mary', p. 180) arrived together with a request for the approval of indulgences for attendance, one of the cardinals asked Cajetan for a reasoned theological opinion on the canonicity of the swoon as a sign for Mary's grief.

The need for clarity arose chiefly from the fact that there was no scriptural basis for the swoon of the Virgin, at least not an authentic one. The source of the tradition was the apocryphal gospel of Nicodemus in the text of the longer Greek recension, in which we read that when she saw Jesus being led to his crucifixion, Mary fainted (10.1) falling backwards to the ground among the weeping women in her company.[5] Conceived in all probability on the model of the swooning of Andromache, who collapsed into the arms of her attending maidens when she first saw Hector's cruelly abused body,[6] the scene of Mary's swoon at her first sighting of Jesus following his arrest entered deep into the spiritual imagination of the Middle Ages and was incorporated into Marian devotional practices, as if it had the full authentication of Scripture. Whether it was spoken, painted or sculpted, the swoon was a sign meant to give rise to a sense of intimacy with the inner sorrow of Mary, which it manifested. Variously visualized by artists and writers of spiritual themes, her swoon was regarded as a cognitive point of access to the nature and depth of Mary's anguish as *mater dolorosa*. Her swoon invited readers, hearers and viewers alike to contemplate the Passion of Jesus through her eyes and to understand it through her pain, in a prolonged empathic meditation on the swoon as a physical sign of her suffering. It also invited them to gain some insight into the nature of Mary's suffering through the experience of their own emotions in the presence of images of overpowering grief. The swoon was an expressive sign of Mary's compassion, etymologically understood as intentional suffering alongside the sufferer, and a stimulus to seek participation in her sorrow in an act of affective piety, as a penitential turn towards meriting redemption.

Eventually the swoon of Mary became an integral part of the penitential culture. It encouraged women to give meaning to their suffering, particularly the suffering of motherhood, by relating it to the suffering of Mary and by interpreting it in terms of sacramental penance. The suffering of motherhood could thus be articulated as an imitation, albeit a pale one, of the suffering of Mary during the Passion of Jesus.[7] It was pale not only on account of the intensity of what Mary had to endure but also on account of the fact that, through her suffering at the death of her son, she symbolically gave birth to the church. This view was based on the traditional interpretation of the woman clothed with the sun (Apoc. 12.1-2) crying out the pain of childbirth, read as Mary's symbolic parturition of the church, which could come into existence only at and through the death of Christ. Mary's suffering at the death of her son was the mystical labour of her motherhood of the church for the salvation of mankind. This view gave rise to the notion that the labour of human motherhood could signify by analogy the labour of Mary and could recall its salvific function. By a metaphorical extension of the physical suffering of childbirth to the suffering of the soul at the moment of confession,[8] when the soul gives birth to a purified form of itself, the semantic field of Mary's suffering was amplified to include men as well as women. Full identification with Mary, however, could naturally be interpreted only as a woman's penitential ideal, for in virtue of their (real or potential) motherhood, women were also living signs of Mary in a way that men could not be. Yet, as we have seen in previous chapters, women, viewed under the aspect of their perceived weakness to temptation, were also signs of Eve. Indeed, under the aspect of their alleged proneness to deceitful temptation, they could also be signs of the devil himself. Their sensual and potentially 'serpentine' nature, attributed to them by a theological reflection of considerable gravity and apparently authenticated by Scripture, had made unredeemed femaleness the gate through which sin and death poured into the world. There were grounds for contrast between the two semiotic associations and hence, as the popularity of the commemorative celebration and artistic representations of our Lady of Sorrows increased, there developed an oppositional movement against its perceived excesses. Cajetan's *De Spasmo*, written as it was in response to an official request for an informed view, is an early contribution to the movement against the excesses of Marian devotional practices focused on the magnitude of her sorrow during the Passion.

The penitential interpretation of the swoon of Mary involves an analysis of suffering in which semiotics is identified with diagnostics, as in one of the most ancient theories of signs as medical symptoms. In this approach to the language of the body, signs are 'compulsive, automatic and non-arbitrary',[9] which is to say that they are involuntary and unintended physical expressions of an inner condition of the subject, to which they are linked by biological continuity. The semiotic aspects of syncope preoccupied theologians who were troubled by the rise in popularity of the swooning of Mary motif, concerned that the image might have unwarranted theological implications for current official doctrines, especially with regard to the granting of indulgences for its liturgical commemoration. The question before Cajetan was what, precisely, did the swoon of Mary signify, since swooning can be taken in two different senses: one technical, as the loss of consciousness caused by a morbid alteration of the body's ability to sustain the experience of suffering; the other popular, as a sudden feeling of weakness and unclear consciousness when one is confronted by unexpected grief, a condition usually relieved by sprinkling cool water on the person's face. Cajetan was first of all concerned with the technical usage of the term, for that was its proper sense, and in order to determine its meaning with precision he consulted Avicenna's treatise on swooning.[10] Avicenna was a fundamental source on the interpretation of syncope as a sign of inner distress and disease. If the problem consisted in finding a proper way of signifying such inner physical corruption as something that actually existed in reality, then surely the image of a swoon could be used to signify it. But the body of Mary, Cajetan argued, though human, was endowed with a special dignity, in virtue of which it was worthy of being the body of the Mother of God, and hence could not have been subject to such internal corruption. In the non-technical use of the word, the temporary loss of control over one's body could be employed to signify a sudden onslaught of emotional suffering, greater than a healthy person can endure. In either case, Mary's swoon would have to be considered a symptomatic signifier pointing the mind of the beholder to a morbid physical condition, or to a grief of a higher order of magnitude than her body could sustain, since excessive suffering tightens the sinews and manifests itself as loss of consciousness.

In this argument, the modern reader may detect an unusual degree of fluidity in the idea of signification, applied to the term *spasmus* as if it were the symptom itself – rather than only its linguistic designation – of the inner state of the Virgin Mary, without giving rise to any consciousness of crossing a disciplinary boundary between language and diagnostics. The reason for the fluidity is that for Renaissance scholars the concepts of sign and symptom were convertible into each other. The philosophical root of their approach to signification is found in Aristotle's treatise *Peri hermeneias* (*On Interpretation*), a work with which Cajetan was very familiar, having edited and completed St Thomas's commentary on it in 1496. There we find that vocal sounds – that is, words – are 'signs of passions in the soul' (16a3), and in this expression signs (σύμβολα) clearly mean symptoms.[11] The classical theory of signs, to which some Renaissance scholars returned, especially in Aristotelian circles, did not distinguish, as we do, linguistic from symptomatic signification.[12] So conceived, signification has a conceptual amplitude that enables easy movement between linguistic and visual signs of the passions suffered by the soul. On this premise, the question of the canonicity of the term *spasmus* does not entail ascertaining its meaning in other theological works but in determining, from Scriptural sources, what passion did Mary in fact suffer in her soul as a witness of her son's Passion. Was her experience of suffering through com-passion such that it caused her to swoon? To this effect, Cajetan cites Simeon's prophecy on the happy occasion of Mary's purification that a sword would one day pierce her heart (Lk. 2.34), taking the Lucan passage in the interpretation of St John Damascene, for whom the piercing sword referred prophetically to the very great pain that Mary would have to bear in witnessing the Passion and death of her son. This interpretation of Simeon's prophecy played an important part in the development of the image of Mary as *mater dolorosa*, routinely depicted in popular piety at first with one sword and later, as her other sorrows were foregrounded, with seven swords piercing her heart.[13]

Swoon artists who wanted to express the intensity of Mary's suffering when she first saw her son on his way to Calvary could thus have recourse to this tradition, which appeared to justify representing Mary's pain by the image of fainting, taken as the proper signifier of the passion of her soul: the suffering of her son so pierced her heart that she fainted. According to the pseudo-Bonaventuran *Meditationes vitae Christi*, it also happened at the foot of the cross, where Mary fell 'inter brachia Magdalene', but the subsequent swoon culture easily multiplied its occurrences.[14] The painted or narrated swoon, however, did not arise naturally from textual interpretation or from the application of official doctrine but from a process of reverse semiosis, which starts with the presumption of an invisible inner signified and posits a likely external signifier, which artists and writers depict as if calling the passion in Mary's soul by its name. This semiotic reasoning, which greatly emphasized the humanity of Mary, was informed by medical and theological knowledge. Such knowledge gave credence to the belief that Mary indeed fainted in witnessing the Passion of her son, and hence suggested using the image of her swoon as a true pictorial signifier of her internal condition. Yet Cajetan rejected this position, on scriptural as well as inferential grounds. Scripturally, the assumption that Mary fainted contradicts the Gospel passage according to which she *stabat iuxta crucem* (Jn 19.25), an expression in which the verb *stabat* means 'stood', as Cajetan illustrates with the aid of various examples (p. 181). Mary could not have fainted in a nearby place and then regained her consciousness and strength minutes later, when the text describes her standing at the foot of the cross to witness even greater suffering. The belief that she fainted was thus refutable on philological grounds. But according to Cajetan, it could also be invalidated by rational argument. The fact that, as a signifier, fainting signifies the experience of suffering does not logically imply that the experience of suffering, however intense, necessarily causes the sufferer to swoon. Cajetan cites the example of Jesus himself, who did not faint during his Passion though the suffering that he had to endure as a man was indeed great. Therefore, though in depictions of the Passion the signified idea is the suffering to which Jesus was subjected, its external signifier is not a swoon. The same thing, Cajetan proposes, was true of Mary: her suffering was certainly intense, but she endured it without fainting.

To prove that it is not appropriate to represent Mary swooning or to believe that she actually did swoon, Cajetan cites the phrase *gratia plena* from the Gospel of Luke (1.28), which he, apparently still unaware of, or unimpressed by, Lorenzo Valla's recent 're-appropriation' of the Greek text, interprets as a statement of the fullness and perfection (*plenitudinem perfectionemque*, p. 181) of Mary's grace.[15] On that premise, he argues, it is not possible to admit that Mary's suffering was such as to cause her to faint. For fainting is also a sign of weakness or morbid deficiency, attributes that would have impeded Mary from attaining the fullness and perfection of grace that she instead did attain. Moreover, excessive suffering causes people to become distraught with emotion and unable to exercise their power to reason. Properly applied, reason allows individuals to have some control over their emotions, which belong to a lower level of being. People who are overcome by suffering reverse the order, allowing their reason to be subdued by their emotions. Mary was definitely all human, and if she had suffered such pain, she would have surely reacted in a human way, that is, by losing control of her ability to reason and hence by failing to understand her own suffering. It would have been inappropriate to attribute to her a suffering of such intensity as to cloud her mind because it would have prevented her from sharing in the

Passion of the Lord, not only emotionally but also intellectually, by discerning God's purpose in it and by keeping the affective aspects of her being under the control of her intellect. Hence, on the basis of Gabriel's salutation *Ave Maria gratia plena* we can safely say that Mary did not suffer a swoon, for that would have revealed her grace to be less perfect than Gabriel says it was, while on the basis of her intellectual participation in the Passion of Christ, we can conclude that her suffering, though intense, did not overpower her mind, allowing her emotions to cause her to lose consciousness. For each of these reasons, the image of the swooning Virgin is not a correct visual sign of her interior experience as a witness of her son's Passion.

Returning to the question whether a celebration of the swoon of Mary as a commemoration of her suffering at the Passion would be canonical, Cajetan says categorically that it would not. Besides the fact that it is based on an apocryphal gospel, the swoon of Mary is an inaccurate sign of the reality that it purports to signify. Indeed 'swoon' is a misnomer, since Mary's physico-spiritual dignity was inconsistent with the human weakness of swooning, whether swooning is understood as a medical sign of disease or as a popular sign of sudden enfeeblement and loss of consciousness. Mary did not swoon, Cajetan concludes, because she could not have swooned. If the church is to commemorate the sorrow of Mary in a feast, let it do so under a more appropriate title and without recourse to a swoon as the signifier of the passion of her soul.

Cajetan understood well an aspect of semiosis that was to be made clear by Peirce. Among his many definitions of the semiotic process, Peirce makes the following statement, which applies well to Cajetan's analysis of the swoon of Mary:

> Suffice it to say that a sign endeavours to represent, in part at least, an object, which is therefore in a sense the cause, or determinant, of the sign even if the sign represents its object falsely. But to say that it represents its object implies that it affects a mind, and so affects it as, in some respect, to determine in that mind something that is mediately due to the object.[16]

In the relationship between sign and the object that it signifies, the object is the causative agent. It gives shape and meaning to the sign by which it purports to be represented, even if in the end the representation should turn out to be false. The swoon does not arise as a sign out of nothing but out of real suffering, which determines it as its sign for the artist. The theologian concludes that the sign represents its object falsely by comparing what the sign suggests to the object as he knows it to have been in reality from his knowledge of scripture and theology. The theologian's path in this process is the reverse of the one followed by ordinary contemplative Christians. He does not move empathically from the visible sign to the invisible object, as they do, but coolly and rationally from the object, whose existence he has established independently, to the image given as its sign. His path reflects the traditional approach to knowledge, which posits metaphysics as the first science and the arts as the last, with the metaphysics of the object determining language and imagery of its sign. That is how he is able to identify that the false element in the representation is due to the artist's not having taken into account at least two things, which show that Mary is related analogically rather than univocally to all other mothers: first, the unique dignity conferred on her by God, as a special grace that guarded her from syncope without attenuating her suffering, and second, her capacity to participate not only emotionally but also intellectually in her son's Passion, which enabled her to see the full significance of her suffering in the context of the redemption, beyond the horizon of her personal situation as a mother.

Once Mary's swoon entered collective consciousness, as an element of a human vocabulary for the intentional signification of a spiritual reality, it became itself a powerful determinant, giving rise in the minds of its users to an intimate understanding of the Virgin that revealed her suffering to resemble their own, the difference being mostly one of degree rather than kind. Their path to enlightenment was antithetical to the one followed by the theologian, proceeding as it did from the visible sign to its invisible object, with the result that in their case metaphysics ended up being determined by language and imagery rather than the other way round. Marian popular culture encouraged affective meditation on the image of the swoon, exploring it in every detail, so as to gain in the process an emotional understanding of the suffering that produced it as its visible sign. By focusing all of their attention participatively onto it, typical devotees determined Mary's suffering by experiencing it penitentially as being partly their own, in a univocal understanding of resemblance that only the empathic imagination can make possible. The usage and interpretation of signs put us always on the razor edge between error and truth, and hence in need of guidance from those who have the authority to provide it. That was, in essence, Cajetan's recommendation to the church.

Cruce erecta

In the religious culture of the Middle Ages, there were two modes of imagining the crucifixion process, described in detail in the *Meditationes vitae Christi*, a composite work once attributed to St Bonaventure but probably written by Johannes de Caulibus on the basis, as Sarah McNamer has shown, of an earlier Italian version, with additional interpolations in Latin by a later Franciscan editor.[17] The first mode, known as crucifixion *cruce iacente*, entails setting the cross down on the ground and making Jesus lie on it to be crucified, at which point the cross would be raised and fixed vertically by inserting the post into a hole in the ground. The second mode, known as crucifixion *cruce erecta*, entailed first fixing the cross vertically and then causing Jesus to climb onto it to be crucified. The two modes, both of which predate the composition of the *Meditationes*, are strikingly different and represent antithetical approaches to the theological role of conative signs of suffering – that is to say, signs that betray the author's deliberate intent to generate a feeling of pathos – in the narrative of the crucifixion.

The *cruce iacente* method has dominated the Christian imagination in the modern period, with its great appetite for the crude realism to which the process lends itself. It greatly emphasizes the human dimension of Jesus as a resisting victim, violently forced onto the cross by cruel executioners. The visual narrative of *cruce iacente* representations of the crucifixion is articulated in a manner intended to give prominence to a theology of the humanity of Jesus, privileging the incarnation over the resurrection as the major premise, and is designed to provoke emotional participation in his suffering. It is a narrative whose point of observation is located in the past, after the flagellation, from which the viewer is invited to consider with empathy the accumulation of Jesus's injuries and torture leading to his painful death on the cross, and, we might expect, the pathos of the swooning Virgin.

The *cruce erecta* method, described in much greater detail in the *Meditationes*, shows Jesus actively participating in his execution, willingly mounting the cross and correctly positioning himself onto it so that his executioners may nail down his hands and feet. It greatly emphasizes the divine dimension of Jesus, approaching his death and collaborating with his executioners with the knowledge that he will soon triumph over it. The visual narrative of *cruce erecta* depictions of the crucifixion is intended to give prominence to a theology of the divinity of Jesus, ultimately privileging the resurrection over the incarnation as the starting premise of its argument, and to elicit in the beholder a sense of hope that redemption is at hand. It is a narrative whose point of observation is located in the future, after the resurrection, from which the viewer is invited to consider the redemptive function of Jesus's sacrifice on the cross. It leads us to expect, not the pathos of a swooning Madonna, but the emotional sobriety of a mother certain that her son is divine as well as human, and that his execution, though a cause of great suffering, is a temporary surrender to death, willingly accepted for the redemption of mankind.

There were early iconographic examples of *cruce erecta* crucifixions in which the figure of Jesus was depicted in more human terms, but the one described in the *Meditationes* represents the basic narrative paradigm for the early modern period.[18] There are many excellent examples of the way this paradigm was used to construct a visual narrative of the crucifixion. Here we will discuss only three of them, selected to illustrate the thematic range of which this mode of envisioning the Passion was capable: Pacino da Bonaguida's illumination of the crucifixion in a manuscript in the Morgan library collection,[19] the Fresco of the crucifixion in the chapel of Sant'Antonio in Polesine in Ferrara and Fra Angelico's depiction of the subject in the convent of San Marco in Florence.

Pacino's illuminated panel depicts the idea of the crucifixion more than the actual process. Although the elements of the composition are all realistically rendered – they are all signs that signify by resemblance – the composition represents a narrative of abstract theological concepts. While the lower part of Christ's body is wrapped in the semi-transparent veil with which Mary had covered his nakedness, his sanctity is marked by a halo and by the absence of wounds, bleeding and other marks of torture and maltreatment since his arrest. The absence of expected signs is therefore itself significant, indicating that, in his vision of the crucifixion, Pacino has artistically transformed the tortured body of Christ into a sign of spiritual perfection. The body of Christ signifies his human nature, but the unblemished appearance of his skin signifies his divine nature. Christ is shown climbing the ladder of his own volition, without prodding, while a soldier offers him a hammer, almost as if he were expected to crucify himself – a gestural sign, no doubt, that the narrative of the crucifixion is the story of the self-sacrifice of God through his human–divine person.

The cross to which Jesus Christ is to be nailed has the shape of a patriarchal cross staff, consisting of a vertical pole with two horizontal crossbars of different length – the long one for the arms of Christ and the short one above it for the inscription (*Iesus Nazarenus Rex Iudaeorum*) ordered by Pilate. In the late medieval period, the patriarchal cross was part of the insignia of higher prelates, including archbishops and cardinals, which is to say the church, as represented by its higher prelates. It was a symbol of their dignity and authority, and, in liturgical processions, it was carried in front of them with the corpus of Christ facing forward as a sign that he is the true hierarch of the church. Depicted thus, the cross is a sign with a triple signifying function, each with a referent in a different narrative. The cross in fact refers Pacino's viewers at once to the

Figure 5 The Crucifixion Pacino da Bonaguida. Creative Commons (Public Domain).

historical event of the crucifixion, to the church as the institution ordained by Christ, and to the liturgical commemoration of the sacrifice of Christ for the redemption of mankind. The first narrative takes place in historical time at a precise moment of the past, the second in continuing time throughout the existence of the church subsequent to the crucifixion and resurrection and the third in the present moment of the liturgy, whenever it is celebrated.

Pacino's painting fuses together the separate times and settings of his three layered narratives into a single meditative moment in front of the cross. In causing this movement in the viewer's mind, it is a pictorial analogue of what narrative theory has been calling a chronotope, since Bakhtin first introduced the concept and the term. A chronotope is a unit of discourse that foregrounds the connectedness of time and space, 'materializing time in space', and that emerges as the centre from which all abstract elements of the narrative, including all ideas and arguments, derive their sense.[20] In pictorial as in verbal narrative, a chronotope is a junction point that all the narratives traverse and from which they derive the crucial part of their meaning. Everything seems to gravitate towards it, because it is the semiotic centre of the composition, without which the rest of the picture would have little meaning. At the chronotopic juncture of narratives, the discovery of meaning is an entirely cognitive achievement, an experience of intellectual rather than affective meditation.

This kind of meditation leads to calm thinking rather than emotional participation and mystical rapture. The mind proceeds slowly, step by step, from the first apprehension of the historical details of the Passion to the abstract principles of which they are signs, articulated as theological precepts by the church. Abstract principles can be visualized as characters performing particular actions, but they can be grasped only as verbal discourse, imagined or real though it may be. The interpretation of pictorial signs consists largely in their translation as discourse.[21] From the calm demeanour of the soldiers on the right and from the friendly gesture of the one holding the hammer up to Jesus, we know that, though they figure literally as characters in the historical narrative of the crucifixion, the soldiers are symbolically characters in the other two narratives as well. In the ecclesiastical narrative they have the benefit of the teaching of the church, in which the signs of the historical crucifixion have already been interpreted as theological discourse and distilled into precepts. In the liturgical narrative, they participate in a ritual ordained and performed for their salvation, and in that narrative the hammer-holding soldier is virtually an altar boy assisting a priest as a figure of Christ in the commemorative celebration of the crucifixion. The chronotopic layering of stories makes the soldiers Christians from the time of the artist who looks to the crucifixion as Christ's freely given ransom of himself for their redemption and who use Pacino's image as a visual aid in their contemplative meditation of this truth.

In the light of this chronotope, the ladder that Jesus is climbing has a special semiotic function in the spiritual exercise of meditative ascent, understood as the mind's climb to communion with God. The seven rungs of the ladder are in all probability signs for the seven gifts of the Holy Spirit, dispositions of the mind, as Bonaventure taught, that enable man to follow the precepts of the church necessary for his ascent to God.[22] All the gifts are necessary, but Pacino pays special attention to the gift of Christian fortitude, and he does this by the dignified composure of the Blessed Virgin Mary. According to Bonaventure, Mary was endowed with Christian fortitude more fully than any other human being, which is why she was able to endure the pain of his Passion. The Blessed Virgin appears 'clothed' with fortitude, and, through her, so does the church.[23] True to this interpretation, Pacino da Bonaguida does not depict her swooning or weeping, but composed and without any physical signs of unbearable suffering, with her sanctity indicated by a bright halo. The Blessed Virgin is the exemplar of fortitude as a character in all three narratives of the visual chronotope. She was blessed with the fortitude that she needed to witness the sacrifice of her son, thereby collaborating with Christ as his coredemptrix, as taught by the church. Christ's ascent up to the arms of the cross, ready to yield himself to death by crucifixion, was depicted by Pacino as an action signifying that he really suffered death on the cross for the sake of mankind, while Mary participated patiently in the sacrifice, with the fortitude to contain her sorrow for having contributed her only son to the economy of salvation.

Located on a wall of the side chapel of the monastery of St Antonio in Polesine, and probably by members of Giotto's school, the Ferrara fresco of a *cruce erecta* crucifixion follows the same narrative paradigm. Jesus is climbing a ladder leaning against the cross to which he will be nailed. The cross itself is not modelled on a staff and hence does not openly allude to the church or the liturgy. Standing to the left of the cross are two soldiers and a Hebrew elder, while on the right there are two other male characters, unconcerned with the crucifixion, engaged in what appears to be the post-crucifixion division of Jesus's garments. As Jesus ascends, one of the two executioners kneeling on top of the horizontal bar of the cross bends down offering him a hand to help him climb, while a soldier pierces his side with a long spear, and a little blood spills from the wound, but Jesus continues to climb with the spear in his flesh, seemingly undisturbed by the injury. His body is depicted in the transfigured mode signified by his halo – the only halo in the fresco – without visible manifestations of suffering and without blemishes of any kind, other than the wound made by the spear. Clearly the chronotope of the cross brings together two narratives: the historical one, telling the viewer what took place on Calvary, and the theological one, describing how Christ had an active role in his crucifixion, to which he freely climbed. Jesus is the central figure of both narratives.

Figure 6 Jesus Mounting the Cross, Chapel of Monastero di Sant'Antonio in Polesine, Ferrara (author's photograph of a wooden reproduction).

The two narratives are superimposed on the figure of Jesus Christ, who is a figure of both narratives at the same time. The rest is about history. The primary didactic purpose appears to be to teach history and simultaneously to help the viewer visualize the event of the crucifixion in the theological context of the redemption. The scene surrounding it on either side of the cross includes a soldier and an agitated patriarch in the foreground on the left and the two calm figures dividing the garments of Jesus in the pastoral landscape on the right. The characters are not static but in the process of expressing emotions and performing actions, and none of them contributes anything of significance to the theology of redemption signified by Jesus's ascent of the ladder. Because much more of the fresco is about the compositional details of the narrative than its theological symbolism, the scene is dramatically richer than the one painted by Pacino da Bonaguida but semiotically less complex.

The semiotic simplicity, however, is limited to the internal configuration of the scene and not to the scene as a whole. For when we consider the scene itself in a semiotic perspective, regarding the entire composition as a single sign, and hence in relation to other possible configurations themselves considered as signs, the artist's depiction of the historical event of the crucifixion reveals itself to be strikingly different from, and hence to position the viewer against, visual narratives such as the one depicted by Pacino da Bonaguida. The crucial difference between them is the deliberate omission of the Virgin Mary from the scene of the crucifixion in the Ferrara fresco. Mary is not present to witness the death of her son. To be sure, of the four evangelists only John (19.25) explicitly mentions her (*mater ejus*) as standing by the cross. The other evangelists do not refer to her explicitly but speak of the many (Matthew) or various (Luke, Mark) women that had followed Jesus to Calvary, and hence lead the reader to the reasonable assumption that his mother was among them, as John says. The *Stabat mater* hymn and the entire penitential and artistic culture that developed around it are based on this scriptural evidence. But the Ferrara fresco ignores both the gospels and the *Stabat mater* tradition and thus avoids giving the Virgin Mary an active role in this visual narrative of the redemption. In the story told by the fresco, there is no such thing as co-redemption. Whatever role Mary had in the life of Jesus as a man before and during his Passion, the fresco does not authorize the viewer to regard her as his collaborator in the redemption. Moreover, the fresco has no women at all in it, the gospels notwithstanding. Their suffering and their affection are consigned to silence and obscurity.

The significance of the omission of the Virgin Mary and other women from the scene comes easily into prominence when we consider that the fresco is located in a monastery of Benedictine nuns, women who had consecrated themselves to God and led a contemplative life of prayer within the monastery walls. Novices from aristocratic families of Ferrara usually arrived with some training in music, which they continued to improve by practice in the choir, but their spiritual education was imparted on the premises. A monastery is an institution with a strict code designed to contain any potential deviations from the norm and to create a sense of corporate unity, away from the world. In such a programme, decorative frescoes on the walls have a formative function, their primary intent being to help the nuns become accustomed to a particular way of visualizing the narratives of the faith, and to use those visualizations as paradigms for their internalization of the theological principles that concerned their lives. As they went in and out of the chapel throughout the day and night to chant the divine office, they had the opportunity to look at the fresco by the entrance and to be instructed by it on how to imagine the scene of the crucifixion. As a tool of spiritual formation, the fresco was meant to condition the way the nuns recalled the historical narrative whenever they thought about it, allowing it to predetermine their basic theological attitude to the idea of redemption.

Scholarship is divided on the influence of literary and dramatic sources on the development of the *cruce erecta* crucifixion in late medieval and Renaissance art, but there can be no doubt concerning the debt of Beato Angelico's fresco of the crucifixion to the pseudo-Bonaventuran *Meditationes vitae Christi*. Whereas other pictorial representations illustrate the motif itself, with some variation of its symbolic components, Beato Angelico's crucifixion in the Dominican Monastery of San Marco in Florence includes so many details from the *Meditationes* that it may be considered a reverse ekphrasis. So exact is the correspondence that the passage on the *cruce erecta* crucifixion in the *Meditationes* reads like a description of the main part of the fresco, almost as if it had been written by someone looking directly at it:

> Now diligently behold the process of crucifixion. Two ladders are accustomed to be placed, one on the one side, the other on the other; upon these, wicked men go up, with nails and hammer; while another ladder is placed in the front, reaching to that part of the cross where the feet are to be nailed. Contemplate now each event. Our Lord may have been compelled by means of this small ladder to ascend the Cross, for He does whatsoever the bid Him, humbly, without resistance or complaint. Having reached the top of the ladder, He turns Himself round, it may be, opens His arms, and extends his hands – so royal and beautiful – and yields Himself up to his crucifiers. . . . Then he who was behind the Cross, took His right hand, and nailed it firmly to the Cross.[24]

The ladders, the crucifiers, the lack of resistance on Jesus's part, the manner in which he has positioned himself to be crucified, the unblemished appearance of his body and the actions entailed by the crucifixion process are all included by Beato Angelico exactly as the Pseudo-Bonaventurian author describes them. It is clear that, in designing his fresco, Beato Angelico used the *Meditationes* as a manual and heeded its suggestion to envisage the crucifixion scene this particular way. The only blood in the scene, so little that it is almost undetected in the first viewing, drips from the right hand of Jesus into which one of his crucifiers has just driven a nail, and it is a sign that this precise instant of the crucifixion narrative is the subject of Beato Angelico's depiction. In human terms, this is an instance of intense drama and suffering, the actual beginning of the crucifixion itself. Beato Angelico, however, has filtered out anything that might provoke an emotional response to the crucifier's treatment of Jesus. His crucifixion *cruce erecta* exhibits throughout the 'calm and concentrated atmosphere' typical of his San Marco frescoes,[25] a mode of prayer focused on the divinity of Christ and on the spiritual significance of the crucifixion. Christ's divinity is also shown by his halo, as is that of the Virgin Mary and Mary Magdalene standing by the cross.

Figure 7 Christ Nailed to the Cross by Fra Angelico and Workshop. Monastero di San Marco, Florence Vincenzo Fontana / Getty Images.

All the elements of the scene come together to create a sense of contemplative calmness in the viewers. Even at the initial moment of the crucifixion, when the first nail goes through his hand, Christ is not a passive victim of his executioners calling empathic attention to his wounds, but the undaunted agent of salvific grace, leading us to meditate on his gift of redemption through the sacrifice of his life as a human being.

All the essential elements of the *cruce erecta* paradigm are there, but the fresco includes a number of other significant details, which do not refer primarily to its theological message but to its composition as a visual narrative. Some of these details refer the viewer to theatrical representations of the crucifixion. The cross is planted into a pedestal draped with a cloth with folds painted to simulate crevices in the rock, but the drape covers only part of the ground, leaving enough of it uncovered to reveal that it is a wooden floor, made of planks positioned orthogonally to the horizontal of the foreground, like those of a platform for the theatrical representation of a Passion play. Mary, comforted by Mary Magdalene, affects only a subdued grimace, while the three men on the right witness the event without any visible excitement. The soldier with his back to the viewer seems very much like a member of the audience watching a play. All of this demonstrates that Beato Angelico conceived the event described in the *Meditations* through the semiotic apparatus of the theatre, going as far as to leave in the fresco visible evidence of his code-mixing for the viewer. Such a melding of artistic codes is a common enough phenomenon in Western culture. 'Life and painting communicate in a number of instances through the theatrical medium,' observes Jury Lotman, because the semiotic code of the theatre, being temporal as well as spatial, occupies an intermediate position between the flow of life and the stillness of images.[26] The possibility of a semiotic *contaminatio* enables theatre to encode life as drama, enriching its signifying power by borrowing from the visual stillness of painting. It also makes possible the importation of drama, including its repeatability, into the frozen instant of a purely visual representation.

Beat Angelico's *contaminatio*, however, is more complex. The cross itself, according to Pere Cartier, who must have intuited the mediation of liturgical performance, suggests the setup of an altar onto which the sacrificial victim climbs towards his executioners with spontaneous acquiescence.[27] The calmness of theological contemplation is further emphasized by the superimposition of an element of verbal script in the form of a banderole rising from the lips of Jesus with the sentence *P(A)T(E)R DIMICTE ILLIS QUIA NESCIU(NT)* (Father, forgive them because they do not know), in which the first and last words are given in abbreviated form, using signs from the contemporary scribal code for the visual representation of speech in sacred works. In the fresco, history is encoded as drama, and drama is semantically augmented by the code of the liturgy and sacred texts. By drawing the theatrical code into the painting, and by enhancing that code with those of the liturgy and sacred texts, Beato Angelico is able to emphasize not only the calmness of theological reflection on the redemption but also the drama of the crucifixion as an iterative spiritual event in the life of the viewer, for whom, in the guise of a liturgical performance, it recurs every time he turns to the fresco with undisturbed contemplative attention.

Yet it would be a serious mistake to assume that theological quietude is the only response elicited by the fresco. Drama is principally a temporal art, and even when it is imported into the stillness of painting, it awakens in the viewer's consciousness images of what happened just before and just after the depicted instant. In his design of the *cruce erecta* crucifixion, Beato Angelico makes Jesus climb to the top of the ladder leaning against the vertical post of the cross to a height considerably higher than the platform to which his feet are to be fixed with a single large nail, as signified by the pre-drilled hole. Although it is not depicted, the next step in the process, immediately present in the imagination of the contemplative viewer, is such a dramatic instant of the Passion that it destabilizes the calmness of the viewer's theological contemplation with a sudden plunge from the realm of reason into the domain of emotion. After fixing Jesus's left hand to the cross, the executioners come down and remove the ladder supporting his feet, at which point his body, held up only by the nails in his hands, suddenly sinks under its own weight, with an instantaneous and savage upsurge of pain.[28] At that point, it would not be unreasonable to envision Mary swooning. The imagined sequel to which the fresco leads the imagination of its viewers throws them into intense emotional agitation, empathically embracing the human side of Jesus Christ's redemptive sacrifice in spiritual counterpoint to the untroubled understanding of the theological message painted on the wall.

Office of the compassion of Mary

The imaginative experience of examining Beato Angelico's fresco leaves the contemplative viewer with material for a complex spiritual meditation, compounded of rational and affective approaches to the idea of redemption. The rational approach, associated mostly with Dominican theology, is a contemplative exercise focused on God's gift of redemption, while the affective approach, championed by the Franciscans, is based on the Passion as the way to redemption. At first consideration, the two approaches to contemplation appear to be in serious contrast and perhaps even to call for a separation between the Christ of Faith and the Jesus of history in the manner of modern debates on the subject, but neither the official Catholic theology of the time nor lay devotional practice appears to have seen the coexistence of the two approaches as a difficulty. We can see this combined approach with complete clarity in the *Officium de compassione Beatae Mariae Virginis*, a liturgy of the hours for the commemoration of our Lady of Sorrows attributed for a long time to St Bonaventure.[29] Since the first celebration of the Feast of the Compassion authorized by the archbishop of Cologne as a local feast in 1423, extended to the whole church by the Franciscan pope Sixtus IV in 1482, the material of the pseudo-Bonaventuran office entered the stream of popular devotion, where it continued to be reprinted, edited and translated throughout the subsequent history of Mariology as a fundamental text of Marian piety, always with the approval of the church.[30] In this textual tradition, in the chapter (*capitulum*) reading for Sext (noon) prayers, we find the two contemplative approaches to the redemption joined into a single meditation on the Passion of Jesus and on the Compassion of Mary. The chapter is short and incisive:

> Erecta cruce Jesus ascendit et extendit brachia, manus et pedes clavantur: quae videns piissima Mater, prae dolore defecit.[31]
>
> (The cross having been raised, Jesus climbed onto it and stretched out his arms, and his hands and feet were nailed down. When his most pious Mother saw this, she swooned for the pain.)

The *cruce erecta* method is the only one mentioned in the office, though, as is to be expected, the text is replete with images of the human aspect of the Passion. Mary collapses, unable to maintain the calmness of the theological posture assigned to her by the artists of the crucifixion with a raised cross. From the simple statement that Mary fainted, the office moves on to the corporate prayer of the Collect, using a text that in this function can be traced back to the Cologne service. Here those who pray invoke the intercession of Mary, recalling immediately the sword of sorrow that pierced her heart when she witnessed the crucifixion of her son, so that, the sword of compunction and the sword of compassion might go through their hearts as well, in order for them to be pierced by the spear of God's love.

The language is obese with metaphors of piercing swords and the desire to suffer along with Mary, to suffer in co-compassion with her or in compassion with Christ twice removed. In this spiritual exercise, the community seeks to suffer by empathic identification with Mary, because this is the process through which the blood of sin may pour out of their hearts, *a pectore nostro*, as a feeling of compassion and contriteness. Far from being antithetical, the *cruce erecta* and *spasmus virginis* motifs, the one from the Christological vocabulary of the redemption and the other from the Mariological symbolism of the compassion, come together into a complex semiotic structure designed to cause and to signify a single spiritual experience, based at once on awareness of the hypostatic union and on knowledge of the essential role of Mary in the redemption of humanity.

8

Imitatio Christi

In advising the nuns of the convent of Santa Marta in Milan on how to use paintings in their spiritual edification, Federico Borromeo instructed them that there were two approaches to the appreciation of sacred art, one contemplative and the other meditative. The contemplative approach sought to appreciate the painting as a whole, noting its coherence as a composition, the beauty and disposition of its colours, and, in general, the harmony by which it is sustained. In the meditative approach, the observer automatically fragments the painting into motifs and details, focuses on one of them and then discourses about it, either mentally by himself or in reality with another person, before returning to perform the same exercise on another part of the painting.[1] Ideally the viewer repeats the pattern until the entire painting has been observed and talked about, either in an interior monologue or in an external dialogue with a fellow observer. We can envisage the final result of the meditative mode as a blending of the painting into expository discourse, in a manner that has much in common with the practice of reading a running commentary on a text. The final product in the resulting verbal–pictorial text is a double-coded discourse created by the fusion of linguistic and visual elements, brought into a relationship of mutual dependence. Either textual form might be considered chronologically and logically primary. If the primary one is the verbal text, the visual one may be considered a pictorial gloss or an illustrative diagram; if the primary test is the visual one, the verbal text may be a meditative exposition and an expanded interpretation of the painting.

The *Veridicus Christianus* (1606) by the Jesuit theologian Jan David belongs to this category of works.[2] It is a book of sacred emblems intertwined with expository and exhortative essays designed to provide answers to 100 questions on how to imitate Christ in one's own life. The imitation of Christ is preparatory to salvation in that it makes the imitator deserving of God's grace and hence worthy of being described as a true Christian, a *Veridicus Christianus*. The essays are written in continuous prose, with some passages indexed in the margin with letters of the alphabet corresponding to similarly labelled details in the accompanying engraving, following a system, originally designed by Jerome Nadal as a contribution to Jesuit pedagogy on meditation.[3] The verbal and visual elements are thus integral parts of a composite text generated by a double code. Of special interest to the present project is David's treatment of question 15, which examines the central issue of the book, reflected in its title, namely, who is worthy of being called a true Christian. Its interest derives from the fact that the essay is accompanied by two engravings, the first is called *Hominis vere Christiani descriptio* and is inserted in the essay as a graphic recodification of some of the ideas expressed in the prose, while the other, called *Orbita Probitatis*, one of the most famous carvings of Theodoor Galle, is included in the appendix, where it figures as the primary visual text on which the main argument of the essay is modelled.

Christ the model

The engraving inserted into the essay shows a man standing under a fruit-bearing tree, holding a cross with his left hand and an open book with his right hand, surrounded by friendly animals and set in a generic countryside. David explains that this emblem represents the type of a true Christian, a man who, in speech and deeds, lives a life that fulfils the promise contained by that designation. He professes the true Christian faith and lives according to its moral principles, as specified in Scripture and taught in the Catechism. A Christian is one who has entered the church through the sacrament of baptism, has learnt to profit from its doctrine and never falls prey to the temptation of ideas and teachings from other sources, *ab Ecclesia Catholica alienis* (p. 44), outside the Catholic Church. But this designation applies equally well to good and bad Christians. Baptism and doctrine are necessary conditions, but they are by no means sufficient. Using the analogy of a tree, David says that the sacrament of initiation and the articles of faith are like the tree's roots, but salvation requires the Christian to put those articles into practice by means of good works, which in the analogy correspond to the good fruits produced by the tree.

Authentic Christians have faith, which they practise and serve by doing works of charity. In Sacred Scripture, good works that can help one earn salvation are designated (*significantur*) by natural signs, such as trees and animals. Accordingly, the accompanying visual text includes a number of such signs to reinforce the message that a true Christian is one who displays the authenticity of his Christianity by imitating Christ in his daily life. What good is there in a name if it is applied to a person who does not embody the essence so designated? The appellation of 'king' applied to a person who does not embody the essence of royalty is an empty sign, and the same is true of any other name, including that of Christian. All such signs are empty if the activities undertaken on a daily basis do not generate the essence that the terms designate. Whether verbal or gestural and ritualistic, such signs are empty forms that must be filled on a continuing basis with acts of virtue that pertain to an authentic Christian life. This does not mean, of course, that the sacrament of baptism is an empty sign, devoid of the grace that it is supposed to convey. It means rather that salvation, which is made possible by the sacrament, also requires an unwavering commitment to an authentic Christian life, and that commitment can be best achieved by consciously imitating Christ in one's daily activities.

The principle that the achievement of salvation necessarily involved the imitation of Christ had roots in both Greek philosophy and the Bible, two sources harmonized into the Christian ethics of Renaissance humanism. In the *Republic* (613a), Plato tells us that by the constant practice of virtue, man likens himself to God, while in the Gospel of St Matthew (5.48), Jesus exhorts all to strive to be as perfect as their heavenly Father. Man rises from his fallen state by trying to liken himself to God, and he achieves this by imitating Christ, who is both God and man. This is a principle that enters Christian thought early in the history of the church and is echoed throughout the tradition.[4] Cajetan observed that, whereas many call themselves Christians and even serve Christ as its ministers, only the elect among them actually imitate him.[5]

A scholar wishing to write a manual on the subject for the ethical edification of students and other readers beyond the school had many sources on which to count for historical information and theological insight. Yet the main text on which David based himself to pose and answer the question 'what constitutes a true Christian?' is the pseudo-Augustinian tract entitled *De vita Christiana*. David's central issue is that one would call oneself a Christian in vain, if he did not also acknowledge the fact that such a designation entailed a profound commitment to imitate Christ: *Christiani nomen ille frustra sortitur qui Christum minime imitatur,* words which David repeats verbatim (p. 44) from the *De vita Christiana*.[6] David answers the question in the last paragraph of his chapter, in which he says that a true Christian is one who is moved by a profound sense of social justice to alleviate the suffering of others, to make their pain his own, to help the poor and to seek nothing for himself, disdaining earthly possessions and honours so that one day he might know glory in the presence of God and the angels.⁷ These and similar descriptions of the attributes of a true Christian, which are for David embodied by Christ in his role as model to be imitated by all who wish salvation, are all taken verbatim from the *De vita Christiana*. Together they form the ethical ideal of attainment for one who is Christian only in name but would like to be one in essence as well. Such acts of virtue and moral disposition are signs that may be used by the readers to recognize authentic Christians in society.

The *De vita Christiana* is a short treatise which was preserved among the works of St Augustine and circulated widely under his name. In the seventeenth century its authorship was attributed to a follower of Pelagius, the English bishop Fastidius, on the basis of manuscript evidence, and that view remained popular for a long time, enjoying some currency even today. But from the turn of the nineteenth century onwards, the authorship of the *De vita Christiana* has been the subject of controversy, being variously attributed to Pelagius himself or to a scholar working under his immediate influence. The question of its authorship remains unresolved, but what is not controversial is that the *De vita Christiana* was not authored by Augustine and was written from a Pelagian perspective. It is not a Pelagian manifesto by any means: its Pelagianism is more in the nature of what it omits to say about the church's teaching on fall and redemption than in what it does say, which is mostly an affirmation of moralism articulated as the need to imitate Christ. There is no doubt that Pelagian anthropology is a tacit substratum of the entire work, including its author's emphasis on man's need to imitate Christ in order to rise from acquired worldliness. Without an explicit denial of the historical transmission of original sin and of the necessity of grace, the line of demarcation around Pelagian moralism is difficult to draw, since on the orthodox side of the line the fascination of worldliness may well be considered a consequence of the fall. Moreover, since the work was thought authored by Augustine, the exhortation to imitate Christ was not suspect and could be easily extracted for use in a handbook of Christian spirituality, for which to be a true Christian one must first of all be baptized and live within the teachings of the Catholic Church.

In Christian Latin, *imitatio* comes with a wealth of associations, including some from the theory and practice of painting, which was generally theorized in terms of imitation. A painter was one who imitated nature, using lines and colours to reproduce its semblance on a flat surface. David was especially interested in painting *ad vivum*, that is, painting by an artist who imitated reality by observing a living model posing directly in front of him. When this Latin phrase was applied to the production of images of non-human referents, such as botanical subjects, the artist was thought to have painted them while closely observing the referents or visualizing them after careful observation. A painting of the Virgin Mary with a lily, for example, was a painting of a woman serving as the artist's sitter, holding a lily in her hand and poised as the Virgin. *Ad vivum* painting professed to be true to life because it was based on the empirical observation of a model and purported to record accurately all that the artist could actually see.[8] This type of painting, in which the referent, or its visualization after careful scrutiny, is always materially linked to the artist by direct vision, has been rightly called indexical, using Peirce's term for signs that presuppose a natural or causal continuity between the referent (cause) and its signifier (effect).[9] The artist's ideal goal, however, is to produce images that may be perceived by the viewer to be related to their referents by complete verisimilitude, that is, iconic signs that are related to their referents by perfect resemblance. The images of *ad vivum* painting are thus iconic signs, for viewers interested only in the quality of the depiction, but also indexical signs, for viewers curious to relate that quality to the production process.

David was concerned especially with the way that the artist used his brushes and paints to imitate his model for the purpose of visualizing and depicting his real subject, and it is with this paradigm in mind that he speaks of true Christians as imitators of Christ. In chapter 15 of the *Veridicus Christianus*, David asks his readers to visualize other Christians as painters in the process of painting an image of Christ, by observing him directly as their sitter:

> Effinge itaque pictores plurimos ad tabellas suas sedere, & in Christum oculos coniicere, vt debitis eum coloribus adumbrent; sive sancte in terris conuersantem, siue orantem in horto, siue denique flagellatum, crucem gestantem, aut etiam Cruci affixum: interim pictorum alij, loco iam dictorum, pingerent Christum vel adoratum a magis, vel aquam in vinum mutantem, vel multiplicantem panes, vel ingressu Hierosolymitano triumphantem, vel in monte Thabor splendore gloriae radiantem, & eiusmodi speciosa, grata, placentia; ... alij, quod peius est, pro Christo Iudam proditorem delineent & effingant: alij (horreo scribens) etiam cacodaemonem in cordis suis tabella, pro Christo, depingere non erubescant, interim Christi exemplar contemplantes; vt pictores effigiem cuiuspiam efficturi, viuum solent prototypon inspicere. Qui vero horum omnium Christum optime expresserit, ille optimus eiusmodi pictor & Christianus censendus est. (p. 45)

> (Visualize also several painters sitting in front of their canvasses with their eyes fixed on Christ in order to imitate him with the right colours, either in sacred

conversation on earth or praying in the garden, or indeed being scourged, carrying the cross or nailed to the Cross. In place of these painters, visualize at the same time others, who might paint Christ either being worshipped by the magi, or changing water into wine, or multiplying loaves of bread, or entering Jerusalem in triumph, or radiant in the splendour of glory on mount Tabor, and other beautiful and grateful pleasantness of the same type. ... And, worse, others that might sketch and portray the traitor Judas instead of Christ. On the canvas of their hearts, others – what horror in writing about it – also paint the devil in place of Christ and feel no shame in contemplating Christ as their model, like painters who customarily look at a living model when they are intent on painting someone's likeness. But among all of these, the one who may be considered an excellent painter and Christian alike is the one who represents Christ truly.)

Christ is figured as the model whose attributes the faithful need to follow if they are truly interested in moving from apparent to real Christianity, allowing the indexical condition of being in his presence to mould their lives according to his example. The artists paint the model, placing him in the guise and poise of the historical Jesus, in scenes easy to visualize from a general knowledge of the gospel narrative. Thus, the model may be visualized at various stages of Jesus Christ's ministry and Passion, including the final one of being nailed to the cross. By asking a contemporary Christian to imitate Christ in his own life, David did not mean to suggest that those in search of salvation should undergo the same Passion or should be able to perform miracles. Though presented on the canvas of the imagination by means of signifiers of the historical events, the model to be imitated in life and traced on the soul is not the historical figure of Jesus Christ, but an image of him that, in the tradition of the faith, has embodied the virtues that all must follow in order to become human beings worthy of heaven, virtues that constitute the defining characteristics of a true Christian. The practice of these virtues is the answer to the question of what Christ means, or should mean, to them, in the *hic et nunc* of their lives. This is essentially the pastoral version of the tropological exegesis of the gospel, the search for the personal message of conversion and moral guidance that readers may take away from the text. We are reminded of a comment by Kierkegaard, who said that, behind every visible verse of Scripture there is an invisible one exhorting the reader to go and do likewise.[10] That verse is written with the invisible signs of the virtues that can take the reader from inauthentic to authentic Christianity.

Christ-the-model to be imitated, in other words, is itself a sign, and hence the imitation of it reproduced on the canvas of the imitators' soul – *in cordis suis tabella* – is the sign of a sign. What is more, the sign of Christ as model is difficult to decipher, requiring as it does the right predisposition of faith, which is why when they look at Christ the imitators see different things. Some look at the sign for Christ and see Judas as the invisible *signatum* of the model while others see the devil himself. Besides indicating that the interpretation of signs is a subjective activity fraught with risks of error, the plurality of significations is itself a sign of the heterogeneity of the Christian community, which includes in its midst even those who see Christ only to be reminded of the Antichrist.

The metaphor of the soul as a painter's canvas and the analogy between imitating Christ in one's life and imitating an object in a painting of it have roots in early Christian spirituality. In his exposition of Mary's words *Magnificat anima mea Dominum* (Lk. 1.46), Origen, for example, likens the soul to a canvas on which true Christians make every effort they can to depict Christ, though some manage, however, to reproduce only an imperfect image, each in accordance with his unique ability to bring himself closer to God in the way he lives his life.[11] St Gregory of Nyssa, in his theology of the iconicity of man, goes as far as to portray God as a painter and man as the canvas on which he paints his own likeness in the act of creation, while in his dialogue on the nature of the soul he compares at length the soul to the canvas on which the artist uses different colours to represent the beauty of the object whose image he wishes to depict.[12] In the *Veridicus Christianus* the analogy of the soul as a canvas is retained in the figure of *cordis tabella*, the canvas of the heart, but the analogy of the painter is transferred from God to man, who must visualize himself making every effort to paint the image of Christ in his heart by the exercise of virtue.

Christian probity

David outlines the path through which Christ may be imitated in the *Orbita probitatis*, or a pathway to probity, which he appended to the *Veridicus Christianus*. The entire section is meant to have an Augustinian character, and for the author the Augustinian canon includes the spurious *De vita Christiana*. The *Orbita probitatis* is introduced by a quotation from Augustine's *Confessions* (12.29) in capital letters large enough to cover the entire first page: *Tolle, lege; tolle, lege. Arrripi, apervi, legi in silentio capitulum, quo primum coniecti sunt oculi mei* ('take it and read it, take it and read it. I took it, I opened it and I read in silence the first verse that fell under my eyes'), words with which Augustine begins to speak about his conversion, upon hearing a voice telling him to pick up the Bible and begin reading the verse he happened to focus upon. By placing them as a one-page epigraph at the beginning of the section, David conveys the message that he wants his *Orbita probitatis* to be approached as a handbook for conversion from inauthentic to authentic Christianity. The argument is presented as an extended gloss on his treatment of the Christian life as the conscious imitation of Christ:

> Quemadmodum praecellens aliquis pictor, omni sua industria ad viuum conatur exprimere, quod sibi ex arte imitandum praesumserit; ita illa homini Christiano incumbit cura, vt Christum Saluatorem nostrum in vita sanctaque conuersatione imitetur, & in se ad viuum quasi delineatum exhibeat. (p. 353)
>
> (Just as any excellent painter makes every effort to express from a living model what he presets for himself to imitate with his art, so it is incumbent on a Christian to show the same care in imitating Christ our Saviour with the sanctity of his life and conduct, displaying his outline in himself almost as a living model.)

Painting an image of Christ in one's heart or on one's soul is an exercise of the imagination rendered possible by the visual culture of the time, which encouraged reliance on structured fantasizing in the effort to get closer to God. But achieving a transformation of the self through improved conduct is a practical exercise that can result only from a rational decision to behave as Christ would behave if he were in the same situation. In the *Orbita Probitatis* David provides his readers with help on both fronts: a visual aid to prompt their imagination and a manual on what to do, and what to avoid doing, in their daily lives.

The manual does not hold any surprises. It is a cento of extracts from Holy Scripture, theology, hagiography and prayers, compiled to reinforce, with examples and a more detailed articulation, the argument advanced on the essence of the true Christian. Among the examples cited are St Anthony and St Francis (pp. 359–60), who disdained earthly possessions to embrace poverty, and St Augustine for his conversion upon reading a verse in the Bible, in an extensive treatment on the quotation already given on the title page of the appendix (p. 362). On the significance of reading the Bible, David even quotes from the Gospel of St Luke (4, 16–20) the example of Jesus reading in the synagogue, from the book of Isaiah the passage on proclaiming the good news to the poor and downtrodden (pp. 366–7). From these and numerous other examples, we can see that the practice of virtue is nothing other than the practice of compassion, charity and human solidarity. While doing precisely that, learning to detest vice and yielding to the promptings of virtue, one becomes a better imitator of Christ, *exactior Christi imitator* (p. 359), with his conduct and a more talented painter of the Christian virtues on his soul than the ancient master of the art, Apelles.[13] The saints and biblical figures cited as examples are not meant to represent themselves and to enrich the manual with fragments of biography. Rather they are meant to be signs of the different forms in which virtue can be exercised and perceived to its highest degree, signs that *significando causant* by their power to redirect the mind towards a form of human fellowship that could be endorsed by Christ. Together they form a code for the articulation of the authentic anthropological message of Christianity. In addition to communicating ethical ideals, these holy signs can cause the readers to act virtuously by inspiring them to pursue the particular course of action for which each saint is known in the Christian tradition. Their semiotic function is both to reveal and to edify.

As far as composition is concerned, the chapters appear somewhat disjointed from each other, without the logical interdependence of inferential discourse. Each chapter may be read independently of the others, its message being largely self-contained. They are brought together by simple aggregation into a whole, as a globe of Christian virtues surrounding the individual with signs of the different possibilities of being that lie at hand. An advantage of such a design is that it invites the reader to enrich the text with other exempla from literary memory and practical experience. Viewed under this aspect, the *Orbita probitatis* is an assemblage of signs, each with its own story to tell and all held together by the same pragmatic intent – namely, the moral lesson that the reader should strive to disdain vice and embrace virtue, even as Christ would.

The visual aid accompanying the text is an engraving by the distinguished Flemish artist Theodoor Galle. It is called 'Aspicientes in auctorem fidei' (looking at the author of faith), a quotation from St Paul's Epistle to the Hebrews (12.2), and it bears the logo 'Christiani nomen ille frustra sortitur, qui Christo minime imitatur' (he calls himself in vain a Christian, if he does not imitate Christ), cited, as we have already seen, from the very popular *De vita Christiana*. The engraving depicts a scene that resembles an art class in an outdoor setting. Dressed in a religious tunic, a barefoot Christ stands on a hillock, bearing his cross on a shoulder, while around him ten artists, each seated in front of an easel, are either fixing their gaze upon him or have already scrutinized him (*aspicientes*) as their model and are engaged in the process of painting him (*imitatur*) *ad vivum* on their canvasses. The artists are in the presence of the referent whose image they want to reproduce.

Galle's engraving lends itself to a meditative approach, in Cardinal Borromeo's sense of the word, particularly since it appears to have been conceived almost in its entirety as a reverse ekphrasis of the instruction issued by David to his readers when he asked them to visualize Christians as imitators of Christ through the

Figure 8 Orbita Probitatis by Theodoor Galle. Engraving in Veridicus Christianus by Jan David, 1606, p.351. ETH-Bibliothek Zürich, Rar 8222, https://doi.org/10.3931/e-rara-34430 / Public Domain.

analogy of painters imitating their model. The ancient practice of translating a work of art into a verbal text was frequently reversed by Renaissance artists, who painted scenes and figures by transforming a written text into a visual one.[14] Working in this tradition, Galle composed a picture closely based on chapter 15 of the *Veridicus Christianus*. This exercise implies the possibility of replacing the verbal code with the visual one, and vice versa, in a representation of the same object. The shared principle of imitation makes this exchange possible and intelligible. But a third code, the dramatic code of life, is also based on the principle of imitation. Its main signifying elements are body and spirit, language and conduct, and intellect and imagination, all of which, just as in Aristotle's definition of tragedy for the stage, can transform a state of being into the imitation of a serious action, albeit only in fiction. In real life, imitating Christ means undertaking a transformative action of great magnitude, an action that takes the imitator closer and closer to his model, to the point of making him a virtually identical copy.[15] Galle's viewers are asked to imitate the artist who imitates Christ so well in the foreground. Be ye followers of me, he seems to be saying with Paul, even as I am of Christ (1 Cor. 11.1).

Except for one of them, all of the depicted artists are shown sketching scenes and figures visually unrelated to the appearance of the model in front of their eyes. The one exception is the artist intent on reproducing *ad vivum* what he actually sees in front of him, namely Christ bearing his cross. He is a representation of the perfect Christian, the model that Galle's viewers ought to follow. The others, however, seem intent on subverting the *ad vivum* principle. While they appear intent on scrutinizing their model for details, with their gaze fixed upon him or on their canvas, they actually paint scenes suggested to them by the identity of the model as Christ but not visually related to him as he stands before them. It is not possible to identify most of the sketches with any degree of certainty, since they are in the process of being completed and only a few details are visible, but it is clear that some of the figures already on canvas refer the reader to other episodes of the Gospel narrative, as indicated earlier by David: the wedding feast at Cana on the top left, for example, the payment of Judas with a bag of coins a little below, and the adoration of the Magi on the top right. Others, however, do not appear to be taken from the life of Jesus as told in the gospels but from different texts of the faith, as, for example, the sketch of the devil at the bottom left corner of the engraving, and the sketch, immediately to the right, of what is possibly the last judgement, when Christ will return to pronounce his final sentence on all.[16] Such an approach to Galle's engraving has a clear catechetical function, inviting reflection on the significance of the different depictions in terms of their relationship to Christ the Saviour, in the gospels and in the life of the reader.

For the proper exercise of that function, especially with respect to young and inexperienced readers, David devised a mechanical aid for re-reading the text and meditating on the details of its images, a sort of interactive general index to the work. He provides the instructions for its design and assembly in the epilogue. The apparatus is a simple paper model of the *Orbita probitatis*, in which *orbita* is literally interpreted as a wheel similar to the wheel of fortune visually and conceptually familiar from iconography and literature. A perforated disc is mounted at the centre on a larger sheet with references to the individual sections of the *Veridicus Christianus* and labelled with the Gospels at the four corners, each functioning as a cardinal point of the moral universe in which the reader is called to dwell. By turning the disc, the reader is taken to a particular section of the work to re-read the passage and meditate on the engraving. Through this operation, the reader may generate a sign of any particular virtue to practice and the corresponding vice from which to turn away. The mechanism can thus regenerate the entire work as a semiosphere of moral rectitude, a world of indexical signposts of exempla giving the reader a new goal for reflection every time that he enters it with the honest desire to transform himself spiritually in the process.

This spiritual development is accomplished in the process of imitation, which leads to knowledge of self and God at the same time. The Christian imitator is exhorted to profit from the practice of virtue so that he may represent in himself, as if on canvas, Christ as his model or prototype: *vt Christum veluti prototypon suum in se ipse velut in tabula repraesentet* (p. 353). Since to imitate Christ in one's life is to transform oneself into an imitation of Christ, and since this type of imitation is analogous to the kind of imitation involved in creating a painting, the new person thus depicted is an image of the imitator's new self, transformed by the imitation, and simultaneously an image of Christ as the prototype of the true Christian. The Renaissance *topos* that every artist paints himself is literally true of the art of imitating Christ, because that is in fact the objective. In the metaphorical discourse of the work, self-portrayal is a form of character building and self-formation through a radical modification of conduct and attitude. The process of constructing a new self and an image of Christ at the same time involves a complex dynamic of cyclical semiosis. Faith and the Catechism first enable the individual to posit an image of Christ as model, a sign of the virtues that the reader should strive to embody, the *signatum*; he then consciously imitates that sign with his conduct, imprinting a personal version of it in his soul, wherein it shapes his spiritual attitude and transforms him internally into a bearer of both the *signum* and its *signatum*, which together form the ideal of personal attainment in Christian spirituality. The term *orbita probitatis* may thus be taken both as the path to follow in order to achieve Christian probity and as the trace left on the soul once that goal has been reached.

9

Signum magnum

'Signum magnum apparuit in caelo' (a great sign appeared in heaven). These are the words with which the author of the book of Revelations (12.1) introduces the woman clothed with the sun, with the moon under her feet and a crown of stars on her head. In the Christian imagination, this great sign stood for the Blessed Virgin Mary under her aspect of Queen of Heaven and, with the rise of Mariology, became a reference type for the semiotization of historical struggles against the forces of evil, all ultimately interpretable as echoes of Mary's role in the economy of salvation. Moreover, as we have already seen, in the typology that related her to Eve, Mary was presented as the serpent defeater ordained by God to reverse the process set in motion by the fall, according to the text of the Vulgate. These two aspects of the sign of Mary were abundantly present in the liturgy and in the arts, and they continued to be celebrated with increasing devotion even when Mariology came under serious theological attack. The two signs of the Virgin were frequently brought together into a single pictorial, verbal or musical image of the Queen of Heaven trampling the serpent of Eden.

Two of the most famous examples of this Mariological celebration are the antiphons *Ave Maris Stella* and *Salve Regina*. Both refer to Mary in her capacities as Queen of Heaven and antitype of Eve, and to mankind who, as inheritors of the sin of Eve, are in need of Mary's help as they make their way through this vale of tears. The *Salve Regina* addresses Mary directly as queen in the opening verse and focuses on her merciful nature, asking her, as the advocate of mankind, to intercede on behalf of all so that all may be delivered from the exile into which the fall has sent them. In describing this role, the hymn presupposes a sort of parallelism with Christ, something that the Jesuit Francois Coster in his meditations on the text (1587) developed at length, further popularizing the idea of her collaboration with Christ for the salvation of mankind.[1] *Ave Maris Stella* was equally famous, in popular as well as in settings by distinguished composers. It refers indirectly to the Queen of Heaven by the term *stella*, which identifies her with the polar star, and it refers directly to her status as antitype of Eve, by stating explicitly that Mary, through the angelic salutation *Ave*, reverses the name of Eva, just as she makes possible the reversal of the fall. As star of the sea, she helps all sailors on the ocean and all travellers in the sea of life. The identification of Mary as a guiding star facilitated the secularization of the antiphon, which eventually became, for example, the national anthem of the Acadians in Canada, where it is still sung at national assemblies, though only the initial verses and the refrain are still heard in Latin.[2]

At the height of the anti-Mariological preoccupation of theology, Federico Della Valle combined the two aspects of the great sign and made them the basis of his two biblical tragedies *Iudit* and *Ester*, dramatizations of key episodes in the biblical narratives of Judith and Esther, both of whom saved their people from certain destruction. Though written some time earlier – *Iudit* as early as the late 1590s – these two tragedies were published together as a single volume in 1627. Judith, however, is more closely related to the main themes of this book, and so the focus of this chapter will be on *Iudit*. The book of Judith, on which Della Valle's tragedy is based, is the story of a beautiful widow who triumphs in a world of pusillanimous men. Her decapitation of Holofernes, the leader of the Assyrian army that held the city of Bethulia under siege, has been made famous by composers, playwrights and painters, especially the latter, with whom the book of Judith found great favour in the sixteenth and seventeenth centuries. In these artistic representations and in Della Valle's play, Judith is a sign of idealized womanhood: she is pious, intelligent, courageous and vigorous to the extreme, and she enjoys the deference of the Jewish male community for possessing those traditional male virtues in much greater measure than a man. Her idealization reverses the social hierarchy of the real world, for Iudit is as far from the real widows of the Counter-Reformation as the literary shepherds and shepherdesses of contemporary pastoral poetry were from the sheep farmers of the time.

In the technical literature on pedagogy – that is, the science of changing children into adults compatible with the aspirations of society as a whole – the theme of the natural inferiority of women is so common as to render unnecessary all documentation. It is sufficient to say that the vast majority of those who wrote on the intellectual nature, social place and correct behaviour of women adhered to the severe teaching of the fathers of the church, whose misogyny had turned women into temptresses and had explained away as symbol all scriptural celebrations of sensuality (such as the Song of Songs) and women (such as Judith) that could not be easily reduced to examples of lust.[3] The proof text for the perceived inferiority of women was the account of the creation of Eve from Adam's rib. The much less primitive account of creation in Genesis (1.26-27), which told how God made humanity both male and female without suggesting that there was a hierarchy between them or that only the male was created in his image, was passed over in silence in the social teachings on the matter and never found its way into mainstream Christian iconography and sacred theatre. To the scandalous possibility of an egalitarian philosophy and theology of gender, the most enlightened men of the time preferred to walk in the footsteps of the fathers and in the company of Plato and Aristotle, who had all taught that the nature of women lagged far behind that of men.[4] As Ludovico Della Torre put it in his *L'idea della madre di famiglia*, the biblical Judith was simply an anomaly willed by God.[5] That is how she was understood throughout the exegetical tradition: Judith was an exception because she was a typological promise of the future coming of Mary.

Della Valle adheres to this tradition, and in his dedication, which he addresses to the Queen of Heaven, he states most emphatically that he took Judith and Esther as historical adumbrations of Mary. Conceived along the lines of a medieval *accessus ad auctores*, the dedication, brief though it is, has the function of a preface designed to provide the reader with the interpretative paradigm necessary for a proper interpretation and appreciation of the text:

Altissima Reina de' Cieli

Furo tuo ombre queste donne, i cui gran fatti figurati in versi presenta al tuo divino piede umana confidenza; presuntuosa troppo, s'altamente non professasse la presunzione. Trema la mano porgendo, ma è stimolato l'animo a porgere: e se la grandezza della maestà risospinge, i meriti dimandano e la benignità alletta: né altra più potendo in forte voglia debolissima creatura, porge, prega, e adora. Tu, eccelsa pregata e adorata, vedendo che umiltà tua somma amica dona, e donando invoca la tua amicissima pietà, permetti che Iudit e Esther, se fur già dette tue figure, si dicano anche cose tue. E come d'impetrata mercè dando umilmente grazie, ti riadora la supplice Fattura del tuo gran Figlio. Fed.[6]

(Most High Queen of Heaven

Since these women once foreshadowed you, I have the human presumption to lay at your divine feet their great deeds figured in verse. But I would presume too much if I also did not loudly confess my presumption. My hand trembles in making this offer, but my soul urges me to make it. And though I am held back by the greatness of your majesty, your merits call me forward and your goodness is inviting. As I am unable to do anything else, which I would ardently wish despite my great weakness, I offer, I pray and I adore. You, exalted, prayed to, and adored, seeing the offer coming from humility and profound devotion, invoking your own most loving mercy, suffer that *Iudit* and *Esther*, who have been called your prefigurations, may also now be said to belong to you. And thanking you, most humbly, for your grace, I, a suppliant creation of your great Son, continue to adore you. Fed.)

It is most unfortunate that, in the still standard and otherwise excellent critical edition of Della Valle's works by Pietro Cazzani, the dedication to the Virgin has been removed from its proper place, where it was meant to be seen by the reader before the text of the plays, and buried in the notes at the end of the volume, amid all manner of philological and contextual information (p. 442). When Della Valle chose to dedicate his two plays to the Queen of Heaven, he was not only making a rhetorical gesture expressive of his personal devotion to Mary, though he certainly did that, but also making a statement about their contents, suggesting how to read them. His first point is that, in his plays, the biblical heroines Esther and Judith must be considered types of Mary, and he makes the case by using the technical vocabulary of typology, in which the Latin *umbra* and *figura*, both equivalent to the Greek *typus*, all meaning type, were considered synonyms for the first element of a typological correlation, whose meaning could became complete only when the second element, the antitype, arrived on the scene. The typological meaning of the Latin terms is discernible, at least in part, in the English terms 'foreshadowing' and 'prefiguration'. At the very opening of his dedication, Della Valle, translating the Latin terms into Italian, says that Judith and Esther were *ombre* of Mary, and he repeats that statement using the term 'figure' near the end of the passage. This statement is by itself a sufficient indication of the Mariological significance of the dedication, which may be regarded as programmatic, in the sense that it represents the strategy followed by the author in writing the text of both plays. Della Valle's reader was about to embark on a reading experience in which the language and events associated with the protagonists must be considered as signs that carry the typological promise of future fulfilment by their antitype, the Blessed Virgin Mary. The salvific functions that Judith and Esther have in the history of the Hebrew people include the promise, of which they are unaware, that the significance of their heroic actions will be revealed by, and fulfilled in, the action undertaken by Mary as God's collaborator in his plan for the redemption and salvation of all mankind.

Della Valle's second point is that in his verses he turned the heroic deeds of Judith and Esther into types. The expression *figurati in versi* means that the great deeds have been recorded as poetry, but, coming as it does immediately after Della Valle's presentation of Judith and Esther as types of Mary, it also carries the meaning that, in the poetry, the deeds are presented as *figure* or types of other events in the history of salvation. Everything, then, associated with the two characters should be regarded as an anticipatory sign of a greater gesture of liberation by a greater woman, still to come at some point in the future. The entire dramatic action, in other words, was constructed typologically, with Mary as the great sign of liberation at the other end of the relationship. This typological understanding of the actions of Judith and Esther is based on a well-established exegetical tradition that goes back several centuries. Still it has a great impact on the reader, chiefly on account of the manner and timing of Della Valle's statement. The manner is that of a prayer of gratitude by a devotee of the Blessed Virgin, cast as a personal letter, signed with an abbreviated form of the author's first name, Fed(erico). It is laden with signs of great emotion and imbued with the rhetoric of humility, typical of the affective side of devotion, though that is by no means a sign of insincerity. The timing is the period of great controversy over the cult of Mary, in the wake of the Council of Trent, which confirmed her intercessory role and the canonicity of the book of Judith, against powerful Protestant arguments to the contrary.[7] The 'figured' deeds of the two heroines automatically signify this climate of hostility as well as the biblical events themselves and the co-redemptive action of Mary.

In this hermeneutical process, Della Valle makes use of a concept of signification that is simultaneously prophetic and recollective but embodied by a person, an object or an action that also has an independent signifying function in the present. Della Valle offers us some insight into the concept of sign involved in typology in the opening scene of *Esther*. There, by the magic of theatrical personification, a cloud descends onto the stage to deliver the prologue, prompting the audience to assume the appropriate attitude for a satisfactory reception of the play and for the intended interpretation of its message. By its presence as a speaking character, the cloud lets the audience understand, somewhat playfully, that they are about to step into a world of signs, where things are, and yet are not only, what they appear to be. To begin with, says the cloud, the audience may be surprised to be addressed by a cloud, speaking to them like a human being, but that is only because they have never looked at themselves from the perspective of clouds, to which all human beings seem to have a cloud in them and to communicate the way clouds do. If you could only look at yourselves from such a perspective, says the cloud, 'nubi anco vi vedrete' (you would also see yourselves as clouds). That does not mean that when clouds look at human beings, they see clouds instead of people. It means, rather, that they see clouds in the people, the way people look at clouds and, without losing any awareness of their materiality as clouds, see images of people in them:

> chi non vede là su, nel nostro cielo,
> uomini figurarsi
> talor, con testa e braccia e petto e spalle
> e 'n ciascun membro a voi ben somiglianti,
> quali dritti, quali torti,
> quai nani e quai giganti? (p. 96)
>
> (who does not see at times up there, in our sky, men taking shape, with head and arms, chest and shoulders, and resembling yourselves in every member, some straight and other crooked, some dwarfs and some giants?)

In the act of perception, clouds become hosts to transient signs, and, at that point and to that extent, they carry not only information about their own essence as clouds but also the meaning of the images that others see in them. The operative concept here is *seeing in* rather than *seeing as*. When we read the words of a narrative, we do not normally anchor our consciousness to the material makeup of the individual letters joined together on the page but penetrate immediately to the meaning of the words, and it is the flow of meaning that we follow in the reading process. The same thing is true of our perception of representational paintings, which we do not normally see as variously shaped blotches of coloured paint, adjacent to each other on a flat surface, but figures in perspective and scenes that resemble reality. Representational signs presuppose the idea of seeing as rather than in, since the thing seen must be seen to stand for something else. Not so with clouds: we see images in them and co-substantial with them, temporarily shaped like something else. For observers that discern shapes in them, the clouds carry two meanings at the same time: the meaning of their own being as clouds and the meaning of the images seen in them. Such images are not representational in any conventional way and cannot reveal their presence without the imaginative collaboration of the observer, nor, once they are present to consciousness, can they reveal their full meaning as signs of something else if the observer is not subjectively invested in discerning that meaning.[8] They have, however, a textual character, in that they embody messages awaiting recognition and interpretation.

What the cloud prologue offers us is a semiotic base for understanding the prognosticative structure of the history of salvation, the fact that history is punctuated with signs hidden in language, imagery and events discovered at a later stage. To appreciate this idea more fully, we shall turn to Della Valle's construction of his main characters, especially Iudit. From a semiotic perspective, Iudit is very much like a cloud, in that we are called upon to see *in* her the presence of another, namely the Blessed Virgin Mary. After addressing the audience directly, asking them to recognize the fact that some matters are beyond human comprehension and hence should not be subjected to interrogation, the angel invokes Judith's presence, calling her out, as if from another ontological realm. As a historical figure from the past, Iudit does not exist until she is summoned to step into the present by appearing on stage:

> Esci, immagine bella
> D'altra di te più bella, ancor non nata
> Ma innanzi il tempo e gli anni
> Negli alti abissi del gran Ciel formata! (p. 6)
>
> (Come forth, o beautiful image of another more beautiful than you. She is not yet born, but in the great depth of heaven she was formed before time and before the years!)

Judith was a very beautiful woman: the entire narrative of her decapitation of Holofernes is based on the power of her beauty, to which he yields and by which he is duped. Della Valle, however, does not speak of her beauty as such but of the fact that she is a beautiful image of a more beautiful woman that is still somewhere in the future. Iudit is presented as a sign of Mary, but she does not for that reason cease to be meaningful as the widow Judith. Both meanings are present simultaneously in her, one corporeally and the other as an adumbration of someone still to come. Similarly, her person embodies two expressions of beauty, her own and Mary's, though her beauty is presented as the beauty of an image and hence revealed only in the light of the greater beauty of the referent of that image. Mary's greater beauty illuminates Iudit's from the future, in the here and now of Iudit's personal history, as seen by her summoning angel.

In so far as she is a sign for Mary, Iudit has a temporal semiotic structure. She points our minds forward in time to the mother of Jesus, but she also points us backwards to the moment at the beginning of human history, between the prelapsarian period, when there was still no need for redemption, and post-lapsarian time, when God's plan for the redemption of mankind had to be set in motion. Though she will be born in the future, Mary was conceived by God in the past, before 'the years', that is, before human history, which is marked in years. Yet in the here and now of her history, in virtue of which she can assume the role of a Marian sign unbeknownst to her, she is her own person, a beautiful and heroic Jewish widow with a plan to liberate Bethulia by killing Holofernes.

As a signifying structure, the image embodied by Iudit clearly reflects St Augustine's concept of time, in which memory and anticipation figure as the present time of the past and the present time of the future (*Conf.* 11.20). In itself, the present time is Iudit's kairos or the crucial moment of her liberating action. The present time of the past is the recollection of God's promise that a woman will one day crush the serpent's head (Gen. 3.15). The present time of the future is the anticipation of Mary's role as co-redemptrix.

The prologue angel specifies that, though it has this temporal structure, the Marian sign embodied by Iudit is not easy to see. The image of Mary must be seen in Iudit the way shapes are seen in clouds, in which they are concealed and where they await discovery. Hidden in the heart of Iudit, Mary prays:

> Ella nel seno tuo nascosa prega
> Ed a voce si cara
> Il fortissimo Eccelso
> Quasi giunco si piega:
> Tutto dà, nulla niega. (p. 6)

(Concealed in your breast, she prays, and to so dear a voice, the high almighty bends like a rush, granting all and denying nothing.)

The image of Mary expressed in these lines contrasts with, and complements, what we know of Iudit, who will soon need to act at first like a seductress and then like a warrior to save her people. Mary is indeed invisible to conventional observers, who are intent on identifying signs by seeing objects as something else rather than by seeing signs inside the objects themselves, and drawing them out imaginatively for contemplation. Mary is hidden in Iudit's heart, where she prays with so sweet a voice that God denies her nothing. Her beauty, for which the angel first praised her, is now extended to the sweetness of her voice, which is a metaphor for the power of her prayer. The aspect of Mary that is signified here is that of advocate of mankind, who is able to soften God's heart and cause him to respond mercifully to the needs of those on whose behalf she is interceding. In the Italian literary tradition known to Della Valle, Dante offers perhaps the most famous examples of Mary's intercessory role by which Della Valle might have felt prompted to stress her advocacy. In the *Purgatorio* we are told of her intercession on behalf of the fallen Ghibelline warrior Buonconte da Montefeltro, though he managed to invoke her by mentioning only her name before dying (*Purg.* 5.101), and, on a grander scale, in the last canto of the *Paradiso*, St Bernard asks Mary to intercede for the wayfarer, so that he may be granted a mystical vision of God (*Parad.* 33.25-27). In Della Valle's play,

Mary intercedes for Iudit from within her heart, in which the author presents her as present in every respect except the material one, in accordance with the promptings of typology.

Typology denotes at once a mode of hermeneutics and a providentially ordained principle governing the structure of history, in which two distinct events, represented by two different signs, render each other intelligible by means of latent prophecy and recapitulation. Hermeneutical typology requires that the items to be correlated in reciprocal explanation share a metaphysical quality. In Della Valle's play, the correspondence is far more complete than would be required by simple typology. In spirit, Mary is present in Iudit, not merely in a shadowy way, by which she could be signified by Iudit without either being aware of the relationship, but in a real manner, since Mary is fully cognizant of the task that Iudit has to face, which is the reason why she prays that Iudit may have the strength and courage to accomplish what she is setting out to do. Mary is already present in Iudit's heart long before her corporeal manifestation in history.

This emphatic statement of the reality of Marian typology at the basis of Iudit takes the principle of metaphysical correspondence further than the exegetical tradition. The assumption in Della Valle's reasoning is that the Virgin has existed in God's mind since the beginning of time. She existed first as a preincarnate spirit, actually and fully present in the souls of her biblical types, including the crusher of the serpent of Eden, Judith and Esther, all foreshadowing her future coming into history. At that preordained time she came into being materially as the mother of Jesus, inextricably linking the transcendental and historical dimensions of her being in the same person. This assumption brings Della Valle's devotion close to the idolatrous worship of Mary, since it raises her almost to the level of Christ, for, on the one hand, it implies a distinction between the Virgin of faith and the Mary of history, a distinction that – strictly speaking – is possible only for the historical Jesus and the second person of the Trinity, and, on the other hand, conceives the Virgin of the faith as a female analogy of Christ, or, more precisely, the Christ of the early apologists, who identified him with the preincarnate Logos, ephemerally present in human consciousness as a shadow of the true God prior to his advent as the historical Jesus, when he became Jesus the Christ.

Although he did not work out the implications of his assumption, Della Valle clearly had a Christological idea of Mary, and he was no doubt drawn into this line of thinking by two sacred texts that were much debated in the Counter-Reformation. The first of these was the beginning of the Hail Mary, a prayer officially introduced into the breviary in 1568. It contained the familiar phrase from the angel's salutation at the Annunciation (Lk. 1.28), *Ave Maria, gratia plena*, which, despite the philological objections raised by Valla and Erasmus, was interpreted as already meaning 'full of grace' in the original Greek, rather than simply 'accepted into grace', and this complete theological idealization of her being could have encouraged a devotee to regard her as a perfect analogue of Christ in her relation to the rest of humanity. The second text was the messianic prophecy in the book of Genesis (3–15), which in the Hebrew original states that *he* – that is, the messianic descendant of Adam and Eve – shall crush the head of the serpent, whereas in the Vulgate St Jerome had rendered the pronoun as *she*, thereby providing a Scriptural basis for the evolving belief in the eschatological role of Mary. Luther, Zwingli and Calvin had all strongly objected to the translation, but the church stood firmly behind the authority of the Vulgate and the exegetical tradition.[9]

These considerations enable us to understand the apocalyptic nature of Iudit's assassination of Holofernes in Della Valle's tragedy, for in addition to relating the book of Judith to contemporary debates on Mariology, Della Valle also eschatologized its narrative into a representation of the final defeat of Lucifer in his struggle with God at the end of time. The angel of the prologue is very explicit:

> Pugnerai, vincerai, e 'l tuo gran fatto
> Sarà lieta figura
> D'altra pugna più dura
> Di più chiara vittoria,
> Principio a maggior bene
> Ministra a maggior gloria. (p. 6)

(You will battle, you will win, and your great deed shall be the happy prefiguration of harsher battle and greater victory, the beginning of a greater good and minister of a greater glory.)

Della Valle uses typology to make the future, rather than the past, relevant to the present, to give shadowy presence here and now to the events of the cosmic end, when the serpent will emerge from the abyss for the final contest with its maker. At strategic points in the dramatic action, Della Valle characterizes Holofernes as a perfect antitype of Lucifer, as the self-exalted rebellious angel who would be God. In this interpretation of Holofernes, Della Valle follows a hermeneutical line authorized by Rabanus Maurus and made popular by such works as the *Speculum humanae salvationis*, in which Holofernes is typologically linked to the serpent of Genesis in the guise of the dragon of the Apocalypse.[10] A Cambridge manuscript of the *Speculum* includes an illustration that neatly summarizes the entire tradition and could easily pass for an iconographic representation of Della Valle. It shows Mary standing next to Judith while the latter drives a spear into the dragon's mouth.[11] In other manuscripts of the *Speculum* Judith appears surrounded by the instruments of the Passion – the *arma Christi*, or the arms with which Christ defeated the devil – while she slays a dragon (Vienna copy) or a bound devil (Darmstadt copy), images that explicitly provide a crucial role for her in the economy of redemption.

Whereas inauthentic Christians may consider eschatology exclusively a doctrine of the cosmic end, the time of the apocalyptic upheaval of the created order prior to the coming of the Kingdom, true believers know that, with respect to personal salvation, the eschaton of history is also here and now. They can live the present as eschatological time because their incorporation into the mystical body of Christ or the ecclesiastical community mediating their salvation enables them to foretaste the Kingdom of God through the medium of faith. Iudit's struggle against Holofernes has, therefore, a historical dimension and an apocalyptic one, the struggle with the Assyrians symbolizing the opposition of Rome to the spreading of Protestantism, which denied the Catholic devotion to Mary, and called the church the whore of Babylon, the very abode of the serpent. As the biblical Judith, Iudit is an *exemplum* of heroic piety in history, and as a type of the Virgin Mary, she foreshadows her eschatological triumph. Iudit fights the serpent with the ruthlessness that the historical and eschatological settings demand, and she uses her wisdom, her eloquence and her beauty – all qualities which she already has in the Vulgate – to ensnare the enemy, to lead him where she can decapitate him.

In Iudit's great prefiguration of the end, Our Lady is typologically turned into a femme fatale,[12] who seeks out the enemy and assumes the poise that can best make him feel the magnetism of her physical beauty. She prepares herself for the task by enhancing her beauty with a flattering attire and an ingenuous expression, so that she may be irresistible to the eye of any male beholder. No one desires to or can shield himself from her haunting beauty. The first to experience her effect on the men she meets is a soldier, the chorus leader, and then all the Assyrian characters, each commenting that a more attractive woman is nowhere to be found on earth. Her beauty, they feel, is ample compensation for the rigours of war. At the dinner on the eve of the battle, in the warm sensuality of food and wine, she sits in mock innocence and vamps the senior officers one by one, as they fall prey to her strategy – *difficile inter epulas servatur pudicitia*, had taught

St Jerome.[13] Her main target, however, is Holofernes, who is totally inebriated with her beauty as well as wine. Iudit mercilessly watches him fall victim to her wiles: her beauty is the seal of his fate.

In a moment of dramatic irony, it is Holofernes himself who comments most accurately on the situation: 'Gran macchina è bellezza' (beauty is a great machine, p. 67), he says, without fully realizing the significance of his words. In the early seventeenth century, the word 'macchina' denoted principally a war machine and was used metaphorically with connotations of devious machinations, so much so, in fact, that the Crusca dictionary of 1612 includes it and so defines it only under the general entry of 'macchinazione' or crafty scheme.[14] All the wiles of the whore of Babylon and the insidiousness of the serpent become Iudit's instruments of victory for God. In this, Iudit is a femme fatale in the etymological sense of the word as well. Fate, of *fatum* in Latin, means that which has been said, from the verb *fari*. In the context of the type-antitype structure of history, this can only refer to the fact that what was said by the type is a prophecy of the antitype. In the Vulgate, the prophecy is God's promise that the deliverance of humanity from the power of the serpent will be by a woman, who will crush its head. Iudit is the prophesied femme fatale, issuing typologically from the lips of God, and she is bound by the prophetic order of history to fulfil that promise. To this purpose she deploys the full machinery of her beauty, to suggest that union with her is the ultimate erotic delight, much like the wanton woman-serpents that we met in the pictorial representations of the fall. Iudit carefully mimics the harlot and the serpent, using their insidiousness to lure Holofernes into vulnerability and to hold him spellbound till the fatal and fated moment of his beheading. That is how she crushes the head of the great serpent.

To accomplish this great task Iudit makes use of a code of mendacious signs, which appear to signify one thing but actually mean another, and she does so in order to gain control of her beholder's behaviour. Her appearance, her gestures and her actions *significando causant*, moving her interlocutor closer and closer to his perdition. In doing so, Iudit turns her body into a text that speaks to Holofernes of a sensuality worthy of his greatness, but only if it is read superficially, the only way in which he can read it. Under the spell of her beauty, his mind can only focus on her. She fills his being with phantasms of her body and suggestions of erotic delight till he yields to his concupiscence with abandon, seeking the full gratification of his senses. To this effect he calls to his aid his eunuch Vagao who, as the agent of his pleasure, gladly consents to painting verbal images of Iudit's body, turning a material text into ekphrastic poetry, while Holofernes listens to him as if to a rhapsodic reader giving an oral performance of the text. As he visualizes what he hears, Holofernes surrenders to the erotic power of the language and fantasizes himself in sexual union with her. As I picture her in my mind, he says to the eunuch, 'l'abbraccio anco e la stringo e già la godo' – that is, I embrace her tightly and I enjoy her (p. 48).

Inebriated as he is by the sense of his own greatness, Holofernes cannot see that Iudit has structured her body and behaviour as an ironic text, on the psychology of diabolical temptation, as described, for example, by St Thomas in the *Summa Theologica* (IaIIae.80.2; IIIa.41.1). Iudit's calculated fascination over Holofernes appears to be, first, a controlling influence over his intellect, since she stimulates his imagination to create phantasms on which his intellect is drawn to muse with satisfaction, and, second, an actual exercise of power over his will, since, by igniting his erotic instincts, Iudit disorients his thoughts and presents herself to him as his most desirable object, swaying him from his military resolutions. She puts on the appearance of and behaves like many of the women on trial for witchcraft in the author's time and like the female serpents of Eden depicted by Raphaël and Michelangelo in the Vatican or by the anonymous restorer of the sculptural relief of the temptation on the portal of the Virgin in Notre-Dame Cathedral. Yet it is the latter that is particularly illuminating as a comparandum, for the trumeau of that sculpture, in addition to the bare breasted maiden serpent with an innocent demeanour, includes a statue of Mary. Wearing the crown of the Queen of Heaven, the Virgin stands tall with one foot over the head of the maiden serpent, forming a perfect analogy for the two typological referents signified by Iudit.

Holofernes's eunuch Vagao is himself under Iudit's spell, and while he thinks that he is serving the interests of his master, he actually serves Iudit's, contributing unknowingly to his downfall. In the apparent plot of the tragedy, as it unfolds in the mind of Holofernes, Vagao carries out the function of his assistant, helping him reach his objective or the sexual possession of Iudit. But in the real plot, which emerges on stage only at the moment when Iudit decapitates Holofernes, Vagao has the role of an unwitting servant of Iudit, working hard to the detriment of his lord by unconsciously bringing him into her trap and helping her to kill him. In both plots he describes Iudit to his lord in the refined baroque mode of chiaroscuro eroticism. In his description of her for Holofernes, Iudit plays with the passions of her observer, concealing and unconcealing parts of her body, and arousing him by apparently innocent suggestions. She places his imagination somewhere between consciousness of beauty concealed and consciousness of sensuality released. She oscillates with calculated perfection between virtue and vice, with the skill of a seasoned actress. She uncovers herself by pretending to cover herself better, and invites sexual advances while affecting modesty.[15]

Of course, we never actually see Iudit putting on the performance described by Vagao, and neither does Holofernes. The text places us before a scene with two men, one of whom, like a skilled rhapsode, recites a rehearsed piece for the entertainment of the other. Iudit is here imagined by the author to be the way she might be imagined by Vagao, who, in turn, verbally exhibits her the way his lord would like to see her in his own imagination. She is a trope of a trope of a trope, or a sign of a sign of a sign. Her presence in this powerful scene, in which the seduction of Holofernes is ostentatiously paraded before us, is ultimately relegated to the realm of language. Here she takes shape as a male phantasm of female sexuality, veiling and unveiling herself at the same time, and inciting passion for her body in Holofernes's mind and in his eunuch's speech.

As a function of Vagao's imagination, Iudit is far from being the great sign of the Apocalypse, other than by the rhetoric of inversion, for here she is the type that she pretends to be in order to accomplish her great deed. Beneath her performance as an insidious harlot, Iudit is a heroic figure whose role is recapitulative and proleptic at the same time, pointing the readers forward to

Figure 9 Judith and Holofernes, 1599, by Michelangelo Merisi da Caravaggio (1571-1610), oil on canvas, 145x195 cm. Photo by DeAgostini/Getty Images.

the great sign that appeared in heaven just prior to the cosmic defeat of evil by the Queen of Heaven, and yet pointing them backwards to the image of the serpent defeater promised in Genesis, which was itself the first prophecy of the great sign at the end of time. By virtue of semiotics of typology, Iudit participates in that part of the work of redemption that concerns the defeat of Lucifer. By decapitating Holofernes, she recapitulates the messianic prophecy of Genesis, and she anticipates the slaying of the dragon in the Apocalypse.

Yet it is the great sign that has the greatest impact on Della Valle's creative imagination in constructing the character of Iudit. The Queen of Heaven, for whom Della Valle wrote his tragedy, appears on the first page, as the recipient of his dedication. The angel who speaks the prologue tells us, moreover, not only that Iudit is a prefiguration of the Virgin but that the Virgin is actually already in her, doing what she does best in contemporary Mariology, namely invoking God's help on behalf of humanity. From within Iudit's heart, Mary guides, and gives eschatological meaning to her actions. The *signum magnum* from the edge of the future acts like a final cause that draws Iudit's actions forward in the historical time of Bethulia and, by the logic of typology, in the cosmic time of Genesis and the Apocalypse, as the end points of the history of redemption.

10

The starry saints

The Christian imagination visualizes the universe as a cosmic assemblage of signs, confusing to an individual who is foreign to the community of faith but semantically and logically coherent to all others, who are held together by its embrace. The chapter is about the effort of the mind to overcome that confusion, by elevating the symbols of the Christian faith to the role of master code, revealing the will of God in the economy of redemption. Thematically this chapter is a study of the semiotic relationship between the Bible and the book of nature, the two books of God to be read under the tutelage of theologians and scientists respectively. Reading either book enables the mind to return to God, unless the reader is prevented from reaching this goal by reading instructors and reading methods foreign to the task.

The focus of the chapter, around which a number of these ideas gravitate, is Julius Schiller's Christianization of the night sky, in his *Coelum stellatum Christianum*. First published in Augsburg in 1627, this is a celestial atlas in which the night sky is conceived as a gigantic vault, a curved surface bestrewn with points of light joined into figures representing the narratives of Christianity and the teachings of the church as well as the latest advances in astronomical observation. Schiller recoded the constellations as Christian signs, retracing the Zodiac houses as the constellations of the twelve apostles, and covering the two hemispheres with figures of saints, patriarchs and events from Scripture and sacred history. He did so in collbration with Jakob Bartsch, the astronomer who checked the scientific details; Johann Matthias Käger, the artist who drew the constellations; Kaspar Schecks, the scientific expert who positioned the stars for the engraver; Lucas Killian, the engraver who transferred the images and stars onto copper plates; and Andreas Aperger, the printer who published the atlas itself – all men of considerable distinction in their respective fields. But at different stages of the project, Schiller had sought the assistance and advice of various others, most notably the ageing Johann Bayer, who had himself published a famous stellar atlas, the *Uranometria* (1603), generally regarded as a great accomplishment in celestial cartography. Schiller had assembled a team of very talented men to work with him on an atlas designed for the greater glory of God and the church, *tam triumphantis quam militantis* (p. 2), the community of faith entrusted to the care of the Pontiff and the clergy, operating on earth with the help and guidance of the community of saints in heaven.

The atlas consists of large and detailed maps of the stars, in which the constellations are reconfigured as allegories of Christian narratives. It is conceived as the intersection of scientific, theological and aesthetic views of the vault separating the material universe from heaven. My purpose in this chapter is to examine a few salient aspects of that intersection, in relation to the spiritual and semiotic culture of the Counter-Reformation and in the context of the baroque aesthetic, with which that culture was concomitant and by which it was imbued. Schiller's celestial globe of catasterized Christianity rotates paternally about the earth, with all of mankind under the attentive eye of the Archangel Michael, Lucifer's great conqueror, looking down from the constellation that delineates his beautiful figure brandishing a flaming sword, just below the North Star. The Constellatio Sancti Michaelis is the first in Schiller's atlas, where it has replaced Ursa Minor. As a circumpolar constellation, it never sets below the horizon, circling the globe, just below the clear light of Mary, the *signum magnum*, watching over all from the North Star, with which she is identified. In this spectacular display of semiotic creativity, stargazers and astronomers could view the constellations as coded messages of the loving inspiration of the saints and the enlightening guidance of theology, silently pointing out to all how to rise from their fallen state. Thus, from the edge of the universe, on the boundary between the material and the spiritual orders of reality, the champions of the faith watch over the affairs of men, offering stargazers guidance in their quest for knowledge and understanding, including self-knowledge and self-understanding.

Like all stargazers acquainted with star lore, Schiller turned his eyes to the night sky and saw points of light come together to form the outlines of the animals and characters of ancient myths that had long given shape to the constellations. A devout Catholic who reflected assiduously on ways of strengthening the faith, Schiller considered these figures an enduring obstacle to the work of the church in expounding and proclaiming the glory of God:

> Diu jam est, Beneuole candideque Lector, cum non sine animi dolore indignationeque contemplor, purissimam illam et sydeream Coeli faciem, cuius est gloriam Dei jugiter enarrare, et opera manuum eius annunciare, non solum Gentilium superstitiosa caecitate, olim, idololatricis perniciosissimique exempli

fabulis et imaginarijs monstris bestijsque, temere confusissimeque deturpatam ac infamatam; sed nec post exortum Iustitiae Solem, in hunc vsque diem abstersam.[1]

(For a long time now, benevolent and honest reader, I have been contemplating, though not without suffering and indignation in my soul, how that purest and sidereal face of heaven, whose role it is to expound forever the glory of God and to proclaim the work of his hands, was not only befouled and defamed long ago, heedlessly and confusedly, by the superstitious blindness of the pagans, with idolatrous fables and fantastical monsters and beasts of a most pernicious example, but neither was it wiped after the birth of the Sun of Justice, to our own day.)

In addition to lamenting the endurance of pagan culture, Schiller explains that the purpose of his project is to contribute to the dissemination and strengthening of the faith. All of creation proclaims the glory of God, not least the celestial vault, which is for Schiller the visible face of heaven itself, the outer surface of the empyrean perceivable from within the created order, marked with luminous signs that point the mind to their Creator and to the abode of the blessed on the other side of space and time. Ancient culture, however, has shamed and defaced that surface by superimposing on the stars signs in the shape of animals, signifying fables of wickedness and idolatry. They were surely taken by Satan from works of poetry, says Schiller, and raised to the stars to cause great offence to God.[2]

The face of heaven is the first of two metaphorical representations of the celestial vault designed to prepare the reader for the argument that sustains Schiller's atlas. The image of the face of heaven is a personification of heaven that invites the reader to contemplate the sky the way one contemplates the face of a human being, reading it as a physical expression of the invisible essence within. As the face of heaven, the night sky expresses the essence of heaven or the glory of God, though that expression is covered up by idolatrous symbols and immoral narratives designed to draw the mind away from God, turning its gaze onto the contemplation of deeds that befoul the contemplative act itself. Schiller sees nothing worth saving in pagan culture and claims, with zeal and conviction, that surviving fragments of pagan beliefs, even when reduced to poetic images, are a formidable impediment to the pursuit of faith.

The second metaphorical representation is architectural. Schiller says that the sky is the vestibule of heaven, its entrance court opening onto the physical world below. There is much happening in this image. While its primary signification is heaven as such, its secondary signification is the earthly paradise, often depicted with an exit through which Adam and Eve were expelled into the world of historical space and time. This image is recalled by Schiller from the iconography of the fall to help his readers visualize the work of Satan: having been banished from heaven itself, Satan moves about it on the outside, where 'at least in his vestibule he might emulate the Almighty with obstinate treachery'.[3] Satan's acts of treachery include raising to the stars the fables of the ancient pagans, already used under his inspiration by poets and astrologers to insult God and to lead mankind away from him, reversing the course of individual attempts to rise from the fall. Satan thus imparts contempt for faith in Christ and promotes the imitation of the foul deeds celebrated among the stars.

Such a celebration stands not only against the Christian faith but also against reason itself. The coding of the book of nature as a book that perpetuates the memory of pagan superstitions, particularly those that carry demonic suggestiveness, points to the need to replace the traditional signs of the constellations with Christian symbols. It seemed urgent to Schiller to recode the constellations with narratives that can counter the effect of the received tradition of star lore and can lead stargazers back to God in heaven. He sought inspiration from the Bible and he found it in the book of Daniel, where we read that the learned and teachers of justice shine with the brightness of the firmament (Dan. 12.3). The greatest need for corrective changes concerned the familiar circumpolar constellations. When stargazers of Schiller's time turned their eyes towards the north celestial pole, to set their orientation on sea and land by the North Star and by the constellations that never fall below the horizon, they automatically saw two bears (Ursa Minor and Ursa Major), one of them with the end of its tail on the North Star itself, and a gigantic snake or dragon. Yet the pious tradition had long identified the Blessed Virgin Mary not only with the moon, above which she is normally depicted, but also with Polaris. In the popular imagination, the hymn *Ave Maris Stella* identified her with both the *signum magnum* of the final apocalypse and the North Star, the one sure signpost that could help all travellers find their way. In the context of Christian spirituality, however, finding one's way can ultimately mean only finding one's way back to God, overcoming the distance created by the fall.

In Christian culture one could find the hieroglyphs, as Schiller sometimes calls his starry signs, with which to combat the residue of a literary culture that continued to exercise fascination over the minds of good Christians, drawing them away from the truths of the faith. The hieroglyphs to be seen when we look at the stars in the sky, he states clearly, ought to consist 'of blessed spirits and men of extraordinary sanctity'.[4] Thus, Schiller began re-coding the points of light on the screen of the sky, regrouping them into fifty-one constellations and providing Christian labels and imagery for them. Starting with Polaris he redrew Ursa Minor as the Archangel Michael, and proceeded this way until he covered the entire celestial globe. He reconfigured the twelve Zodiac signs as the twelve apostles,[5] surrounding the universe with their teaching, as the first transmitters of the message of Christ. He covered the southern hemisphere with narratives from the Old Testament, and the northern hemisphere with stories from the New Testament and the lives of the saints who played a significant role in the history of the church, all watching over mankind with care from the outer limits of reality. Viewed in its entirety, Schiller's atlas is the replacement of the traditional cartographic text of the sky with a Christian one, on the assumption that the Christian reader would naturally find it a better representation of the book of nature, the reading of which should best reveal the glory of its creator

Figure 10 Constellation of the Archangel Michael (Ursa Minor). Engraving in *Coelum Stellatum Christianum* by Julius Schiller, 1627. Used with permission from Felice Stoppa (www.atlascoelestis.com/).

and direct the mind of the stargazer towards heaven. The *Coelum stellatum Christianum*, both as a book and as an envisaged celestial globe, is a veritable semiosphere of Christianity, a closed domain of interrelated signs that enable Christians to make sense of the universe and of life in it.

The assumption behind this operation is that the relationship between the sign and its referent is not a necessary one, since the same referent can be described with different cultural vocabularies. Indeed, Schiller himself notes that, even within his own system, Polaris can be related either to the Archangel Michael, or to the other figures in the stars, the way, he explains, that the same altar can be used to celebrate the solemnities of more than one saint (p. 9). Schiller's approach is consistent with the new organization of culture that emerged at the end of the Renaissance. Foucault observes that whereas in the sixteenth century one asked 'how it was possible to know that a sign did in fact designate what it signified', in the seventeenth century the corresponding question was 'how a sign could be linked to what it signified'.[6] Renaissance culture approached the first question through the concept of resemblance, from the similarity of iconic correspondence to the similitude of analogical correlation. Post-Renaissance culture faced the second question by means of a conception of language as an art of naming and renaming, with different vocabularies. The asterisms along the equatorial path of the sun constitute the essence of the book of nature, coded as the Zodiac strip by the ancients and as the apostles by Schiller.

A simple model for such trans-codifications was briefly outlined by the contemporary Dominican philosopher Tommaso Campanella, who, in an autobiographical reflection, had recourse to the language of scribal and textual criticism, taking the idea of the book of nature one step further into metaphor. Campanella regarded reality as God's autograph book of nature and the world views of different philosophers as copies or transcriptions of that autograph made from the different perspectives from which they read the original, some misreading it and others reading it correctly.[7] We may judge how truthful each copy is only by collating it with the original, that is, by scrutinizing nature itself and correlating our own observations and interpretations with those found in the world views of others. Concerning the arrangement and movement of the planets, for example, geocentric and heliocentric representations of the world are two different versions of the divine autograph that lies below the stars. The same heavenly bodies and the same physical movement are signified by different vocabularies from different vantage points, each claiming to offer a true representation of the original and to enable a more accurate visualization of God's blueprint.

The question is somewhat more involved when the representation itself is meant to reflect articles of faith and to exercise influence rather than to teach the workings of the physical world. Here it is also necessary to speak of the trans-signification of the book of nature, or the transformation of its semiotic value, so that while a new Christian figure is a sign for a constellation, the constellation so depicted is a sign for the narrative from which the figure is taken and for the theological principle that it carries, in the interpretation authorized by the church. In the process of trans-signification, the original referent, or the original object of signification, becomes itself a sign for an invisible referent in sacred history and theology, awakening it to active presence in the observers' consciousness and educating them on how to rise from their fallen state. Schiller's trans-signification is meant to reverse the effect of the traditional depiction of the constellations and to celebrate the Christian faith at the same time.

The great constellations just south of Polaris, Ursa Minor, Ursa Major and Draco appeared to Schiller as a clear manifestation of the wickedness inherent in traditional star lore, and he sought to create a semiotic text that would negate it. The area around the celestial North Pole, which for Schiller is almost the pole of eternity and heaven (*aeternitatis quasi et beatarum sedium diximus cardinem*, p. 8), is surrounded by a gigantic reptilian sign. In Christian culture, this sign can only be interpreted as the devil, the ancient serpent exhibiting himself among the stars in the vestibule of paradise, having been expelled from Eden. There, among the stars, the serpent – alias the rebellious angel overcome by the Archangel Michael and represented typologically by Holofernes – will be defeated as the Antichrist in the final struggle at the end of time. It makes excellent sense, then, to transform Ursa Minor into the Archangel Michael, wielding the flaming sword of his victory, immediately above the serpent, as the divine hero of the angelic struggle that took place in heaven before the beginning of historical time. The fact that the last star of this constellation is the sidereal sign of Mary raises the symbolism one step higher, presenting Mary as the enemy of the serpent to which God alludes in the Vulgate text of Genesis.

From his position by the North Star, the Archangel Michael extends his protection to the large constellation of Ursa Major, transformed by Schiller into the Navicula Petri, or St Peter's bark, saved by Jesus from a storm: *navicula autem in medio mari jactabatur fluctibus* (Mt. 14.24). In the traditional interpretation of this gospel passage, the *navicula* was generally glossed as a sign for the church, and the interpretation still survives in modern languages that call the main body of the church its *nave*. Though at times she finds herself in a storm, buffeted by waves of persecution, the church, so signified, does not sink but remains always visible, like the circumpolar constellation in which it is figured as a sign for the harbour that human beings should reach in order to enter their celestial homeland, *coelestis patriae portum* (p. 9). The seven bright stars of the constellation, a sign for the Holy Spirit through the attribute of his seven gifts, recall the seven fat cows of Genesis 41, which are themselves a collective sign of the seven oxen (*triones*) in the term *septentrionem*, a name for the North, from which the Blessed Virgin keeps the evil one at bay, as the first and brightest star of the constellation of the Archangel Michael.

In his construction of the circumpolar constellations, Schiller worked with a concept of pictorial and theological discourse that engages the reader in the pursuit of multiple semiotic strategies. The process of signification includes two essential steps. Having interpreted Draco as a pagan sign for the devil, Schiller generates, by an inverted analogy, a series of new signs that tacitly overturn the ones designating the constellations encircled by Draco. The new signs carry multiple new references, all of them converging on the idea of salvation. But they also retain a memory of the old meaning as the negative justification of the new ones. This semiotic approach to the stars is consistent with a concept of language development current in the early seventeenth century, as a practice of sign creation that deflects old significations.[8] The sidereal text on the celestial vault thus constitutes narratives and ideas that reflect sacred history and construct a different world view, which is expected to circulate as a valid picture of reality, both astronomical and theological. Like verbal language, the idiom of the stars does not reflect the essence of what it designates but constructs an image of it, rich with biblical recollection and theological reflection.

Schiller's atlas is based on two familiar principles: that nature can be conceived of as a book whose pages are covered with symbols, and that a community is held together by its symbols. The symbols are not fixed once and for all, and they are not tied to reality as names that carry the full essence of the things they signify. As natural philosophers and artists transcribe God's autograph (in Campanella's sense of the term), other sets of symbols can replace them. Indeed, there can be a plurality of signs, none of which exhausts completely the thing that it signifies, there always being some residue of meaning not covered by the new symbols. The excess of signification therefore invites new naming, which, in turn, contributes to the development or consolidation of a world view. Schiller was prompted by such principles to create a semiotic code out of the narratives of the Bible and the church, using it to interpret the night sky as an expression of the glory of God and, at the same time, to promote Catholicism by surrounding the community with a sphere of allegorical signs designed to reinforce the world view contained in its official teachings.

Star symbolism is open to interpretation and redrawing because the signs themselves are pictures in the mind rather than on the vault of the sky, which displays only points of light. The constellations are groupings of stars linked by imaginary lines into recognizable configurations. They may be differently visualized, invested with different narrative messages, appropriated by different ideologies, and presented as a didactic discourse from heaven. The sky is thus a screen on the outer surface of the celestial globe, covered with floating signifiers that may change shape and meaning, depending on the culture in which they are rooted. The Ptolemaic and Copernican cosmologies are two different ways of unravelling the same mystery of the paths of the planets in the sub-astral world, each cosmology with its own interpretation of the divine plan and its own theology of the place of man in the universe. Indeed, to the extent that it is still in need of decipherment, the book of nature is a book of signifiers with indeterminate significations. This is a major premise of post-Renaissance culture, a premise common to aesthetics, science and religion. If nature is conceived as a book, then the discernment of its meaning, in whole or in part, can be figured as the intellectual process for the recognition and reading of signs. For Galileo, the book of nature was written in mathematical symbols and formulas, many of which are visible only to the intellect of a properly trained scientist. Schiller was concerned with the pages of the book that are visible to the imagination of all contemplating the night sky, pages that early Western culture had covered with images of animals and mythological characters. In his celestial cartography, Schiller laboured to release the night sky from the code of Greek and Babylonian mythology by transcribing its pages as the narratives and teachings of Christianity.

The chief purpose of celestial maps drawn without symbolic imagery – maps, that is, showing only the constellations, individual stars and their magnitudes, all properly labelled – was to enable astronomers and stargazers to identify and navigate different areas of the sky. The maps served as charts on which to record new observations. They were also tools for assigning, in a systematic way, names to newly discovered stars, identifying them by their order of magnitudes and their location in a constellation. From a purely astronomical point of view, Schiller's maps were perhaps the most accurate and up to date in the field, with respect to both number and relative position of the stars. The *Coelum stellatum Christianum*, for example, is the first atlas to record the great nebula of Andromeda, which in Schiller's scheme figures on the edge of the constellation of the Holy Sepulchre. For the representation of the stars in the northern and southern celestial hemispheres, each viewed as a whole, Schiller used hemispherical projections, whereas for each of the fifty-one constellations that form the substance of his atlas, he used trapezoidal projections, in accordance with established methods for the representation of large and small spherical areas on a flat plane surface.[9]

To be sure, Schiller's maps fulfil their scientific purpose, but, covered as they are with images, they were primarily designed to condition the way in which stargazers might use the constellations to reflect on their personal lives and on history – not mythological history, but the history of salvation. In an age in which astrology had not yet been discredited by science, Schiller offered stargazers a way of rethinking the traditional belief in the influence of the stars as the moral inspiration of the saints and the theological guidance of the church. This theological purpose is clearly visible in Schiller's depiction of the constellation of Noah's Ark, his version of the ship of the Argonauts. It is by far the most prominent non-Zodiacal constellation in Schiller's southern hemisphere. The Roman Catechism presents Noah's Ark as the most important allegory of the Old Testament, recommending that priests use it as a source of instruction. The Catechism says,

> It was built by the command of God, in order that there might be no doubt that it was a symbol of the Church, which God has so constituted that all who enter therein through baptism, may be safe from danger of eternal death, while such as are outside the Church, like those who were not in the ark, are overwhelmed by their own crimes.[10]

As a sign, the Ark is related to its referent by being physically joined to it. For precisely that reason, later in the century the logicians of Port Royal offered the Ark as an eminent example of signs conjoined to things. Noah's Ark, 'signe de l'Église', they say in their chapter on the concept of signs, 'était jointe à Noé et à ses enfants qui étaient la véritable Église de ce temps-là'.[11]

For the same reason, the dominant non-Zodiacal constellation in Schiller's northern hemisphere is the river Jordan, or the allegory of baptism, the sacrament that incorporates individuals into the Christian community and hence into the church. Indeed, the Catholic Church taught, *nulla salus extra ecclesiam* (there is no salvation outside the church). To the extent that the church, understood under the aspects of its government and magisterium, is a corporate metaphor for its pope, cardinals and bishops, the Ark places them on the celestial vault as well. The suggestion for this, and its ultimate justification, may be found in the decrees of the Council of Trent. In their twenty-second session, the fathers acknowledged that those who have dedicated their lives to the service of the church are naturally perceived by the rest of the Catholic community to occupy a higher position, in virtue of their authority as teachers and their role as leaders. This is why, the council decreed, priests must conduct themselves in an exemplary manner, in accordance with the standards enacted by Pontiffs and Councils. The faithful who seek from the church instruction in piety and spiritual guidance will naturally consider them models to imitate, patterning much of their own lives on the examples of clerics. The council had specified that all the signs of exemplary conduct should be displayed by clerics, including behaviour, conversation, dress, gait, so that they may be taken as signifiers of religiousness and might impress all as worthy of veneration.[12] The constellation of Noah's Ark, prominently displayed in the sky, was therefore also a semiotic of decorous comportment for the clergy that administered the church and carried out its teaching.

Schiller's Christian cartography was at the time an entirely logical development for both science and religion. A map of the celestial vault is the spatial counterpart of the calendar, not only in the scientific sense that the latter could not be constructed without the former but also in the practical sense of their intended function, which is to enable us to find orientation in time and space. However, while stellar cartography had still an entirely mythological appearance, the calendar was also a device for spiritual orientation. The Christian dominance of the calendar in the Renaissance is so well known as not to require any comment – suffice it to say that the calendar was then little more than a list of saints, in relation to which it was possible to determine when to worship and when to attend to other matters. Unlike modern calendars, which fix temporal location by means of abstract and equal segments of neutral time, sixteenth- and seventeenth-century calendars were still only a matter of fixed and movable liturgical events, in which differences in time were viewed and calculated as a function of specific days of worship.

Yet in a curious mixture of Christian and pagan symbolism, the calendar makers of the time routinely included the symbols of the Zodiac next to the names of the months, not only on wall calendars, which had just been introduced and which were getting popular very quickly, but also in books of hours, for prayer and meditation rather than the practical tasks of daily living.[13] No doubt these symbols had become so trite as not to represent any risk of religious distraction, not even when they were printed in such a spiritual setting, but it is perfectly reasonable to expect that in the militant climate of the time someone should desire to Christianize the Zodiac everywhere, on calendars, on maps of the heavens, and in the imaginations of all stargazers, so that when they looked at the night sky, they should also see the saints that gave structure and meaning to the days of the year.

It is interesting to note at this point that the Roman Catechism severely reprimanded parents who insisted on giving their children classical pagan names, and instructed that one of the functions of baptism was to enable the child to acquire the name of a saint, of a person 'of eminent sanctity' so that he might be stimulated by his name to imitate him in the practice of virtue. Though its scale is different and the subjects in question are stars rather than children, the operation undertaken by Schiller was essentially the same: to rename the constellations, to give them new images in the likeness of the saints, to force astronomers to give Christian names to new stars, all on the assumption that this would slowly but systematically remove from the culture's field of awareness all traces of the non-Christian symbolism that had been traditionally associated with the observation of the stars. The elevation of objects and human beings to the stars, as the final step in the creation of a living mythology through an operation of allegorical catasterism, involves a complex form of visual signification, which is based on the possibility of hybridizing concepts and images from various sources, and which therefore flourishes best in a culture where the arts and sciences are not consciously kept apart but are purposely brought together, in the pursuit of goals that they cannot achieve by working alone. The epistemological conditions that make this possible and the institutional ones that make it desirable are conspicuous aspects of the culture of the baroque period, a culture whose components transfuse readily into each other, giving rise to hostilities when the light coming from one area shows errors in the other, but also and more frequently bringing about an enrichment of each other's creative potential by osmosis. Such conditions are presupposed by the baroque aesthetic, which invents opera by bringing together drama, music and art, engaging them in a single creative act, an aesthetic that creates fantastic fountains by superimposing dance on sculpture and architecture. The pictorial recasting of the constellations belongs to this class of phenomena. In the factual language of cultural history, the baroque aesthetic may be described as an aesthetic of collaborative creativity, but in terms of the analytical thought forms of intellectual history, it is an aesthetic of the intersection of concepts from various discourses, an inevitable aspect of the consilience of culture.

The concept of 'allegorical catasterism' as a living mythology implies that the creation of such a mythology presupposes a homogeneous culture of signs, a culture in which sensible images are consciously given the function of signification as similes on a popular level. Unless this is already present at the popular level, a new mythology remains an individual's dream and would never have any hope of becoming a living mythology for society, a mythology that can be used to give structure and meaning to new ideas and new discoveries. Mythological catasterism aspires to be the generative and formative base of world views, at the popular level, though it naturally begins at the top, with the scientists, the philosophers and the theologians themselves. According to Plato, we all recognize that the starry heaven is a sight of great beauty, a magnificent surface decorated with mythical figures that fire up the imagination with their narratives. Those narratives, however, must not be mistaken for the truth that lies beyond the visible surface of reality. They are only an epistemological instrument in our quest for real knowledge. Philosophers and scientists must use 'the blazonry of the heavens as . . . diagrams drawn with special care and elaboration by Daedalus or some other craftsman or painter' (*Rep.* 529d).

In a famous passage of his analysis of icons, Charles Sander Peirce noted that, in their purest forms, icons are located on the border of semiosis, where they stand to lose their status as signs and, in the consciousness of those who perceive them, meld with the objects that they were meant to represent.[14] Such borders may be located anywhere but are chiefly found in works of science and art, whose referents can so engross the mind that we momentarily lose sight of the fact that the icons that we are contemplating belong to a different ontological order than that of the things they represent. Diagrams and images are different types of icons, the resemblance of the one being limited to the relative location of individual points in both the object and the drawing, whereas that of the other is limited to the mimetic similarity of colour and line between an object in space and its depiction on a plane surface. Yet when they serve as effective cognitive channels to objects of a compelling nature, they lead to an experience in which the sign and its referent are inseparable. The individual maps of the constellations were first created as diagrams that grouped into recognizable shapes the otherwise unrelated points of light in the firmament, just as had always been done throughout the astronomical tradition. Then the diagrams were turned into symbolic figures each invested with its own narrative and all forming the grand narrative of Christianity. These figures, however, retained some of the diagrammatic character of the first drawings, since they were not paintings but line drawings with transparent profiles.

Among iconic signs, diagrams stand out as signs that allow their restructuring by the erasure of some of their lines and the addition of other lines, uniting other points and making available other cognitive possibilities. The essence of diagrammatic reasoning is that such signs can lead us to the intuition of new ideas that can cause us to modify the signs themselves. Schiller formed the constellation of Eve by joining the stars of three separate constellations (Apus, Chamaeleon and Volans), and he formed the constellation of the Magi by breaking up the image of Hercules into three separate figure diagrams. In most other cases he altered the diagrams of the received tradition by relating their stars to others in the same constellations with whatever lines seemed necessary to profile the new figures. The process is made possible by the principle that the signification of diagrams is a matter of construction and reconstruction rather than direct reference. Constellation diagrams can be varied at will, by linking some stars rather than others. The same is true of the allegorical figures that could be constructed on the diagrams, since they could be reconceived as narrative projections of another culture.

Schiller reconceived them as functions of Christianity and had them drawn as iconic signs on the screen of the night sky, itself to be considered a complex iconic representation of the faith. He was fully aware of the fact that contemporary stargazers were accustomed to looking at the sky through the traditional signifying mechanism. Schiller, however, was able to use this starting condition as the first stage of what he hoped would be a transformative way of beholding the night sky. Looking from their internal point of view at the area of the sky that had been traditionally known as the constellation of Orion, stargazers would probably first locate the three stars of his belt, joining them with an imaginary straight line from zeta to delta rising on the right. They would then drop straight lines from zeta and delta to the lower stars of the constellation, namely beta and kappa, which mark, respectively, the left and right foot of the hunter. At that point they could visualize lines extending upwards from the end points of the belt to the stars alpha and gamma, which mark, respectively, Orion's left and right shoulders, joining them to lambda, the star that indicates the location of his head. Finally, they would shift their gaze slightly to the right to locate the stars profiling Orion's shield, joined to the rest of the figure by a line produced rightward from the star gamma on his shoulder. By means of this operation they would construct as an invisible diagram a skeletal structure on which to visualize the body of the hunter holding up his shield with one hand and wielding his weapon with the other.

Schiller's transformation of that diagram begins with a lateral inversion of the pattern. In order for them to see St Joseph where others saw Orion, Christian stargazers would have to assume an external point of view, looking at the stars as if they were fixed to the outer rather than the inner surface of a globe. By taking this step, they would reverse the orientation of the diagram. The new permutation signified a cultural and spiritual reversal, a veritable conversion from a traditional way of relating to the stars to one that carried the essence of Christian doctrine. In the new version of the diagram, the three stars previously taken as markers of Orion's belt rise to the left, leading the eye to the outer left edge of the constellation. Only at that point could Schiller's stargazers begin to transform the skeletal figure of Orion into one suitable to sustain that of St Joseph. By the end of the process, the traditional image of the hunter holding a shield and ready to strike appeared like that of an elderly man kneeling on a cloud, near the instruments of his trade, and holding a twig of lilies.

The risk involved in such an operation is that of mistaking immanence for transcendence, under the illusion that the material reality of the stars is actually the spiritual reality of which they are a manifestation. Plato had already seen that danger, and issued a clear warning in the *Republic*. The beauty and orderliness of the night sky should not mislead us into thinking that real beauty and truth lie in their material makeup. 'The blazonry of the heavens', Socrates observed, is no more than a stepping stone to the truth and beauty that lie beyond, the eternal forms that are out of reach to perception (*Rep.* 529d). Schiller's Christian constellations are meant to be no more than that – a stepping stone to the beauty and truth in the spiritual realm beyond the stars. Schiller is very explicit about this. When we think about the stars and planets in the firmament, we naturally think of the figures into which they have been organized and the poetic narratives associated with them. But our minds, says Schiller, 'must be raised not to poetic vanities but to the living and true God and his saints'.[15]

Schiller understood well both the diagrammatic character of sidereal signs and the risk of the ontological confusion entailed in their contemplation, as Plato warned. Yet, if the pleasure of contemplating a Christian allegorical figure represented an educational opportunity, the shift of the focus of consciousness from the sign to its referent is the condition for the experience of transcendence in the world of immanence. In this design, Schiller was aided by at least three aspects of contemporary culture: first, the conviction that the community is held together by a bond of sensible signs, something which had always been true in Catholicism and which, as we remarked in other chapters of this work, had been recognized by St Augustine and reasserted by the Catechism of the Council of Trent;[16] second, the sense that material reality is a cyphered message, something which we certainly know to be true of the baroque in science, witness Galileo's concept of the book of nature; and third, the conviction that language is a system of artificial and material signs through which we grasp abstract ideas by analogy, an idea fundamental to the culture of Catholicism, and especially so in the baroque period, in which it was disseminated by the Roman Catechism in its section on sacramental theology.[17]

These conditions, theoretical and historical, favoured Schiller's catasterism of the saints and enabled his readers to imagine transcendence. The Roman Catechism had stated that figures of the saints, of crosses and other sacred objects were artificial signs with the power to signify the sacred but not with the magical power to accomplish what they signified, which is a prerogative only of the sacraments.[18] Therefore, so long as one did not fall prey to the temptation of sacramental empowerment, the allegorical catasterism of the saints could be sanctioned by the church, for which it was a desirable cultural acquisition because of the great multitude of people that were bound to be positively affected by it. Stargazers who configure images of saints where the eyes see only distant stars perform a signifying action that remains wholly within the privacy of their minds and any experience of moral conversion that they may undergo is produced entirely by that action rather than by any sacramental power of the signs themselves.

The immanence of that action, however, does not mean that the experience has no social dimension. On the contrary, it is a special prerogative of allegories to speak with the voice of an entire community. The personal conversion that they seek to bring about is always a return to the ways of the community, real or idealized though the community may be. Allegory can hardly be conceived other than as a function of community discourse. Its ideological thrust is necessary to reaffirm the values of a society. Allegory is, among other things, an instrument for the annexation of individuals to a community, held together, as Augustine had said, by its sensible signs.

These considerations enable us to approach in a meaningful way what is by far the most interesting aspect of Schiller's maps, namely the convex direction of their curvature. In the seventeenth century stellar maps could be constructed as flat projections of either a concave or a convex surface, the stars being imagined either on the inside or on the outside of a geocentric globe. In either case, the globe figured as the boundary of reality, or as Kepler once defined it, echoing the book of Psalms, *extendens caelum sicut pellem* (103.2), as the skin of the world[19] beyond which it was not possible to venture with the imagination and remain in the realm of material reality.

In the context of a pagan world view, the direction of the curvature could not have any serious consequences: the map was simply a practical instrument without metaphysical implications. But when the signs had been transformed into Christian allegories, the situation was quite different, since beyond the physical world there was the world of divine transcendence. The 'skin of the universe' has its concave surface in the physical reality of nature and its convex surface in the metaphysical reality of heaven. Geometrically, a convex surface is one that bulges towards the point of observation and therefore implies the possibility of a vantage point on the other side of space. From a vantage point on the earth, an observer looking at the stars will see them configured on a concave screen, but when he visualizes them on the basis of Schiller's maps, he sees them depicted on the convex surface of a globe, very much the way he would see the different countries on a terrestrial globe. The difference is that the convex image of a constellation is a mirror image – that is, a laterally inverted image – of the one seen in the sky. A stargazer who needs to identify the smaller stars framed by a constellation must look for the main stars of a constellation, the ones that determine its shape, and invert their positions laterally on either side of the centre line of his field of vision, before he can make effective use of Schiller's map. This is a difficult operation with no scientific value. It is much easier to shift the observer's perspective by imagining oneself on the other side of the stars, as if occupying a position in heaven but on the line actually linking him from the earth to the stars, a line that marks his centre of focus. When he imaginatively looks at the constellation from this new perspective beyond the convex bulge, he also sees himself on the surface of the earth in the act of stargazing, simultaneously positioning himself in and out of the picture that he is contemplating.

This imaginative inversion of curvature in the hermeneutical act subsequent to the observer's sensory perception of the stars is an operation into which Schiller invested a great deal of energy. For contemporary typographers it was much easier to create plates with the stars on flat projections of a concave surface, quite simply because this was the more common way of representing them. In order to represent them with Schiller's laterally inverted constellations, they had to produce counterproofs of regular prints in which the stars were represented as viewed from the earth. By the seventeenth century, printing of counterproofs was an established practice, but that did not make it less laborious or less expensive. In effect Schiller had the typographers produce a set of regular prints, one for each constellation, and then use the prints as printing plates by pressing upon each of them a second sheet of paper before the ink had the opportunity to dry. The resulting image on the new sheet is an exact mirror reflection of the regular one serving as a printing plate.

By showing the Christianized constellations in this manner, Schiller is offering a stargazer the fiction that he can project himself into the realm of transcendence and imaginatively assume the perspective of the saints in heaven beyond the bulge, even as he retains his human vantage point as a man looking at the stars from the surface of the earth within the bulge. An analogous experience is well represented in the *Merchant of Venice*. Lorenzo can look up and see only the concavity of the starry sky as the outer boundary or the ceiling of physical reality, but when he says to Jessica 'Look how the floor of heaven / Is thick inlaid with patens of bright gold' (1.5), he imaginatively shifts his point of observation to a place outside the curvature of space, from which he must look down to see the stars. When this situation is regarded as a lived experience of single individuals in a community of believers gazing in a clear night at the Christianized sky, we observe, in the first place, the individuals vicariously overcoming both the immanence of their efforts and the material limitations of their being, by apparently projecting their consciousness into the region of transcendence. In the second place, we know that the dialectical movement of their consciousness from the concavity of the real starry heaven to the convexity of the one that shapes their fictionally transcendent experience of it is ultimately a form of introspection, since, when they assume the divine point of view beyond the bulge, through the transparency of the saints they should see themselves in the act of looking up. Here the saints frame for them their imaginative projection of themselves as observers seeking the experience of transcendence, as a community which is already in a fictional heaven, an imaginative church Triumphant rather than a real Church Militant.

In the third place, we note that whereas, to the consciousness of the earthbound observers, the saints are points of access to the realm of transcendence, with which they appear to be co-substantial and in unmediated contact, to the consciousness of the pseudo-transcendent observers they appear far below and separated by an infinite chasm, almost as if the globe of the universe were looked at from heaven through the wrong end of the telescope. Although the saints have been rarefied and raised to the edge of reality by the allegorical process, they are still on this side of the boundary, knowable only as men and women of this world, their faces made visible to the imagination by the light of stars rather than the light of glory.

Aesthetically, this experience of consciousness, in which the mind is given the illusion of contact with transcendence through an action that is exclusively immanent, an experience in which our focus of awareness is made to slide back and forth between our physical and our imaginative power of vision, in which the constellations of the saints figure as a gateway to heaven and yet are as far from heaven as light is from glory, in which the inner and the outer surfaces of reality oscillate in our consciousness, and in which what we observe is our act of observing itself, in a manner that allows the observer to be simultaneously in and out of the picture – all of this in Schiller's *Coelum stellatum Christianum* is exquisitely baroque, in conception and in execution. It is a phenomenon made possible by a culture sustained by the effort to lock together into a single creative act science, art, philosophy and religion, on the principle that when they come together they enlighten each other's path and enrich each other to opulence, while when they come apart they inhibit each other's movement and impoverish each other's creativity.

Notes

Chapter 1

1 St. Thomas Aquinas, ST 3a.60.2, in the Leonine edition, *Summa Theologiae, cum commentariis Thomae De Vio Caietani ordinis praedicatorum* (Rome: Typographia Polyglotta, 1888-1906), Tertia pars, p. 5.
2 See, for example, Timothy Beal, 'Reception History and Beyond: Toward the Cultural History of Scriptures', *Biblical Interpretation* 19, nos. 4–5 (2011): 357–72, James S. Bielo, *The Social Life of Scriptures: Cross Cultural Perspectives on Biblicism* (New Brunswick: Rutgers University Press, 2009), Marianne Schleicher, 'Artifactual and Hermeneutical Use of Scripture in Jewish Tradition', in *Jewish and Christian Scripture as Artifact and Canon*, ed. Craig A. Evans and Daniel Zacharias (London: TT Clark, 2009), James W. Watts, 'The Three Dimensions of Scriptures', *Postscripts: The Journal of Sacred Texts and Contemporary Worlds* 2, nos. 2–3 (2006): 135–59, Colleen McDannell, *Material Christianity: Religion and Popular Culture in America* (New Haven: Yale University Press, 1995).
3 A number of people worked on the Catechism in the years of its compilation, but the principal authors were Leonardo Marini, archbishop of Lanciano; Muzio Calini, archbishop of Zara, Egidio Foscherari, bishop of Modena and the Portuguese Dominican Francisco Fureiro. Cf. John A. McHugh's and Charles J. Callan's 'Introduction' to the *Catechism of the Council of Trent for Parish Priests*, trans. John A. McHugh and Charles J. Callan (Rockford: Tan Books, 1982), p. xxiii.
4 Jacques Maritain, 'Sign and Symbol', trans. Mar Morris, *Journal of the Warburg Institute* 1, no. 1 (1937): 2.
5 Stanislao Fioravanti, 'L'opera di Innocenzo III nello sviluppo della dottrina eucaristica', in *De sacro altaris mysterio, Il Sacrosanto mistero dell'altare*, ed. Stanislao Fioravanti (Città del Vaticano: Libreria Editrice Vaticana, 2002), p. xli.
6 Innocent III, *De sacro altaris mysterio, Il Sacrosanto mistero dell'altare*, ed. Stanislao Fioravanti (Città del Vaticano: Libreria Editrice Vaticana, 2002), PL 217, col. 881. My translation.
7 On the historical development of the concept of sign, see John Deely, *The Arc of Semiotic Development* (Ottawa: Legas, 2016).
8 John Deely, *Four Ages of Understanding* (Toronto: University of Toronto Press, 2001), chapters 7–9.
9 Tommaso De Vio, *Epistolae Pauli et aliorum apostulorum ad Graecam veritatem castigatae* (Paris: Ioannem Foucjer, 1542), p. 375 on Hebrews 1.

10 The idea became popular, being eventually used by Bosserel (1615) in his review of Peter Fonseca's *Institutionum dialecticarum libri octo* (1564): 'significare autem est aliquid potentiae cognoscenti repraesentare, ut sensui, phantasiae, intellectui,' John Deely, *Introducing Semiotic: Its History and Doctrine* (Bloomington: Indiana University Press, 1982), p. 167.
11 Tuomo Aho and Mikko Yrjonsuuri, 'Late Medieval Logic', in *The Development of Modern Logic*, ed. Leila Haaparanta (Oxford: Oxford University Press, 2009), p. 32 and Joshua P. Hochschild, 'Logic or Metaphysics in Cajetan's Theory of Analogy: Can Extrinsic Denomination be a Semantic Property?', in *The Immateriality of the Human Mind, the Semantics of Analogy, and the Conceivability of God*, ed. Gyula Klima and Alexander W. Hall (Cambridge: Cambridge Scholars Publishing, 2011), p. 64.
12 Maritain, 'Sign and Symbol', p. 3.
13 See, for example, Paul Helm, *John Calvin's Ideas* (Oxford: Oxford University Press, 2004), p. 196f.
14 On the idea of convergence in communication theory, see H. Giles, N. Coupland and J. Coupland, 'Accommodation Theory: Communication, Context and Consequence', in *Contexts of Accommodation*, ed. H. Giles, N. Coupland and J. Coupland (Cambridge: Cambridge University Press, 1991), pp. 12–21.
15 Cajetan, Commentary on Gen. 9.16.
16 Cajetan, Commentary on Mt. 16.2-4.
17 Cajetan on Rom. 1.20: *ita ut sint inexcusabiles*.
18 Cajetan on *Summa Theologica* 1.1.10, p. 26.
19 *Comentaria in De ente et essentia* (1495), sect. 8. 'by means of accidents of the signified thing as well as by common and essential properties'.
20 Ibid.
21 The principle was established by Aquinas in *Summa Theologica*, Suppl. Q. 45, where he says that the bride and groom who cannot express consent by speaking can do so with gestures, which will have the value of words.
22 All quotations in English are (with revisions) from the *Catechism of the Council of Trent* (1982). Latin quotations are from the Leipzig edition *Catechismus ex Decreto Concilii Tridentini ad Parrochos* (Leipzig: Tauchnitz, 1856).
23 *Catechism of the Council of Trent* (1982), p. 143; *Catechismus ex Decreto Concilii* (1856), p. 114.
24 St Augustine, *De doctrina Christiana*, Corpus Christianorum, Series Latina, XXXII (Turnhout: Brepols, 1962), 2.1.1.7.
25 Deely, *Introducing Semiotic*, p. 18.
26 On these developments see, Francesco Bottin, 'Teoria dei segni e logica tardo-medievale', *Miscellanea medievalia* III, no. 1 (1980): 498–503.
27 *Catechism of the Council of Trent* (1982), p. 145; *Catechismus ex Decreto Concilii* (1856), p. 115.

28 *Catechismus ex Decreto Concilii* (1856), p. 115.
29 Ibid., p. 120.
30 *Catechism of the Council of Trent* (1982), p. 143; *Catechismus ex Decreto Concilii* (1856), p. 114.
31 Roman Jakobson, *Word and Language* (Paris: Mouton, 1971), p. 395.
32 Claude Lévi-Strauss, *Structural Anthropology*, trans. Claire Jacobson and Brooke Grundfest Schoepf (New York: Basic Books, 1963), p. 48.
33 *Catechismus ex Decreto Concilii* (1856), p. 115.
34 Ibid., 115; *Catechism, Catechism of the Council of Trent* (1982), p. 145.
35 In *De venatione sapientiae,* as cited by Meyer-Baer, *Music of the Spheres and the Dance of Death: Studies in Musical Iconology* (Princeton: Princeton University Press, 1970), p. 346.
36 *Catechismus ex Decreto Concilii* (1856), p. 116.
37 Ibid., 119; *Catechism of the Council of Trent* (1982), p. 149.
38 'In nullam autem nomine religionis, seu verum, seu falsum, coagulari homines possunt, nisi aliquo signaculorum vel sacramentorum visibilium consortio colligentur,' *Contra Faustum*, 19.11.
39 Edward Schillenbeeckx, *Christ the Sacrament of the Encounter with God, The Collected Works*, vol. 1 (London: Bloomsbury, 2014), p. 159.
40 Gregory Nagy, *Poetry as Performance* (Cambridge: Cambridge University Press, 1996), p. 55.
41 *Catechismus ex Decreto Concilii* (1856), p. 114; *Catechism of the Council of Trent* (1982), p. 172.
42 'Nam aliquis effectus repraesentat solam causalitatem causae, non autem forma eius, sicut fumus repraesentat ignem,' ST 1.45.7.
43 'Convenit hoc proprie fieri in metaphysica et logica, eo quod utraque scientia communis est, et circa idem subiectum quodammodo,' *Expositio super librum Boethii De Trinitate*, ed. B. Deecher (Leiden: Brill, 1995), 2.2.a.1, on which see Antonino Stagnitta, *Laicità nel Medioevo italiano: Tommaso d'Aquino e il pensiero moderno* (Roma: Armando, 1999), p. 194.
44 Giambattista Vico, *Scienza nuova*, ed. Fausto Nicolini (Bari: Laterza, 1928), and Vico, *New Science*, trans. T. G. Bergin and M. H. Fisch (Ithaca: Cornell University Press, 1968), par. 400.
45 Vico, *Scienza nuova,* and Vico, *New Science*, par. 205.

Chapter 2

1 'Prima che Cristo incarnasse e anco prima al principio del mondo, e anco prima che il mondo fusse formato, egli s'ingegnò d'essere adorato. Nel paradiso terrestre

egli tentò per essere adorato, la prima nostra madre Eva, in forma di serpe col viso d'una bella donna e dissele: Eritis sicut Dii scientis bonum et malum'. Bernardino da Siena, *Prediche volgari* (Siena: Land e Alessandri, 1853), p. 127.

2 Petrus Comestor, *Historia Scholastica - Libri Genesis* (Middleton: Perfect Library, 2019), p. 20.

3 Raffaello Borghini, *Il riposo*, ed. and trans. H. S. Lloyd, Jr (Toronto: University of Toronto Press, 2012), p. 101.

4 Durand, *Guillelmi Duranti Rationale divinorum officiorum*, Corpus Christianorum Series Latina, ed. Anselme Davril and Timothy M. Thibodeau (Turnhout: Brepols, 1995–2000), 1.3.4; translation from William Durand, *The Rationale divinorum officiorum of William Durand of Mende*, Prologue and Book 1, trans. Timothy M. Thibodeau (New York: Columbia University Press, 2007), p. 34.

5 On the evolution of reading practices in this period, see Paul Saenger, 'Reading in the Later Middle Ages', in *A History of Reading in the West*, ed. Guglielmo Cavallo and Roger Chartier, trans. L. G. Cochrane (Amherst and Boston: University of Massachusetts Press, 1997), pp. 120–6.

6 Christiania Whitehead, *Castles of the Mind: A Study of Medieval Architectural Allegory* (Cardiff: University of Wales Press, 2003), p. 55.

7 For a detailed account of the date of production and installation, see James Beck, *Jacopo della Quercia*, vol. 1 (New York: Columbia University Press, 1991), pp. 108–12.

8 Irenaeus, *Against Heresies*, V.17.3, in *The Writings*, vol. 2 (Edinburgh: Clark, 1871), p. 102.

9 In his commentary on Gen. 4.15-16, Bede offers a very clear statement of the principle of *in bono et malo* signification on the basis of the context: 'it is customary in the Scriptures not only for evil things to be signified by good men but also at times for good things to be signified by wicked men.' See Bede, *On Genesis* (Liverpool: Liverpool University Press, 2008), p. 315 and cf. C. B. Kendall's introduction, p. 18.

10 'Poi parve a me che la terra s'aprisse / tra ambo le ruote, e vidi uscirne un drago / che per lo carro su la coda fisse' (*Purg.* 32, 130–2).

11 For an aesthetic and scientific analysis of the issues involved in this kind of empathic response, see David Freedberg and Vittorio Gallese, 'Motion, Emotion and Empathy in Esthetic Experience', *Trends in Cognitive Science* 11, no. 5 (2007): 201.

12 In all probability, it was carved by Geoffroy Dechaume in 1854 – cf. Michael Camille, *The Garogoyles of Notre-Dame: Medievalism and the Monsters of Modernity* (Chicago: The University of Chicago Press, 2009), p. 255. On the dating of the restoration, see William N. Hinkle, 'The Cosmic and Terrestrial Cycles on the Virgin Portal of Notre-Dame', *The Art Bulletin* 49 (1967): 287. The restoration is

frequently mistaken for the original from the thirteenth century – see, for example, Maria Giuseppina Muzzarelli, 'Adamo, Eva e "la serpenta"', in *La storia e le immagini della storia*, a cura di Matteo Provasi e Cecilia Vicentini (Roma: Viella, 2015), p. 83; Gillian M. E. Alban, 'The Serpent Goddess Melusine: From Cursed Snake to Mary's Shield', in *The Survival Myth, Singularity and Alterity*, ed. David Kennedy and Paul Hardwick (Newcastle upon Tyne: Cambridge Scholar's Press, 2010), p. 36; Angela Giallongo, *La donna serpente: Storia di un enigma dall'antichità al XXI secolo* (Bari: Dedalo. 2013), p. 215; Gillian M. E. Kelly, 'The Metamorphoses of the Eden Serpent: From Cursed Snake to Mary's Shield', in *The Survival Myth, Singularity and Alterity*, ed. David Kennedy and Paul Hardwick (Newcastle upon Tyne: Cambridge Scholar's Press, 1972), caption of figure 8.

13 E. Viollet-le-duc, *On Restoration* (London: Low and Searle, 1972), pp. 22ff.
14 *Rationale divinorum officiorum* 1.3.22, trans. Thibodeau, p. 39.
15 Vico, *Scienza nuova* and Vico, *The New Science*, par. 794.
16 Cf. Constantin Teleneau, *Philosophia conversionis* (Paris: Schola Lulliana, 2014), p. 474.
17 On reflexivity as a special attribute of iconic signification, see Thomas A. Sebeok, *Signs: An Introduction to Semiotics* (Toronto: University of Toronto Press, 2001), p. 52.
18 Both theories are based on Aristotle's *De Interpretatione* (16a3-4 and 16b9-21); see also E. J. Asworth, 'Language and Logic', in *The Cambridge Companion to Medieval Philosophy*, ed. A. S. McGrade (Cambridge: Cambridge University Press, 2003), pp. 81–2.
19 Cf. *The Canons and Decrees of the Council of Trent*, trans. and intro. Reverend H. J. Schroeder (Charlotte: Tan Books, 1978), p. 21: 'If anyone does not confess that the first man, Adam, when he transgressed the commandment of God in paradise, immediately [*statim*] lost the holiness and justice in which he had been constituted, and through the offense of that prevarication incurred the wrath and indignation of God, . . . let him be anathema.'
20 Petrarch, *Canzoniere* 90.1, in Petrarch's *Lyric Poems: The 'Rime sparse' and Other Lyrics*, ed. and trans. Robert M. Durling (Cambridge: Harvard University Press, 1976), pp. 192–3.
21 On the erotic connotations of exposed armpits in the visual culture of the Renaissance, see François Quiviger, 'Drunkenness, Sex and Desire in Titian's *Bacchanal of the Andrians*', in *Images of Sex and Desire in Renaissance Art and Modern Historiography*, ed. Angeliki Pollali and Berthold Hub (New York and Abingdon: Routledge, 2018), p. 174.
22 *Canons of the Second Council of Orange, AD 529*, Article 1 (Oxford: James Thornton, 1882), pp. 16–17.
23 Tertullian, *Adversus Iudaeos*, in *Opera*, ed. E. F. Leopold (Leipzig, 1841), XIII.19, p. 324.

24 See St Ambrose, *De Isaac et anima* in *Opera omnia*, in *Patrologia Latina*, accurante J.-P. Migne, vol. 14 (Paris: Garnier fratres, 1882), col. 542., and cf, G. M. Lukken, *Original Sin in the Roman Liturgy* (Leiden: Brill, 1973), p. 86.

Chapter 3

1 Jared Wicks, 'Cajetan: A Biographical Essay', in *Cajetan Responds* (Eugene: WIPF and Stock Publishers, 1978), p. 39.
2 The date was recorded by Cajetan in the *editio princeps* of his commentary, *In Pentateuchum Mosis iuxta sensum quem dicunt literalem commentarii* (Rome: Bladum, 1531), p. 81r. All textual references are to this edition, identified in the notes as Cajetan (1531), and will be given by page number in the text. Scribal abbreviations and symbols have been expanded but the original spelling of consonantal and vocalic *u* have been maintained, as has the punctuation. Translations are mine. Most modern scholars have used later editions (especially the 1639 edition), which are easier on the eye but, unfortunately, include arbitrary textual alterations by the editors and omit significant paratextual details, including Cajetan's notes with the dates of completion of each commentary.
3 According to Creighton Gilbert, 'When did a Man in the Renaissance Grow Old?', *Studies in the Renaissance* 14 (1967): 7–32, for most people old age began in the mid-forties and the average life expectancy was in the fifties. The social group with the longest life span must have been *papabili* cardinals, since Renaissance popes, with their average age of death at sixty-four, were among the oldest members of society (p. 31).
4 Cf. Jennifer Ebbeler, *Disciplining Christians: Correction and Community in Augustine's Letters* (Oxford: Oxford University Press, 2012), p. 218.
5 Cf. Monika Ozog, 'Saint Jerome and *veritas hebraica* on the basis of the Correspondence with Saint Augustine', *Vox Patrum* 30 (2010): 511.
6 Jaroslav Pelikan, 'The Two Cities: The Sack of Rome as a Historical Paradigm', *Daedalus* 111, no. 3 (1982): 85–6.
7 The concept was introduced by Harold Bloom in *Anxiety of Influence: A Theory of Poetry* (Oxford: Oxford University Press, 1973).
8 Jerome describes his practice in his *Apology against Rufinus*, in which he says that the 'prudent reader' of the commentary will review all previous opinions on the passage and determine where he stands in relation to them, rejecting the ones that he considers mistaken. Cajetan seems to have had in mind Jerome's practice, and to allude to it polemically, when he defended the opposite practice in his preface to the commentary on the Pentateuch, warning the prudent reader to focus on the text and not on what the sacred doctors had to say about it. On Jerome's method as

a commentator, see Megan Hale Williams, *The Monk and the Book: Jerome and the Making of Christian Scholarship* (Chicago: The University of Chicago Press, 2006), pp. 102–4.

9 The exegetical movement from *common* to *proper* mentioned by Cajetan represents the procedure of disciplined thought. It is the standard itinerary along which reason advances from universal to particular, or from genus to species, or from group to individual. In grammar it takes the form of a movement from common to proper name, since Renaissance scholasticism continued to designate in grammar as 'common' that which was called 'universal' in logic. Cf. Alfonso Maierù, *Terminologia logica della tarda scolastica* (Roma: Edizioni dell'Ateneo, 1972), p. 520. The universal is what may be predicated of all the species in the genus or of all proper names covered by the common noun. Exegesis is largely about the manner of that predication in the text under examination.

10 *De nominum analogia*, 7.75, and cf. Ralph McInerny, *Studies in Analogy* (The Hague: Martinus Nijhoff, 1968), pp. 69–70.

11 Yuri Lotman, *Universe of the Mind: A Semiotic Theory of Culture* (Bloomington: Indiana University Press, 1990), pp. 36–44 and cf. Winfried Nöth, 'Yuri Lotman on Metaphors and Culture as Self-referential Semiospheres', *Semiotica* 161, no. 1 (2006): 250–1.

12 Cf. *Summa Contra Gentiles* 1.9.2.

13 Animal intelligence was usually discussed in terms of their ability to express themselves and to communicate with others in the external world. For an overview of the issues inherited by and explored in the Renaissance, see R. W. Serjeantson, 'The Passions and Animal Language, 1540-1700', *Journal of the History of Ideas* 62, no. 3 (2001): especially pp. 426–7.

14 On the occurrence of *serpere* with *malum*, see the references to classical sources in John Yardley, *Justin and Pompeius Trogus: A Study of the Language of Justin's Epitome of Trogus* (Toronto: University of Toronto Press, 2003), p. 67.

15 'quod sensim serpat, serpentis nomen accepit', Zeno Veronensis, *De spiritu et corpore*, in *Sanctorum Zenonis et Optati opera omnia*, in *Patrologia Latina*, accurante J.-P. Migne, vol. 11 (Paris: Vrayet, 1845), col. 340, *Tractatus* 12.2 and cf. Lukken, *Original Sin in Roman Liturgy*, pp. 47–8.

16 Cf. Claude Penaccio, *Mental Language: From Plato to William of Ockam* (New York: Fordham University Press, 2017), pp. 95–6.

17 *Phaeudrus* 242b-c in *Omnia divini Platonis opera*, Plato-Ficino (Basel: Officina Frobeniana, 1546), p. 448.

18 Cajetan, on Job 1.6, *In librum Job commentarii* (Roma: Bladum, 1535), pp. 3v–4r.

19 On the function of 'orientative principles' in the construction of interpretative arguments, see Agnes Heller, *A Theory of History* (London: Routledge, 2016), especially Chapter 12, 'The Orientative Principles of Historiography'.

20 Much the same reason prompted Harold Bloom to say that the genre of the book of Genesis is children's literature, in Harold Bloom, *The Book of J* (New York: Grove Weidenfeld, 1990), pp. 184–5.

21 I examined forty-eight scenes without a serpent. Here are a few examples, with the source library: Rome, Biblioteca Corsiniana, MS 55.K.2 (Rossi 17), fol. 3v; Toledo, Archivio Capitular MS 10.8, for. 4v; Augsburg, Universitätsbibliothek, Ms 1.2.2.23, fol. 5r; Cologne, Historisches Archiv Best. 7020W*105, p. 12; London, British Library, Sloane MS 361, fol. 5v; Prague, Národní Muzeum MS III.B.10, fol. 3r; Copenhagen, Kongelige Bibliotek GKS 79, fol. 16v; Paris, Bibliothèque nationale de France, Vélins-906, fol. a.3r.

Chapter 4

1 Guinoforto delli Bargigi, *Lo Inferno della Commedia di Dante Alighieri* (my translation) (Marseilles-Firenze: Mossey Molini, 1839), p. 478.

2 On Claude Tholosan and his *Ut magorum et maleficiorum errores* (1437), see Pierrette Paravy, 'À propos de la genèse médiévale des chasses aux sorcières', *Mélanges de l'École française de Rome, Moyen Age - Temps modernes* 91 (1979): 333–79, and Edward Peters, 'The Medieval Church and State on Superstition, Magic and Witchcraft from Augustine to the Sixteenth Century', in *Superstition and Magic in Augustine and Early Modern Europe*, ed. Helen Parish (London: Bloomsbury, 2015), pp. 77–8.

3 On the idea of 'demonic conspiracy' in relation to the elaborated theory, see Julian Goodare, *The European Witch-Hunt* (Abingdon, Oxon and New York: Routledge, 2016), pp. 76–8.

4 Walter Stephens, *Demon Lovers: Witchcraft, Sex and the Crisis of Belief* (Chicago: University of Chicago Press, 2002), p. 53.

5 Innocent VIII, *Summis desiderantes affectibus*, trans. Montague Summers, in Heinrich Kraemer and James Sprenger, *Malleus Maleficarum* (London: Bracken Books, 1996), p. xix.

6 Ibid., p. xxi.

7 Cited in English in Hans Peter Broedel, *The Malleus Maleficarum and the Construction of Witchcraft* (Manchester and New York: Manchester University Press, 2003), p. 3. The Latin original is on p. 9: 'Quod omnes malefice a iuventute carnalitatibus et adulteriis servierunt variis, prout experiencia docuit'.

8 *Malleus Maleficarum*, translated with an introduction, bibliography and notes by Montague Summers (London: Bracken Books, 1996; 1928). All other textual citations are from this edition and are given by page number directly in the text.

9 Paul Bouissac, 'Iconicity or Iconization? Probing the Dynamic Interface between Language and Perception', in *Outside-in – Inside-out: Iconicity in Language and*

Literature, ed. C. Maeder, O. Fischer and W. J. Herlofsky (Amsterdam: Benjamins, 2005), p. 28, and cf. J. Irvine and S. Gal, 'Language Ideology and Linguistic Differentiation', in *Linguistic Anthropology: A Reader,* ed. Alessandro Duranti, 2nd edn (Oxford: Wiley-Blackwell, 2009), p. 403.
10 Goodare, *The European Witch-Hunt,* p. 77.
11 Francesco Maria Guazzo, *Compendium maleficarum* (New York: Dover, 2017), p. 15.
12 Anonymous of Arras, *Recollectio casus, status et condicionis Valdensium ydolatrarum,* translated as *A History of the Case, State, and Condition of the Waldensian Heretics (Witches)* by A. C. Gow, R. B. Desjardins and F. V. Pageau (University Park: Pennsylvania State University Press, 2016), p. 66.
13 Stephens, *Demon Lovers,* p. 53.
14 At least since the thirteenth century, apostasy and *maleficium* were fused into a single crime. Cf. Gary K. Waite, *Heresy, Magic and Witchcraft in Early Modern Europe* (London: Palgrave Macmillan, 2003), pp. 33, 149.
15 *De Maleficiis* (my translation), pp. 132–3.
16 Marcel Danesi, *Signs of Crime: Introducing Forensic Semiotics* (Berlin: De Gruyter, 2014), p. 26.
17 Ibid.
18 Cesare Beccaria, *On Crimes and Punishments* (Indianapolis: Bobbs-Merrill, 1963), p. 33.
19 Michel Foucault, *Discipline and Punish* (New York: Vintage Books, 1995), p. 42.
20 Giovan Battista Gelli, *Commento edito ed inedito sopra la Divina Commedia,* vol. 2 (Firenze: Bocca, 1887), pp. 282–3.
21 Tommaso de Vio Cajetan, *Thomae Aquinate opera omnia,* tomus nonus, *Secunda secundae summae theologiae,* a questione LVII ad questionem CXXII, cum commentarius Thomae de Vio Caietani ordinis predicatorum (Rome: Typographia Polyglotta, 1896), on Aquinas ST 2a.2ae.95.4.
22 Tommaso de Vio Cajetan, *Thomae Aquinatis opera omnia,* tomus quintus, *Pars prima summae theologiae,* a questione L ad questionem CXIX, cum commentarius Thomae de Vio Caietani ordinis predicatorum (Rome: Typographia Polyglotta, 1889), on ST 1a.78.4.

Chapter 5

1 *City of God,* 13.21, translation by Marcus Dods, vol. 1, p. 546.
2 Antonio Glielmo, *Le grandezze della SS. Trinità* (Napoli: Roberto Mollo, 1639). The first edition was published in 1634, but all textual references are to this edition. Variations of the same story, or of part of it, were also told by the Dominican theologian Angelo Nuzza, in his *Quaresimale* (1654), the Franciscan theologian,

Domenico Traversari, also known as Evangelista da Momigno, in his *Diario Quadragesimale* (1646), the composer Angelo Berardi, in *Miscellanea musicale* (1689), and the scholar Giovanni Maria Chiericato in *Le spighe raccolte, cioè annotazioni erudite et erudizioni notate* (1716). The translation of citations from these works is mine.

3 On this interpretation of the word *tuoni* in contemporary music theory, see Gregory Barnett, 'Modal Theory, Church Keys, and the Sonata', *Journal of the American Musicological Society* 51, no. 2 (1998): 249.

4 *On Catechizing the Uninstructed (De Catechizandis Rudibus)*, 22.39-40.

5 Glielmo here refers the reader to the *solfège* names of the notes La (D), Mi (E) and Re (A) to say that what he has in mind, as an example of the lowest form of humanity, are kings guilty of crimes deserving the death penalty. The phrase describing their wretchedness – 'La Miseria dei Re' (p. 682) – contains the notes La, Mi and Re.

6 In Angelo Nuzza's version of the story in *Quaresimale* (1654), the maestro di cappella is the Holy Ghost, 'prefetto di cantori, maestro di cappella' in charge of teaching music to mankind (p. 433). He is also the conductor of the celestial performance, from which he casts out all the angels who followed Lucifer's lead and started singing out of tune (p. 434).

7 In Traversari, *Diario Quadragesimale* (1655), Lucifer was an alto, but he was seized by the desire to sing the soprano part, usurping God's role. Once cast out of the heavenly choir, he went to the earthly paradise 'per rompere la musica e guastare il concerto', and he persuaded Adam to try the soprano part himself, which Adam did and got himself expelled from the chapel of Eden (p. 238).

8 In Traversari's version, mankind began to sing once again of innocence and justice when Mary sang the words of the annunciation *Ecce ancilla Domini* (Lk. 1.38), following which God became man and so 'la musica fu aggiustata' (p. 238).

9 Arcangelo Spagna, 'Discorso', in *Oratorii overo melodrammi sacri con un discorso dogmatico intorno l'istessa materia*, vol. 1 (Rome: Buagni, 1706), p. 3. Further references by page number are to this edition. The translations are mine.

10 The adjective 'dogmatic', used here as a technical designation of the type of theory that the reader is about to encounter, is not one that we are accustomed to seeing in connection with oratorios or other forms of sacred drama, not even in the scholarly literature on the genre. Yet Spagna chooses precisely this term, carefully and without a hint of negativity or audacity. In the early eighteenth century, the term 'dogmatic' did not have the doctrinaire associations that it has in general usage today. It was a technical term that, in whatever context it may have been used, always carried an echo of *dogmatic theology*.

11 Ludovico Antonio Muratori, *Opere* (Milano: Ricciardi, 1964), 'Lettera esortatoria di Lamindo Pritanio ai capi, maestri, lettori e altri ministri degl'ordini religiosi d'Italia', p. 210.

12 John Mitchell, 'Literacy Displayed: The Use of Inscriptions at the Monastery of San Vincenzo al Volturno in the Early Ninth Century', in *The Uses of Literacy in Medieval Europe*, ed. Rosamond McKitterick (Cambridge: Cambridge University Press, 1990 [1998]), p. 194. The article is on pp. 188–225.

Chapter 6

1 *Inferno* XIII 130-151 and XIV 1-3; Giovanni Boccaccio, *Esposizioni sopra la Comedia di Dante* (Milano: Mondadori, 1994), II, pp. 629–30.
2 Paul Tillich, *A History of Christian Thought* (New York: Simon Schuster, 1968), p. 228.
3 Leone De' Sommi, *Quattro dialoghi in materia di rappresentazioni sceniche* (Milano, 1968), p. 14.
4 Sidney Lamb, *Tragedy* (Toronto: University of Toronto Press, 1965), p. 7.
5 Horace Meyer Kallen, *The Book of Job as Greek Tragedy* (New York: Moffat Yard and Company, 1918), p. 7.
6 George S. Goodspeed, 'The Book of Job in Other Literatures, II', *The Old and New Testament Studies* XV, 3–4 (1892): 105–14. The cited passages are on pp. 105 and 109.
7 Tertullian, *Apologeticus* 18.2, *P.L.* 1, col. 434: 'hic enim est verus Prometheus.'
8 *Fasciculus, Fasciculus Morum: A Fourteenth-Century Preacher's Handbook*, ed. Sigfried Wenzel (University Park and London: Pennsylvania University Press, 1989), p. 296.
9 On the relationship between Prometheus and Christian martyrs, an obvious bridge was Martial's *De Spectaculis*, in which the torment of Prometheus on the rock is comparatively invoked in the description of an execution combining the sentences of crucifixion and *ad bestias* in the Coliseum. In a gloss of Farnciscus Bivarius on epigram 7, appended by him to the *Chronicon* of Flavius Lucius Dexter, who mentions a theatrical miming of such an execution, the relationship is made explicit: 'quo martyris cujusdam Christiani passionem veram, simulatam agentis Laureoli Latronis fabulam, refert.' See Flavius Lucius Dexter Barcinonensis, *Chronicon omnimodae historiae,* una cum commentariis Fr. Francisci Bivarii*, in Patrologia Latina,* accurante J.- P. Migne, vol. 31 (Paris: Vrayet, 1846), col. 251.
10 Gregory the Great, *Moralia in Job*, *P.L.* 75, col. 533; Jerome, *Expositio interlinearis libri Job*, *P.L.* 23, col. 1475 ('Job dolens interpretatur Jesus Christus, qui dolores nostros portavit'). The name of Job was etymologized as 'the one who suffers' by Isidore of Seville, *Etimologie o origini*, a cura di Angelo Valastro Canale, vol. I (Torino: Unione Tipografico-Editrice Torinese, 2004), p. 586: 'Iob in Latinum vertitur dolens.'
11 *P.L.* 172, col. 570.

12 Jacques Maritain, *Art and Scholasticism* and *The Frontiers of Poetry* (Notre Dame and London: University of Notre Dame Press, 1962), p. 28.
13 O. B. Hardison, Jr., *Christian Rite and Christian Drama in the Middle Ages* (Baltimore: Johns Hopkins Press, 1965), p. 40.
14 The figures on textual citations are based on Edward Moore, *Studies in Dante*, first series, *Scriptures and Classical Authors in Dante* (Oxford: Clarendon, 1896), pp. 4–5, whereas those on the characters of the *Divine Comedy* are based on the lists compiled by Dorothy Lister Simons, 'The Individual Human *dramatis personae* of the *Divine Comedy*', *Modern Philology* 16 (1918): 371–80.
15 The E text is from the eleventh century, but it was not transmitted in many other copies. However, the text that appeared in the twelfth or thirteenth century (the A text) was copied very frequently, contributing, among other things, to the developing thought on the nature of cruelty; it has come down to us in almost 300 manuscripts. Cf. Daniel Baraz, 'Seneca, Ethics, and the Body: The treatment of Cruelty in Medieval Thought', *Journal of the History of Ideas* 59 (1998): 195–215, see especially p. 210. For a detailed account of the transmission of Seneca's tragedies in the late Middle Ages, see Richard H. Rouse, 'The A Text of Seneca's Tragedies in the Thirteenth Century', *Revue d'histoire des textes* 1 (1971): 93–121; Otto Zwierlein, 'Spuren der Tragoedien Senecas bei Bemardus Silvestris, Petrus Pictor und Marbod von Rennes', *Mittellateinisches Jahrbuch* 22 (1989): 171–96.
16 *Convivio* IV.28.15-19. Edition used: Dante Alighieri, *Il Convivio*, ridotto a miglior lezione e commentato da G. Busnelli e G. Vandelli, seconda edizione (Firenze: Le Monnier, 1968).
17 On the *Dies Irae* see Walter J. Ong, 'Wit and Mystery: A Reevaluation in Medieval Hymnody', *Speculum* 22 (1947): 321. The text of the Mantuan hymn may be found in Jan M. Ziolkowski and Michael C. J. Putnam, *The Virgilian Tradition: The First Fifteen Hundred Years* (New Haven and London, 2007), p. 412.
18 Th. da Celano, *Vita prima*, 83.2-4, in Celano, *S. Francisci Assisiensis Vita et Miracula* (Rome: Desclée, 1906).
19 *Summa Theologiae*, III.83, Cura Fratrum eiusdem Ordinins (Madrid: Biblioteca de Autores Cristianos, 1965), and cf. Salvatore Marsili, *I segni del mistero di Cristo: Teologia dei sacramenti* (Rome: C.L.V. Edizioni Liturgiche, 1987), pp. 257–8.
20 Cf. Hardison, Jr., *Christian Rite and Christian Drama in the Middle Ages*, p. 271.
21 Oscar Mandel, *A Definition of Tragedy* (New York: New York University Press, 1961), p. 114.
22 Ibid., p. 114.
23 Hans Urs von Balthasar, *Theo-Drama: Theological Dramatic Theory*, vol. 1 (San Francisco: Ignatius Press, 1988), p. 71.
24 Maritain, *Art and Scholasticism* and *The Frontiers of Poetry*, p. 28.
25 Robert Fowler, 'The Rhetoric of Desperation', *Harvard Studies in Classical Philology* 91 (1987): 13, argues that speeches of despair were a 'typical feature' of classical

tragedy. On the psychological state of the character conveyed by the syntax of Pier Delle Vigne, see Leo Spitzer, 'Speech and Language in *Inferno XIII*', *Italica* 19, no. 2 (1942): 96.

26 *Epistola CCLVI ad Dominum Papam Eugenium*, in *Patrologia Latina* 182, 463d. The words quoted by St Bernard are 'non est vir fortis, cui non crescit animus in ipsa rerum difficultate'. The modern critical text, by L. D. Reynolds (Oxford University Press, 1991), is 'non est vir fortis ac strenuus qui laborem fugit, nisi crescit illi animus ipsa rerum difficultate'.

27 On rememorative allegory see Timothy M.Thibodeau, '*Enigmata Figurarum*: Biblical Exegesis and Liturgical Exposition in Durand's *Rationale*', *The Harvard Theological Review* 86 (1993): 77–8.

28 On the comic dimension of the Mass, see Hardison, Jr., *Christian Rite and Christian Drama in the Middle Ages*, p. 46.

29 Col. 1.24.

30 The commentaries of Avicenna and Averroes are available in English in Avicenna, *Avicenna's Commentary on the Poetics of Aristotle*, trans. and ed. Ismail M. Dahyat (Leiden: Brill, 1974) and Averroes, *Averroes' Middle Commentary on Aristotle's Poetics*, trans. and ed. Charles E. Butterworth (Princeton: Princeton University Press, 1986).

31 Dimitri Gutas, 'On Translating Averroes' Commentaries', *Journal of the American Oriental Society* 110 (1990): 97. Among transformations of the original text is the notion of *opsis* at 1450a8-10, which is understood by Averroes as 'theoretical investigation', though, as Gutas points out, in the translation by Butterworth it appears as 'spectacle' (p. 98).

32 T. S. Eliot, *Murder in the Cathedral* (Toronto: Kingswood House, 1959), p. 58.

33 The two *devozioni* were first published in Alessandro D'Ancona, 'Due antiche devozioni italiane', *Rivista di filologia romanza* II (1875): 14–19, (*Devotione de Zobiadí sancto*) and pp. 19–28 (*Devotione de Venerdí sancto*). Further references in the text.

34 Durand, *Rationale*, 1.5.

35 On contemporary nudity costumes, see Peter Meredith and John E. Tailby, *The Staging of Religious Drama in Europe in the Later Middle Ages* (Kalamazoo: Medieval Institute Publications, 1983).

36 Balthasar, *Theo-Drama: Theological Dramatic Theory*, vol. 1, p. 86.

37 Durand, *Rationale*, pp. 8ff.

Chapter 7

1 *Quaestiones disputatae de veritate*, 28.2.12.

2 Dated 17 July 1506, it was published in Cajetan's collection *Opuscula et quodlibeta* of 1514 and reissued in various later editions. I used the 1587 edition, *Opuscula*

omnia, tomus secundus (Lugduni: Ex Officina Iuntarum, 1587), pp. 180–1; all references given by page number in the text are to this edition, and their translation is mine. On the textual tradition of the tract, see M.-J. Congar, 'Cajetan et la dévotion à la Compassion de Marie. L'opuscule *De Spasmo*', *Supplément à la Vie Spirituelle* (1934): 144–5. Cajetan had been appointed professor of theology and sacred letters at the University of Rome at the request of Cardinal Oliviero Carafa, Archbisjop of Naples, recently entrusted by the papacy with the protection of the Dominican Order. See Aluigi Cossio, *Il Cardinale Gaetano e la Riforma* (Cividale: Tipografia Giovanni Fulvio, 1902), pp. 63–4.

3. Donna Spivey Ellington, *From Sacred Body to Angelic Soul: Understanding Mary in Late Medieval and Early Modern Europe* (Washington: The Catholic University of America Press, 2001), p. 80; Marina Warner, *Alone of All Her Sex: The Myth and Cult of the Virgin Mary* (London: Pan Books, 1976), pp. 217–18.

4. The estimate of the number of crucifixions with a swooning Mary is found in Nicholas Penny, *National Gallery Catalogues: The Sixteenth-Century Italian Paintings*, vol. 1 (London: National Gallery, 2004), p. 26. On Erasmus, see Jonathan Willis, *Sin and Salvation in Reformation England*, (Abingdon: Routledge, 2016), p. 155. For a useful overview of the swoon throughout the period, see Barry Windeatt, 'The Art of Swooning in Middle English', in *Medieval Latin and Middle English Literature: Essays in Honour of Jill Mann*, ed. Christopher Cannon and Maura Nolan (Cambridge: D.S. Brewer, 2011), pp. 213–30.

5. *The Apocryphal New Testament: Apocryphal Gospels, Acts, Epistles, and Apocalypses*, ed. R. H. James (Oxford: Clarendon, 1924), p. 116.

6. *Iliad* 22.466-472, on which see Dennis R. MacDonald, *The Gospels and Homer* (London: Rowman and Littlefield, 2015), p. 126.

7. Eliana Corbari, *Vernacular Theology: Dominican Sermons and Audience in Late Medieval Italy* (Berlin, Boston: De Guyter, 2013), p. 164.

8. By St Anthony of Padua, for example, in his *Sermones dominicales et festivi* (Padua: Messaggero di S. Antonio, 1979), sermon for the third Sunday after Easter (3.4.11), on which cf. Neff, 'The Pain of *Compassio*: Mary's Labour at the Foot of the Cross', *The Art Bulletin* 80, no. 2 (1998): 269 and Corbari, *Vernacullar Theology*, p. 165.

9. Sebeok, *Signs*, p. 46.

10. *De Spasmo*, in Avicenna's *Canon medicinae*, 3.2.1.

11. *On Interpretation*, Commentary by St Thomas and Cajetan (Milwaukee: Marquette University Press, 1962), p. 23.

12. In addition to Sebeok, *Signs*, pp. 46–8, see especially Deely, *The Arc of Semiotic Development*, p. 48, and Deely, *Four Ages of Understanding*, p. 420.

13. See Maria Marcellina Pedico, *Mater dolorosa: L'Addolorata nella pietà popolare* (Libreria Editrice Vaticana: Città del Vaticano, 2015), pp. 102–3; Carol M. Schuler, 'The Seven Sorrows of the Virgin: Popular Culture and Cultic Imagery in Pre-Reformation Europe', *Simiolus: Netherlands Quarterly for the History of Art* 21 (1992): 5–28.

14 Paragraph 79.48 in the edition by M. Stallings-Taney, attributed to Iohannis de Caulibus, *Meditaciones vite Christi, olim S. Bonauenturo attributae, cura et studio M. Stallings-Taney* (Turnhout: Brepols, 1997), p. 278. Cf. Thomas H. Bestul, *Texts of the Passion: Latin Devotional Literature and Medieval Society* (Philadelphia: University of Pennsylvania Press, 1996), p. 123 and Jessica Boon, 'The Agony of the Virgin: The Swoons and Crucifixion of Mary in Sixteenth Century Castilian Passion Treatises', *The Sixteenth Century Journal* 38, no. 1 (2007): 12–13.

15 Valla's interpretation of *gratia plena* as 'highly favoured' was discovered and published by Erasmus just before Cajetan's tract *De Spasmo*. See Jaroslav Pelikan, *Jesus through the Centuries: His Place in the History of Culture* (New Haven: Yale University Press, 1985), p. 153.

16 Charles Sanders Peirce, *Collected Papers*, vol VI, *Scientific Metaphysics* (Cambridge: Harvard University Press), p. 347.

17 Sarah McNamer, *Affective Meditation and the Invention of Medieval Compassion* (Philadelphia: Penn State University Press), pp. 96–101.

18 For some early examples of *cruce erecta* iconography, see Eörsi, '*Haec Scala Significat Ascensum virtutum*. Remarks on the Iconography of Christ Mounting the Cross on a Ladder', *Arte Cristiana*, no. 85 (1997): 151–66.

19 MS 643, fol. 12v, Pierpont Morgan Library, New York.

20 M. Bakhtin, *The Dialogic Imagination* (Austin: University of Texas Press, 1981), p. 250.

21 On this point, see A. P. McMahon, *Understanding the Medieval Meditative Ascent: Augustine, Anselm, Boethius and Dante* (Washington, DC: Catholic University of America, 2006), pp. 1–2.

22 J. Guy Bougerol, *Introduction to the Works of Bonaventure* (Paterson, N.J.: St. Anthony Guild Press, 1963), p. 129.

23 Bonaventure, '*Collationes de septem donis Spiritus Sancti*', in *Opera omnia*, vol. 5 (Quaracchi: Typographia Collegii Bonaventurae, 1891), p. 3 (*Opera*, vol. 5, p. 480): 'Sicut corpus ornatur ex habitu, ita ornatur anima est ex fortitudine; ideo dicitur indumentum animae; nec solum fortitudo est indumentum animae, vel Virginis gloriosae, immo matris Ecclesiae.'

24 Bonaventure-pseudo, *Life of Christ* (London: Rivingtons, 1888), p. 267.

25 Gerbron, 'The Story of Fra Angelico', *Mitteilungen des Kunsthistorischen Institutes in Florenz* 57 (2015): 308.

26 Yuri Lotman, 'Painting and the Language of Theater: Notes on the Problem of Iconic Rhetoric', in *Tekstura: Russian Essays on Visual Culture*, ed. and trans. Alla Efimova and Lev Manovich (Chicago and London: The University of Chicago Press, 1993), p. 51.

27 Pierre Cartier, *Beato Angelico da Fiesole* (London: John Philp, 1865), p. 220.

28 This stage of the process is described in the *Meditationes*. Cf. in English translation, *Life of Christ*, p. 267: The executioners 'descend from the ladders and removed

them. The Lord hangs down by the weight of His body, supported only by the nails through his hands. Nevertheless, another comes up, and draws down his body by his feet with all his might, and holds them, whilst another drives a nail most cruelly through them'.

29 Bonaventuran editorial and textual tradition. Textual references are to the *Officium septem dolorum B. Mariae virginis* (Vibo Valentia: Pasquale Labadessa, 1961) in use by the lay Confraternita di Santa Maria della Pietà in Maierato, founded in 1687, on which see Antonino Cugliari, *La confraternita di Santa Maria della Pietà in Maierato (Catanzaro)* (Oppido Mamertina: Barbaro Editore, 1984), pp. 31–68. For a review of all such confraternities still in existence in Italy and the popular culture surrounding them, see M.M. Pedico, *Mater dolorosa: L'Addolorata nella pietà popolare*. Città del Vaticano: Libreria Editrice Vaticana, 2015.

30 On the development of the motif of the compassion of Mary, see Jean-Pierre Delville, 'L'émergence de la compassion dans le regard sur la Passion', in *Saluting Aron Gurevich: Essays in History, Literature and Other Related Subjects*, ed. Mazour-Matusevič and Alexandra Scheckel Korros (Leiden and Boston: Brill, 2010), pp. 191–226; Giovanni Farris, 'La *compassio virginis* nel sec. XV', *Quaderni di civiltà letteraria* XXI (1981); A. Luis, 'Evolutio historica doctrinae de compassione', *Marianum* V (1943): 261–85.

31 Bonaventure, *Officium septem dolorum B. Mariae virginis*, p. 28.

Chapter 8

1 Pamela M. Jones, *Federico Borromeo e l'Ambrosiana: Arte e riforma cattolica nel XVII secolo a Milano*, trans. Stefano Galli (Milano: Vita e Pensiero, 1997), p. 55.

2 Ioannes David, *Veridicus Christianus* (Antwerp: Officina Plantiniana, 1606). Page references in the text are to this edition. Citations reproduce the original punctuation and spelling though macron abbreviations have been expanded. All translations are my own.

3 Chipps Jeffrey Smith, *Sensuous Worship: Jesuits and the Art of the Early Catholic Reformation in Germany* (Princeton and Oxford: Princeton University Press, 2002), pp. 42–4.

4 On the imitation of God and Christ, particularly with reference to the early part of the tradition, see Anthony Meredith, S.J. *Gregory of Nyssa* (London: Routledge, 1999), pp. 104ff.

5 Tommaso De Vio Cajetan, *In quatuor Evangelia* (Paris: Guillard, 1540), p. 438, on Jn 12.26: 'sed servire Christo ad imitationem Christi proprium est electis'.

6 Fastidius Episcopus, *De Vita Christiana. Patrologia Latina, PL* vol. 50, col. 385. The *De vita Christiana* was published by J. P. Migne without explanation

as a work by Fastidius in PL 50, but he had earlier published it in PL 40, as an appendix to Augustine's works, observing that its authorship was uncertain. The treatise, however, had been attributed to Fastidius already in the seventeenth century by Lucas Hostensius in *Fastidii Episcopi De vita Christiana liber*, denuo editus et autori restitutus ex fide MS. ex codicis sacris Casinen. Monasterij, opera et studio Lucae Holstenij. Rome: Dragondelli, 1663. For the scholarly debate on the authorship, see Robert F. Evans, 'Pelagius, Fastidius and the pseudo-Augustinian *De vita Christiana*', *The Journal of Theological Studies* 13, no. 1 (1962): 72–98; John Morris, 'Pelagian Literature', *The Journal of Theological Studies* 16, no. 1 (1965): 26–60; W. Liebeschuetz, 'Pelagian Evidence on the Last Period of Roman Britain?', *Latomus* 26, no. 2 (1967): 436–47; Duval, 'Sur quelques manuscrits du *De vita Christiana* portant le nom de Pélage', *Latomus* 64, no. 1 (2005): 132–52.

7 'qui omnibus misericordiam facit; qui nulla omnino mouetur iniuria; qui alienaum dolorem tanquam proprium sentit; cuius mensam nullus pauperum ignorat; qui coram hominibus ingloriosus habetur, vt coram Deo angelis glorietur; qui terrena contennit, vt possit habere celestia; qui opprimi pauperem se patiente non patitur; qui miseris subuenit; qui ad fletum fletibus prouocatur alienis' (p. 45). The source text is *De vita Christiana*, PL vol. 50, col. 400.

8 On the theory and conventions of *ad vivum* paintings, see C. Swan, 'Ad vivum naer het leven, from the Life: Defining a Mode of Representation', *Word Image* 11 (1995): 353–72. David Young Kim, 'The Horror of Mimesis', *Oxford Art Journal* 34, no. 3 (2011): 335, speaks of the style as 'heightened verisimilitude'.

9 Noa Turel, 'Living Pictures: Rereading *au vif*, *Gesta* 50, no. 2 (2011): 164.

10 Soren Kierkegaard, *The Works of Love* (New York: Harper and Row, 1962), p. 61.

11 *In Lucam homiliae*, PG 13, col. 1820, and cf. Luigi Gambero, *Mary and the Fathers of the Church: The Blessed Virgin Mary in Patristic Thought* (San Francisco: Ignatius Press, 1999), p. 79.

12 St. Gregory of Nyssa, *Ascetical Works* (Washington: The Catholic University of America Press, 1967), p. 228; Battista Mondin, *L'uomo secondo il disegno di Dio: Trattato ti antropologia teologica* (Bologna: Edizioni studio domenicano, 1992), p. 158.

13 The ancient source on Apelles' fame is Pliny the Elder, *Historia Naturalis, 35,* 36 pp. 79–97.

14 Frederick A. De Armas, 'Simple Magic: Ekphrasis from Antiquity to the Age of Cervantes', in *Ekphrasis in the Age of Cervantes*, ed. Frederick A. De Armas (Lewisburg: Bucknell University Press, 2006), pp. 14–15.

15 On this point, Walter S. Melion, 'Ut Pictura Lex: Jan David, S.J., on Natural Law and Global Reach of Christian Images', in *The Nomadic Object: The Challenge of World for Early Modern Religious Art*, ed. Christine Göttler and Mia M. Mochizuki (Leiden and Boston: Brill, 2018), p. 177, has cogently argued that the imitation that David has in mind is not just a figure of speech but a perfect likeness.

16 Cf. Jean-Vincent Blanchard, *L'optique du discours au xviie siècle. De la rhétorique des jésuites au style de la raison moderne (Descartes, Pascal)* (Saint-Nicolas: Presses de l'Université Laval, 2005), p. 191, and Smith, *Sensuous Worship*, p. 48. In the bottom right part of the engraving, one of the canvasses shows a woman with wild animals in the foreground. Smith argues that this image and that of the devil signify that the artists' 'inner vision of Christ has been corrupted by sin, by holding the devil in their heart' (p. 48).

Chapter 9

1 François Coster, *De cantico Salve Regina septem meditationes* (Antwerp: Plantini, 1587), pp. 23–34.
2 On this point, see Domenico Pietropaolo, 'L'inno *Ave Maris Stella* fra liturgia e politica nella conversione del Canada', in *Lingue e Testi delle Riforme Cattoliche in Europa e nelle Americhe (secc. XVI -XXI)*, ed. Rita Librandi (Firenze: Cesati Editore, 2013), pp. 93–108.
3 Angela M. Lucas, *Women in the Middle Ages* (Brighton: The Harvester Press, 1983), p. 17.
4 Leonard Swindler, *Biblical Affirmation of Woman* (Philadelphia: The Westminster Press, 1979), pp. 341–51; Plato, *Republic* 5.455c-d and *Laws* 6.781b; Aristotle, *Poetics* 1260a20.
5 In Luigi Valpolicelli, ed., *Il pensiero pedagogico della Controriforma* (Firense: Giuntina-Sansoni, 1960), p. 93.
6 Federico Della Valle, *Tutte le opere*, ed. Pietro Cazzani (Milano: Mondadori, 1955), p. 442. All textual references to Della Valle are to this edition of his works and are given in the text by page number. The translations are my own.
7 Luther had no objections to the title of queen, as long as one did not believe that she could actually respond to prayers addressed to her rather than God. On the whole question, viewed from a historical perspective, see Charlene Spretnak, *Missing Mary: The Queen of Heaven and Her Re-Emergence in the Modern Church* (New York: Palgrave Macmillan, 2004), pp. 151–60.
8 Anne Sheppard, *Aesthetics* (Oxford: Oxford University Press, 1987), pp. 13–15, analyses in detail the difference between 'seeing as' and 'seeing in' in the observation of natural phenomena and in the arts, including painting and drama, showing that 'seeing in' always involves making an 'imaginative projection' (p. 15) into the object of observation.
9 Jaroslav Pelikan, *Reformation of Church and Dogma (1300-1700)* (Chicago: Chicago University Press, 1984), pp. 307–8.
10 Rabanaus Maurus, *PL* 109, col. 546; *Speculum humanae salvationis*, chapter 30.

11 Cf. Warner, *Alone of All Her Sex*, p. 55.
12 This expression is applied to Judith by Swindler, *Biblical Affirmations of Woman*, p. 113.
13 St Jerome, *Select Letters* (Cambridge: Harvard University Press, 1933), p. 386.
14 Crusca, *Vocabolario degli accademici della Crusca* (Venezia: Alberti, 1612), p. 496.
15 See, for example, the following lines, spoken by Vagao to Holofernes: 'Parte discinta e sciolta, / parte ristretta e avvolta, /mentre or s'apre or si copre, / mille vaghezze scopre.'

Chapter 10

1 Julius Schiller, *Coelum Stellatum Christianum* (Augsburg: Aperger, 1627), p. 1. All textual references (with my translations) are to this edition and are given in the text by page number.
2 In attributing the catasterism of immoral fables to Satan, Schiller follows St Justin Martyr, *First Apology* 1.27, see Justin, *First and Second Apologies*, trans. William Barnar (New York: Paulist Press, 1997), p. 38.
3 *in eius saltem vestibulo contumaci perduellione Altissimum aemularetur.* Schiller, *Coelum Stellatum Christianum*, p. 1.
4 *Beatis spiritibus, virisque sanctitate insignibus* (Schiller, *Coelum Stellatum Christianum*, p. 2).
5 Thus he redrew the constellations of Aries, Taurus and Gemini as St Peter, St Andrew and St James the Greater; he reassigned the summer constellations of Cancer, Leo and Virgo respectively to St John, St Thomas and St James the Lesser; he reconceived the summer houses of Libra, Scorpio and Sagittarius as St Philip, St Bartholomew and St Matthew; he re-imagined the first two winter houses of Capricorn and Aquarius as profiles of St Simon and St Judas Thaddeus, while he reconfigured Pisces, the last house of the winter Zodiac, as St Matthias, the elected successor of Judas Iscariot.
6 Michel Foucault, *The Order of Things: An Archaeology of the Human Sciences* (London and New York, 2005), p. 47.
7 Campanella expresses this view in his *De gentilismo non ritendo* (1636), on which see Paola Gatti, *Il gran libro del mondo nella filosofia di Tommaso Campanella* (Roma: Pontificia Università Gregoriana, 2009), pp. 19–20.
8 Cf. Foucault, *The Order of Things*, p. 47.
9 This was the common method for regional maps, John P. Snyder, 'Map Projections in the Renaissance', in *The History of Cartography*, vol. 3, part 1, ed. Edward Woodward (Chicago and London: Chicago University Press, 2007), pp. 378 and 381.

10 *Catechism of the Council of Trent* (1982), p. 107.
11 Arnauld Antoine and Pierre Nicole, *La logique ou l'art de penser* (Paris: Hachette, 1961), p. 38, and cf. Marin, *Food for Thought*, trans. Mette Hjort (Baltimore and London: The Johns Hopkins University Press, 1997), p. 9.
12 *The Canons and Decrees of the Council of Trent* (1978), Sess. 22, 'Decree concerning reform', chapter 1.
13 On the relationship between calendars and zodiac signs, cf. Francesco Maiello, *Storia del calendario La misurazione del tempo, 1450-1800* (Torino: Einaudi, 1994), pp. 112–14.
14 Charles Sanders Peirce, 'On the Algebra of Logic: A Contribution to the Philosophy of Notation', *The American Journal of Mathematics* 7 (1885): 180–202.
15 *mentes nostras non ad poeticas vanitates sed in Deum viuum ac verum, sanctosue eius erigendas,* Schiller, *Coelum Stellatum Christianum*, p. 2. Schiller says this on the authority of Bellarmine's *De ascensione mentis in Deum*, step 8.
16 Augustine discusses the issue in *Contra Faust*. Lib. Ix, c, ii; *The Catechism of the Council of Trent* (1982), p. 149.
17 *Catechism of the Council of Trent* (1982), p. 145.
18 Ibid., p. 146.
19 Johannes Kepler, *Epitome of Copernican Astronomy and Harmonies of the World*, trans. Charles Glenn Wallis (Amherst: Prometheus Books, 1995), p. 15.

Bibliography

Aho, Tuomo and Mikko Yrjonsuuri. 'Late Medieval Logic', in *The Development of Modern Logic*, edited by Leila Haaparanta. Oxford: Oxford University Press, 2009.

Alban, Gillian M. E. 'The Serpent Goddess Melusine: From Cursed Snake to Mary's Shield', in *The Survival Myth, Singularity and Alterity*, edited by David Kennedy and Paul Hardwick, 23–43. Newcastle upon Tyne: Cambridge Scholar's Press, 2010.

Alighieri, Dante. *La Commedia secondo l'antica vulgata*, edited by Giorgio Petrocchi. Milano: Mondadori, 1966-1967.

Alighieri, Dante. *Il Convivio*, ridotto a miglior lezione e commentato da G. Busnelli e G. Vandelli, seconda edizione. Firenze: Le Monnier, 1968.

Ambrose, St. '*De Isaac et anima*' in *Opera omnia*, in *Patrologia Latina* (PL), accurante J.-P. Migne, vol. 14. Paris: Garnier fratres, 1882, cols. 523-560.

Anonymous of Arras, *Recollectio casus, status et condicionis Valdensium ydolatrarum*, in *Quellen und Untersuchungen zur Geschichte des Hexnwhans und der Hexenverfolgung im Mittelalter*, edited by Joseph Hansen, 149-83. Bonn: Georgi, 1901.

Anonymous of Arras. *A History of the Case, State, and Condition of the Waldensian Heretics (Witches)*, edited and translated by A. C. Gow, R. B. Desjardins and F. V. Pageau. University Park: Pennsylvania State University Press, 2016.

Anthony of Padua. *Sermones dominicales et festivi*, edited by B. Costa et al. Padua: Messaggero di S. Antonio, 1979.

Aquinas, St. Thomas. *Questiones disputatae de veritate. Opera omnia*, vol. 22. Rome: Sancta Sabina, 1970.

Aquinas, St. Thomas. *Summa Theologiae, cum commentariis Thomae De Vio Caietani ordinis praedicatorum*. Rome: Typographia Polyglotta, 1888-1906.

Aquinas, St. Thomas. *Summa Theologica*, translated by the Fathers of the English Dominican Province. Claremont: Coyote Canyon Press, 2018.

Aristotle. *On Interpretation*, commentary by St. Thomas and Cajetan, translated by Jean T. Osterle. Milwaukee: Marquette University Press, 1962.

Arnauld, Antoine and Pierre Nicole. *La logique ou l'art de penser*. Paris: Hachette, 1861.

Ashworth, E. J. 'Language and Logic', in *The Cambridge Companion to Medieval Philosophy*, edited by A. S. McGrade, 73-96. Cambridge: Cambridge University Press, 2003.

Augustine, St. *De Catechizandis Rudibus*, translated by S. D. F. Salmond, in *Nicene and Post-Nicene Fathers*, First Series, vol. 3, edited by Philip Schaff, 282-314. Buffalo: Christian Literature Publishing Co., 1887.

Augustine, St. *The City of God*, translated by Marcus Dods. Edinburgh: Clark, 1888.

Augustine, St. Le confessioni, testo a fronte, a cura di Maria Bettetini. Torino: Einaudi, 2002.

Augustine, St. *De Doctrina Christiana*, Corpus Christianorum, Series Latina, XXXII. Turnhout: Brepols, 1962.

Averroes. *Averroes' Middle Commentary on Aristotle's Poetics*, translated and edited by Charles E. Butterworth. Princeton: Princeton University Press, 1986.

Avicenna. '*De Spasmo*', in *Canon medicinae: Avicennae arabum medicorum principis*, Ex Gerardi Cremonensi versione. Venetiis: Apud Iuntas, 1595.

Avicenna. *Avicenna's Commentary on the Poetics of Aristotle*, translated and edited by Ismail M. Dahyat. Leiden: Brill, 1974.

Bakhtin, M. *The Dialogic Imagination*, edited by Michael Holquist, translated by Caryl Emerson and Michael Holquist. Austin: University of Texas Press, 1981.

Balthasar, Hans Urs von. *Theo-Drama: Theological Dramatic Theory, vol. 1: Prolegomena*, translated by Graham Harrison. San Francisco: Ignatius Press, 1988.

Baraz, Daniel. 'Seneca, Ethics, and the Body: The Treatment of Cruelty in Medieval Thought', *Journal of the History of Ideas* 59 (1998): 195–215.

Bargigi, Guinoforto delli. *Lo Inferno della Commedia di Dante Alighieri*. Marseilles-Firenze: Mossey & Molini, 1839.

Barnett, Gregory. 'Modal Theory, Church Keys, and the Sonata', *Journal of the American Musicological Society* 51, no. 2 (1998): 245–81.

Beal, Timothy. 'Reception History and Beyond: Toward the Cultural History of Scriptures', *Biblical Interpretation* 19, nos. 4–5 (2011): 357–72.

Beccaria, Cesare. *On Crimes and Punishments*, translated by Henry Paolucci. Indianapolis: Bobbs-Merrill, 1963.

Beck, James. *Jacopo della Quercia*, vol. 1. New York: Columbia University Press, 1991.

Bede. *On Genesis*, translated by C. B. Kendall. Liverpool: Liverpool University Press, 2008.

Berardi, Angelo. *Miscellanea musicale*. Bologna: Giacomo Monti, 1970, Forni reprint of 1689 edition.

Bernard, St. '*Epistola CCLVI Ad Dominum Papam Eugenium*' in *Epistolae*, in *Patrologia Latina* (PL), accurante J.-P. Migne, vol. 182. Paris: Ex typis Migne, 1859, cols. 463-465.

Bernardino Da Siena. *Prediche volgari*. Siena: Land e Alessandri, 1853.

Biblia Sacra, iuxta vulgata clementinam nova editio. Madrid: Biblioteca de Autores Cristianos, 1977.

Bielo, James S. *The Social Life of Scriptures: Cross Cultural Perspectives on Biblicism*. New Brunswick: Rutgers University Press, 2009.

Blanchard, Jean-Vincent. *L'optique du discours au xviie siècle. De la rhétorique des jésuites au style de la raison moderne (Descartes, Pascal)*. Saint-Nicolas: Presses de l'Université Laval, 2005.

Bloom, Harold. *Anxiety of Influence: A Theory of Poetry*. Oxford: Oxford University Press, 1973.

Bloom, Harold. *The Book of J*. New York: Grove Weidenfeld, 1990.

Boccaccio, Giovanni. *Esposizioni sopra la Comedia di Dante*. Milano: Mondadori, 1994.

Bois, Jacques du. 'A History of the Case, State, and Condition of the Waldensian Heretics (Witches), 1460', in *The Arras Witch Treatises*, edited and translated by A. C. Gow, R.B, 19–79. University Park: The Pennsylvania State University Press, 2016.

Bonaventure. *Officium septem dolorum B. Mariae virginis*, Congregazione di Maria SS. Addolorata in Maierato. Vibo Valentia: Tipografia Pasquale Labadessa, 1961.

Bonaventure, St. *Collationes de septem donis Spiritus Sancti*. Opera omnia, vol. 5, 455–503. Quaracchi: Typographia Collegii Bonaventurae, 1891.

Bonaventure, Pseudo-. *The Life of Christ*, translated by W. H. Hutchings. London: Rivingtons, 1888.

Boon, Jessica. 'The Agony of the Virgin: The Swoons and Crucifixion of Mary in Sixteenth Century Castilian Passion Treatises', *The Sixteenth Century Journal* 38, no. 1 (2007): 3–25.

Borghini, Raffaello. *Il riposo*, edited and translated by H. S. Lloyd Jr. Toronto: University of Toronto Press, 2012.

Bottin, Francesco. 'Teoria dei segni e logica tardo-medievale', *Miscellanea Medievalia* III, no. 1 (1980): 498–503.

Bougerol, J. Guy. *The Works of Bonaventure*, translated by José de Vinck. Paterson, N.J.: St. Anthony Guild Press, 1963.

Bouissac, Paul. 'Iconicity or Iconization? Probing the Dynamic Interface between Language and Perception', in *Outside-in – Inside-out: Iconicity in Language and Literature*, edited by C. Maeder, O. Fischer and W. J. Herlofsky, 15–37. Amsterdam: Benjamins, 2005.

Broedel, Hans Peter. *The Malleus Maleficarum and the Construction of Witchcraft*. Manchester and New York: Manchester University Press, 2003.

Butterworth, Charles E. *Averroes' Middle Commentary on Aristotle's Poetics*. Princeton: Princeton University Press, 1986.

Cajetan, Tommaso de Vio. *In Pentateuchum Mosis iuxta sensum quem dicunt literalem commentarii*. Rome: Bladum, 1531.

Cajetan, Tommaso de Vio. *In librum Job commentarii*. Roma: Bladum, 1535.

Cajetan, Tommaso de Vio. *In Quatuor Evangelia*. Paris: Guillard, 1540.

Cajetan, Tommaso de Vio. *Opuscula omnia*. Tomus secundus. Lugduni: Ex Officina Iuntarum, 1587.

Cajetan, Tommaso de Vio. *De Maleficiis*, in *Opuscula*, 132–3. Antwerp: Keerbergium, 1612.

Cajetan, Tommaso de Vio. *Thomae Aquinatis opera omnia*, tomus quintus, *Pars prima summae theologiae,* a questione L ad questionem CXIX, cum commentarius Thomae de Vio Caietani ordinis predicatorum. Rome: Typographia Polyglotta, 1889.

Cajetan, Tommaso de Vio. *Thomae Aquinatis opera omnia*, tomus nonus, *Secunda secundae summae theologiae,* a questione LVII ad questionem CXXII, cum commentarius Thomae de Vio Caietani ordinis predicatorum. Rome: Typographia Polyglotta, 1896.

Camille, Michael. *The Gargoyles of Notre-Dame: Medievalism and the Monsters of Modernity*. Chicago: The University of Chicago Press, 2009.

Canons of the Second Council of Orange, AD 529. Oxford: James Thornton, 1882.
The Canons and Decrees of the Council of Trent, translated and introduced by Reverend H. J. Schroeder. Charlotte: Tan Books, 1978.
Cartier, Etienne. *Beato Angelico da Fiesole*. London: John Philp, 1865.
Catechism of the Council of Trent for Parish Priests, translated by John A. McHugh and Charles J. Callan. Rockford: Tan Books, 1982.
Catechismus ex Decreto Concilii Tridentini ad Parrochos. Leipzig: Tauchnitz, 1856.
Celano. *S. Francisci Assisiensis Vita et Miracula*, edited by E. d'Alençon. Rome: Desclée, 1906.
Chiericato, Giovanni Maria. *Le spighe raccolte cioè annotazioni erudite et erudizioni notate*. Padua: Corona, 1716.
Comestor, Petrus. *Historia Scholastica - Libri Genesis*. Middleton: Perfect Library, 2019. Reprint of 1543 edition.
Congar, M.-J. 'Cajetan et la dévotion à la Compassion de Marie. L'opuscule *De Spasmo*', *Supplément à la Vie Spirituelle* 38 (1934): 142–60.
Corbari, Eliana. *Vernacular Theology: Dominican Sermons and Audience in Late Medieval Italy*. Berlin and Boston: De Guyter, 2013.
Cossio, Aluigi. *Il Cardinale Gaetano e la Riforma*. Cividale: Tipografia Giovanni Fulvio, 1902.
Coster, François. *De cantico Salve Regina septem meditationes*. Antwerp: Plantini, 1587.
Crusca. *Vocabolario degli accademici della Crusca*. Venezia: Alberti, 1612.
Cugliari, Antonino. *La confraternita di Santa Maria della Pietà in Maierato (Catanzaro)*. Oppido Mamertina: Barbaro Editore, 1984.
Dahyat, Ismail M. *Avicenna's Commentary on the Poetics of Aristotle*. Leiden: Brill, 1974.
D'Ancona, Alessandro. 'Due antiche devozioni italiane', *Rivista di filologia romanza* II (1875): 5–28.
Danesi, Marcel. *Signs of Crime: Introducing Forensic Semiotics*. Berlin and Boston: De Gruyter, 2014.
David, Ioannes. *Veridicus Christianus*. Antwerp: Officina Plantiniana, 1606.
De Armas, Frederick A. 'Simple Magic: Ekphrasis from Antiquity to the Age of Cervantes', in *Ekphrasis in the Age of Cervantes*, edited by Frederick A. De Armas, 13–31. Lewisburg: Bucknell University Press, 2006.
Deely, John. *Introducing Semiotic: Its History and Doctrine*. Bloomington: Indiana University Press, 1982.
Deely, John. *Four Ages of Understanding*. Toronto: University of Toronto Press, 2001.
Deely, John. *The Arc of Semiotic Development*. Ottawa: Legas, 2016.
Della Valle, Federico. *Tutte le opere*, edited by Pietro Cazzani. Milano: Mondadori, 1955.
Delville, Jean-Pierre. 'L'émergence de la compassion dans le regard sur la Passion au moyen age: Franciscanisme et mentalité populaire', in *Saluting Aron Gurevich: Essays in History, Literature and Other Related Subjects*, edited by Mazour-Matusevič and Alexandra Scheckel Korros, 191–226. Leiden and Boston: Brill, 2010.

De' Sommi, Leone. *Quattro dialoghi in materia di rappresentazioni sceniche*, edited by Ferruccio Marotti. Milano, 1968.

Durand, William. *Guillelmi Duranti Rationale divinorum officiorum*, Corpus Christianorum Series Laina, edited by Anselme Davril and Timothy M. Thibodeau. Turnhout: Brepols, 1995–2000.

Durand, William. *The Rationale divinorum officiorum of William Durand of Mende*, Prologue and Book 1, translated by Timothy M. Thibodeau. New York: Columbia University Press, 2007.

Duval, Yves-Marie. 'Sur quelques manuscrits du *De vita Christiana* portant le nom de Pélage', *Latomus* 64, no. 1 (2005): 132–52.

Ebbeler, Jennifer. *Disciplining Christians: Correction and Community in Augustine's Letters*. Oxford: Oxford University Press, 2012.

Eliot, T. S. *Murder in the Cathedral*, edited by H. Voaden. Toronto: Kingswood House, 1959.

Ellington, Donna Spivey. *From Sacred Body to Angelic Soul: Understanding Mary in Late Medieval and Early Modern Europe*. Washington: The Catholic University of America Press, 2001.

Eörsi, Anna. '*Haec scala significat ascensum virtutum*. Remarks on the iconography of Christ Mounting the Cross on a Ladder', *Arte cristiana*, no. 85 (1997): 151–66.

Evans, Robert F. 'Pelagius, Fastidius and the pseudo-Augustinian *De vita Christiana*', *The Journal of Theological Studies*, New series, 13, no. 1 (1962): 72–98.

Farris, Giovanni. *La compassio virginis nel sec. XV*, Quaderni di civiltà letteraria, vol. 31. Savona: Sabatelli, 1981.

Fasciculus. Fasciculus Morum: A Fourteenth-Century Preacher's Handbook, edited by Sigfried Wenzel. University Park and London: Pennsylvania University Press, 1989.

Fastidius Episcopus. *De vita Christiana liber*, denuo editus et autori restitutus ex fide MS. ex codicis sacris Casinen. Monasterij, opera et studio Lucae Holstenij. Rome: Dragondelli, 1663.

Fastidius Episcopus. *De vita Christiana. Patrologia Latina (PL)*, accurante J.-P. Migne, vol. 50. Paris: Ex typis Migne, 1865, cols. 3383–402.

Fioravanti, Stanislao. 'L'opera di Innocenzo III nello sviluppo della dottrina eucaristica', in *De sacro altaris mysterio, Il Sacrosanto mistero dell'altare*, edited by Stanislao Fioravanti, xi–xlii. Città del Vaticano: Libreria Editrice Vaticana, 2002.

Flavius Lucius Dexter Barcinonensis, *Chronicon omnimodae historiae*, una cum commentariis Fr. Francisci Bivarii, in *Patrologia Latina*, accurante J.- P. Migne, vol. 31. Paris: Vrayet, 1846, cols. 50-574.

Foucault, Michel. *Discipline and Punish*, translated by A. Sheridan. New York: Vintage Books, 1995.

Foucault, Michel. *The Order of Things: An Archaeology of the Human Sciences*. London and New York: Routledge, 2005.

Fowler, Robert. 'The Rhetoric of Desperation', *Harvard Studies in Classical Philology* 91 (1987): 5–38.

Feedberg, David and Vittorio Gallese. 'Motion, Emotion and Empathy in Esthetic Experience', *Trends in Cognitive Science* 11, no. 5 (2007): 197–203.

Gambero, Luigi. *Mary and the Fathers of the Church: The Blessed Virgin Mary in Patristic Thought*. San Francisco: Ignatius Press, 1999.

Gatti, Paola. *Il gran libro del mondo nella filosofia di Tommaso Campanella*. Roma: Pontificia Università Gregoriana, 2009.

Gelli, Giovan Battista. *Commento edito ed inedito sopra la Divina Commedia*. Firenze: Bocca, 1887.

Gerbron. 'The Story of Fra Angelico', *Mitteilungen des Kunsthistorischen Institutes in Florenz*, 57. Bd. H. 3 (2015): 292–319.

Giallongo, Angela. *La donna serpente: Storia di un enigma dall'antichità al XXI secolo*. Bari: Dedalo, 2013.

Gilbert, Creighton. 'When did a Man in the Renaissance Grow Old?' *Studies in the Renaissance* 14 (1967): 7–32.

Giles, H., N. Coupland and J. Coupland. 'Accommodation Theory: Communication, Context and Consequence', in *Contexts of Accommodation*, edited by H. Giles, N. Coupland and J. Coupland, 1–69. Cambridge: Cambridge University Press, 1991.

Glielmo, Antonio. *Le grandezze della SS. Trinità*. Napoli: Roberto Mollo, 1639.

Goodare, Julian. *The European Witch-Hunt*. Abingdon, Oxon and New York: Routledge, 2016.

Goodspeed, George S. 'The Book of Job in Other Literatures, II', *The Old and New Testament Studies* 15 (1892): 105–14.

Gow, Andrew and Lara Apps. *Male Witches in Early Modern Europe*. Manchester: Manchester University Press, 2003.

Gow, A. C., R. B. Desjardins and A. F. V. Pageau. *A History of the Case, State, and Condition of the Waldensian Heretics (Witches)*, 18–79. University Park: The Pennsylvania State University Press, 2017.

Gregory the Great. *Moralium libri sive expositio in librum B. Job*, in *Patrologia Latina*, accurante J.-P. Migne, vol. 75. Paris: Ex typis Migne, 1862.

Gregory of Nyssa. *Ascetical Works*, translated by Virginia Woods Callahan. Washington: The Catholic University of America Press, 1967.

Guazzo, Francesco Maria. *Compendium maleficarum*, translated by E. A. Ashwin. New York: Dover, 2017.

Gutas, Dimitri. 'On Translating Averroes' Commentaries', *Journal of the American Oriental Society* 110 (1990): 92–101.

Hardison, Jr. O. B. *Christian Rite and Christian Drama in the Middle Ages*. Baltimore: Johns Hopkins Press, 1965.

Heller, Agnes. *A Theory of History*. London: Routledge, 2016.

Hinkle, William N. 'The Cosmic and Terrestrial Cycles on the Virgin Portal of Notre-Dame', *The Art Bulletin* 49 (1967): 287–96.

Hochschild, Joshua P. 'Logic or Metaphysics in Cajetan's Theory of Analogy. Can Extrinsic Denomination be a Semanric Property?' in *The Immateriality of the*

Human Mind, the Semantics of Analogy, and the Conceivability of God, edited by Gyula Klima and Alexander W. Hall, 61–92. Cambridge: Cambridge Scholars Publishing, 2011.

Innocent III. *De sacro altaris mysterio, Il Sacrosanto mistero dell'altare*, edited by Stanislao Fioravanti. Città del Vaticano: Libreria Editrice Vaticana, 2002.

Innocent VIII. *Summis desiderantes affectibus*, translated by Montague Summers, in Heinrich Kraemer and James Sprenger, *Malleus Maleficarum*, xix–xxi. London: Bracken Books, 1996.

Irenaeus. *The Writings*, translated by A. Roberts and W. H. Rambaut, vol. 2. Edinburgh: Clark, 1871.

Irvine, J. and S. Gal. 'Language Ideology and Linguistic Differentiation', in *Linguistic Anthropology: A Reader*, edited by Alessandro Duranti, 2nd edn, 402–33. Oxford: Wiley-Blackwell, 2009.

Isidore of Seville. *Etimologie o origini*, a cura di Angelo Valastro Canale. Torino: Unione Tipografico-Editrice Torinese, 2004.

Jakobson, Roman. *Word and Language*. Paris: Mouton, 1971.

James, R. M. (ed.). *The Apocryphal New Testament: Apocryphal Gospels, Acts, Epistles, and Apocalypses*. Oxford: Clarendon, 1924.

Jerome, St. *Expositio interlinearis libri Job*, in *Patrologia Latina*, accurante J.-P. Migne, vol. 23. Paris: Garnier fratres et J.-P. Migne successores, 1883, cols. 1475-1586.

Jerome, St. *Select Letters*, translated by F. A. Wright. Cambridge, MA: Harvard University Press, 1933 (Loeb Classical Library).

Jones, Pamela M. *Federico Borromeo e l'Ambrosiana: Arte e riforma cattolica nel XVII secolo a Milano*, translated by Stefano Galli. Milano: Vita e Pensiero, 1997.

Martyr, St. Justin. *First and Second Apologies*, translated by William Barnard. New York: Paulist Press, 1997.

Kallen, Horace Meyer. *The Book of Job as Greek Tragedy*, edited by George F. Moore. New York: Moffat Yard and Company, 1918.

Kelly, Henry Ansgar. 'The Metamorphoses of the Eden Serpent During the Middle Ages and Renaissance', *Viator, Medieval and Renaissance Studies* 2 (1972): 301–28.

Kepler, Johannes. *Epitome of Copernican Astronomy* and *Harmonies of the World*, translated by Charles Glenn Wallis. Amherst: Prometheus Books, 1995.

Kierkegaard, Soren. *The Works of Love*, translated by Howard and Edna Hong. New York: Harper and Row.

Kim, David Young. 'The Horror of Mimesis', *Oxford Art Journal* 34, no. 3 (2011): 335–53.

Kraemer, Heinrich and James Sprenger. *Malleus maleficarum*, translated by Montague Summers. London: Bracken Books, 1996.

Lamb, Sidney. *Tragedy*. Toronto: University of Toronto Press, 1965.

Lévi-Strauss, Claude. *Structural Anthropology*, translated by Claire Jacobson and Brooke Grundfest Schoepf. New York: Basic Books, 1963.

Liebeschuetz, W. 'Pelagian Evidence on the Last Period of Roman Britain?' *Latomus* 26, no. 2 (1967): 436–47.

Lotman, Yuri. *Universe of the Mind: A Semiotic Theory of Culture.* Bloomington: Indiana University Press, 1990.

Lotman, Yuri. 'Painting and the Language of Theater: Notes on the Problem of Iconic Rhetoric', in *Tekstura: Russian Essays on Visual Culture*, edited and translated by Alla Efimova and Lev Manovich, 45–55. Chicago and London: The University of Chicago Press, 1993.

Lucas, Angela M. *Women in the Middle Ages.* Brighton: The Harvester Press, 1983.

Luis, A. 'Evolutio historica doctrinae de compassione', *Marianum* V (1943): 261–85.

Lukken, G. M. *Original Sin in Roman Liturgy.* Leiden: Brill, 1973.

Luther, Martin. *Sämmtliche Schriften*, vol. 1. St. Louis: Concordia Lutheran Publishing House, 1880.

MacDonald, Dennis R. *The Gospels and Homer.* London: Rowman and Littlefield, 2015.

Maiello, Francesco. *Storia del calendario: La misurazione del tempo, 1450–1800.* Torino: Einaudi, 1994.

Maierù, Alfonso. *Terminologia logica della tarda scolastica.* Roma: Edizioni dell'Ateneo, 1972.

Mandel, Oscar. *A Definition of Tragedy.* New York: New York University Press, 1961.

Marin Louis. *Food for Thought*, translated by Mette Hjort. Baltimore and London: The Johns Hopkins University Press, 1997.

Maritain, Jacques. 'Sign and Symbol', translated by Mar Morris, *Journal of the Warburg Institute* 1, no. 1 (1937): 1–11.

Maritain, Jacques. *Art and Scholasticism* and *The Frontiers of Poetry*, translated by J. W. Evans. Hardison: University of Notre Dame Press, 1962.

Marsili, Salvatore. *I segni del mistero di Cristo: Teologia dei sacramenti.* Rome: C.L.V. Edizioni Liturgiche, 1987.

McDannell, Colleen. *Material Christianity: Religion and Popular Culture in America.* New Haven: Yale University Press, 1995.

McInerny, Ralph. *Studies in Analogy.* The Hague: Martinus Nijhoff, 1968.

McMahon, A. P. *Understanding the Medieval Meditative Ascent: Augustine, Anselm, Boethius and Dante.* Washington, DC: Catholic University of America, 2006.

McNamer, S. *Affective Meditation and the Invention of Medieval Compassion.* Philadelphia: Penn State University Press, 2010.

Melion, Walter S. 'Ut Pictura Lex: Jan David, S.J., on Natural Law and Global Reach of Christian Images', in *The Nomadic Object: The Challenge of World for Early Modern Religious Art*, edited by Christine Göttler and Mia M. Mochizuki, 149–86. Leiden and Boston: Brill, 2018.

Meredith, Peter and John E. Tailby. *The Staging of Religious Drama in Europe in the Later Middle Ages.* Kalamazoo: Medieval Institute Publications, 1983.

Meyer-Baer, Kathi. *Music of the Spheres and the Dance of Death: Studies in Musical Iconology.* Princeton: Princeton University Press, 1970.

Mitchell, John. 'Literacy Displayed: The Use of Inscriptions at the Monastery of San Vincenzo al Volturno in the Early Ninth Century', in *The Uses of Literacy in Medieval*

Europe, edited by Rosamond McKitterick, 188–225. Cambridge: Cambridge University Press, 1990.

Mondin, Battista. *L'uomo secondo il disegno di Dio: Trattato di antropologia teologica*. Bologna: Edizioni Studio Domenicano, 1992.

Moore, Edward. *Studies in Dante*, first series: *Scripture and Classical Authors in Dante*. Oxford: Clarendon, 1896.

Morris, John. 'Pelagian Literature', *The Journal of Theological Studies*, new series, 16, no. 1 (1965): 26–60.

Muratori, Ludovico Antonio. *Opere*. Milano: Ricciardi, 1964.

Muzzarelli, Maria Giuseppina. 'Adamo, Eva e "la serpenta"', in *La storia e le immagini della storia*, a cura di Matteo Provasi e Cecilia Vicentini, 83–101. Roma: Viella, 2015.

Nagy, Gregory. *Poetry as Performance*. Cambridge: Cambridge University Press, 1996.

Neff, Amy. 'The Pain of *Compassio*: Mary's Labour at the Foot of the Cross', *The Art Bulletin* 80, no. 2 (1998): 254–73.

Nöth, Winfried. 'Yuri Lotman on Metaphors and Culture as Self-referential Semiospheres', *Semiotica* 161, no. 1 (2006): 249–63.

Nuzza, Angelo. *Quaresimale*. Venice: Storti, 1654.

Ong, Walter J. 'Wit and Mystery: A Reevaluation of Medieval Hymnody', *Speculum* 22 (1947): 310–41.

Origen. *Homeliae in Lucam*, in *Patrologia Graeca*, accurante J.-P. Migne, vol. 13. Paris: Ex Typis Migne, 1862, cols. 1801-1900.

Ozog, Monika. 'Saint Jerome and *veritas hebraica* on the Basis of the Correspondence with Saint Augustine', *Vox Patrum* 30 (2010): 511–19.

Pacino da Bonaguida. MS 643, fol. 12v, Pierpont Morgan Library, New York.

Panaccio, Claude. *Mental Language: From Plato to William of Ockham*. New York: Fordham University Press, 2017.

Paravy, Pierrette. 'À propos de la genèse médiévale des chasses aux sorcières: Le traité de Claude Tholosan, juge dauphinois (vers 1436)', *Mélanges de l'École française de Rome, Moyen Age - Temps modernes* 91 (1979): 333–79.

Pedico, Maria Marcellina. *Mater dolorosa: L'Addolorata nella pietà popolare*. Libreria Editrice Vaticana: Città del Vaticano, 2015.

Peirce, Charles Sanders. 'On The Algebra of Logic: A Contribution to the Philosophy of Notation', *The American Journal of Mathematics* 7 (1885): 180–202.

Peirce, Charles Sanders. *Collected Papers, volumes VI: Scientific Metaphysics*, edited by Charles Hartshorne and Paul Weiss. Cambridge: Harvard University Press, 1935.

Pelikan, Jaroslav. 'The Two Cities: The Sack of Rome as a Historical Paradigm', *Daedalus* 111, no. 3 (1982): 85–91.

Pelikan, Jaroslav. *Reformation of Church and Dogma (1300–1700)*. Chicago: Chicago University Press, 1984.

Pelikan, Jaroslav. *Jesus through the Centuries: His Place in the History of Culture*. New Haven: Yale University Press, 1985.

Pelikan, Jaroslav. *Mary through the Centuries: Her Place in the History of Culture*. New Haven: Yale University Press, 1996.

Peters, Edward. 'The Medieval Church and State on Superstition, Magic and Witchcraft from Augustine to the Sixteenth Century', in *Superstition and Magic in Augustine and Early Modern Europe*, 52–90, edited by Helen Parish. London: Bloomsbury, 2015.

Petrarch. *Petrarch's Lyric Poems: The 'Rime sparse' and Other Lyrics*, edited and translated by Robert M. Durling. Cambridge: Harvard University Press, 1976.

Pietropaolo, Domenico. 'Vico e la tradizione dell'*ut pictura poesis*', in *Letteratura italiana e arti figurative*, 719–26, edited by A. Franceschetti. Firenze: Olschki, 1988.

Pietropaolo, Domenico. 'L'inno *Ave Maris Stella* fra liturgia e politica nella conversione del Canada', in *Lingue e Testi delle Riforme Cattoliche in Europa e nelle Americhe (secc. XVI -XXI)*, 93–108, edited by Rita Librandi. Firenze: Cesati Editore, 2013.

Plato. *The Collected Dialogues*, edited by Edith Hamilton and Huntington Cairns. Princeton: Princeton University Press, 1980.

Plato-Ficino. *Omnia divini Platonis opera*, translated by Marsilio Ficino. Basel: Officina Frobeniana, 1546.

Quiviger, François. 'Drunkenness, Sex and Desire in Titian's *Bacchanal of the Andrians*', in *Images of Sex and Desire in Renaissance Art and Modern Historiography*, edited by Angeliki Pollali and Berthold Hub, 169–80. New York and Abingdon: Routledge, 2018.

Rosemann, Philipp W. *Omne Agens Agit Sibi Simile: A Repetition of Scholastic Metaphysics*. Leuven: Leuven University Press, 1996.

Rouse, Richard H. 'The A Text of Seneca's Tragedies in the Thirteenth Century', *Revue d'histoire des textes* 1 (1971): 93–121.

Saenger, Paul. 'Reading in the Later Middle Ages', in *A History of Reading in the West*, edited by Guglielmo Cavallo and Roger Chartier, translated by L. G. Cochrane, 120–48. Amherst and Boston: University of Massachusetts Press, 1997.

Schillenbeeckx, Edward. *Christ the Sacrament of the Encounter with God, The Collected Works*, vol. 1. London: Bloomsbury, 2014.

Schiller, Julius. *Coelum Stellatum Christianum*. Augsburg: Aperger, 1627.

Schleicher, Marianne. 'Artifactual and Hermeneutical Use of Scripture in Jewish Tradition', in *Jewish and Christian Scripture as Artifact and Canon*, edited by Craig A. Evans and Daniel Zacharias, 48–65. London: T&T Clark, 2009.

Schuler, Carol M. 'The Seven Sorrows of the Virgin: Popular Culture and Cultic Imagery in Pre-Reformation Europe', *Simiolus: Netherlands Quarterly for the History of Art* 21, no. 1/2 (1992): 5–28.

Sebeok, Thomas A. *Signs: An Introduction to Semiotics*. Toronto: University of Toronto Press, 2001.

Serjeantson, R. W. 'The Passions and Animal Language, 1540–1700', *Journal of the History of Ideas* 62, no. 3 (2001): 425–44.

Shakespeare, William. *The Merchant of Venice*. Folger Shakespeare Library. New York: Simon & Schuster, 2011.

Sheppard, Anne. *Aesthetics*. Oxford: Oxford University Press, 1987.

Simons, Dorothy Lister. 'The Individual Human *dramatis personae* of the *Divine Comedy*', *Modern Philology* 16 (1918): 371–80.

Smith, Chipps Jeffrey. *Sensuous Worship: Jesuits and the Art of the Early Catholic Reformation in Germany*. Princeton and Oxford: Princeton University Press, 2002.

Snyder, John P. 'Map Projections in the Renaissance', in *The History of Cartography*, vol. 3, part 1, edited by Edward Woodward, 365–81. Chicago and London: Chicago University Press, 2007).

Spagna, Arcangelo. *Oratorii overo melodrammi sacri con un discorso dogmatico intorno l'istessa materia*. Rome: Buagni, 1706.

Spitzer, Leo. 'Speech and Language in *Inferno XIII*', *Italica* 19, no. 2 (1942): 81–104.

Spretnak, Charlene. *Missing Mary: The Queen of Heaven and her Re-Emergence in the Modern Church*. New York: Palgrave Macmillan, 2004.

Stagnitta, Antonino. *Laicità nel Medioevo italiano: Tommaso d'Aquino e il pensiero moderno*. Roma: Armando, 1999.

Steinberg, Leo. 'The Glorious Company', in *Art about Art*, edited by Jean Lipmann and Robert Marshall, 8–31. New York: Dutton, 1978.

Stephens, Walter. *Demon Lovers: Witchcraft, Sex and the Crisis of Belief*. Chicago: University of Chicago Press, 2002.

Swan, Claudia. '*Ad vivum, naer het leven*, from the Life: Defining a Mode of Representation', *Word & Image* 11 (1995): 353–72.

Swindler, Leonard. *Biblical Affirmations of Woman*. Philadelphia: The Westminster Press, 1979.

Teleneau, Constantin. *Philosophia conversionis*. Paris: Schola Lulliana, 2014.

Tertullian. *Adversus Iudaeos*, in *Opera*, edited by E. F. Leopold, Pars III, 291–329. Leipzig, 1841.

Tertullian. *Apologeticus*, in *Patrologia Latina*, vol. 1. Paris: Migne, 1844, cols 257-536.

Thibodeau, Timothy M. '*Enigmata Figurarum*: Biblical Exegesis and Liturgical Exposition in Durand's *Rationale*', *The Harvard Theological Review* 86 (1993): 65–79.

Tillich, Paul. *A History of Christian Thought*. New York: Simon & Schuster, 1968.

Turel, Noa. 'Living Pictures: Rereading *au vif*', *Gesta* 50, no. 2 (2011): 163–82.

Valpolicelli, Luigi, ed. *Il pensiero pedagogico della Controriforma*. Firense: Giuntina-Sansoni, 1960.

Veronensis, Zeno. *De spiritu et corpore*, in *Sanctorum Zenonis et Optati opera omnia*, in *Patrologia Latina*, accurante J.-P. Migne, vol. 11. Paris: Vrayet, 1845, col. 338–45.

Vico, Giambattista. *Scienza nuova*, edited by Fausto Nicolini. Bari: Laterza, 1928.

Vico, Giambattista. *The New Science*, translated by T. G. Bergin and M. H. Fisch. Ithaca: Cornell University Press, 1968.

Viollet-le-duc, E. *On Restoration*. London: Low and Searle, 1875.

Waite, Gary K. *Heresy, Magic and Witchcraft in Early Modern Europe*. London: Palgrave Macmillan, 2003.

Warner, Marina. *Alone of All Her Sex: The Myth and Cult of the Virgin Mary*. London: Pan books, 1976.

Waterschoot, Werner. 'Emblemataliteratuur uit de Officina Plantiniana in de zeventiende eeuw', *De Gulden Passer* 74 (1996): 451–69.

Watts, James W. 'The Three Dimensions of Scriptures', *Postscripts: The Journal of Sacred Texts and Contemporary Worlds* 2, nos. 2–3 (2006): 135–59.

Wenzel, Sigfried. *Fasciculus Morum: A Fourteenth-Century Preacher's Handbook*. University Park and London: Pennsylvania State University Press, 1989.

Whitehead, Christiania. *Castles of the Mind: A Study of Medieval Architectural Allegory*. Cardiff: University of Wales Press, 2003.

Wicks, Jared. *Cajetan Responds*. Eugene: WIPF and Stock Publishers, 1978.

Williams, Megan Hale. *The Monk and the Book: Jerome and the Making of Christian Scholarship*. Chicago: The University of Chicago Press, 2006.

Windler, Leonard. *Biblical Affirmation of Woman*. Philadelphia: The Westminster Press, 1979.

Yardley, John. *Justin and Pompeius Trogus: A Study of the Language of Justin's Epitome of Trogus*. Toronto: University of Toronto Press, 2003.

Ziolkowski, Jan M. and Michael J. Putnam. *The Virgilian Tradition: The First Fifteen Hundred Years*. New Haven and London, 2007.

Zwierlein, Otto. 'Spuren der Tragödien Senecas bei Bernardus Silvestris, Petrus Pictor und Marbod von Rennes', *Mittellateinisches Jahrbuch* 22 (for 1987) (1989): 171–96.

General Index

NOTE: Page references in *italics* indicate figures.

abstraction   36
active sign   5
Adam. *See* fall, the
agony in the garden of
    Gethsemane   121–5
allegorical catasterism   192–3, 195–6,
    197–8
anagoge   115
analogy   1
  classical tragedy   111–12
  labour of Mary   134
  nature of sacrament   18
  serpent (*serpere*) and devil   52–3,
    54–5, 60
  soul as canvas   159
Angelico, Fra
  depiction of crucifixion   141, 147–50
animals. *See also* serpent
  figurative uses   50–1
  intelligence   52, 207 n.13
antecedence   4
antiphon
  Ave Maris Stella   165–6, 184
  Salve Regina   165
anxiety of influence   49, 206 n.7
Aperger, Andreas   181
apostasy   78, 209 n.14
Aquinas, Thomas. *See* Thomas Aquinas,
    Saint
argument from fittingness   51–2
arbitrariness   12–13
Aristotle   163, 167
  catharsis   118–19
artificial sign   3–4, 12–13, 14
arts. *See also* fall, the; Passion
  and Catholic Church   97–8
  representation of Judith   166
  spiritual edification   26–7, 28–9,
    36–7, 131, 163
  superiority over language   25–6

Athenian/classical tragedy   107, 110,
    111–12
Augustine, Saint   6, 48, 90, 102, 195, 196
  notion of sacrament   2, 4, 5
  notion of sign   11–12, 16, 17–18, 41
  notion of time   172
authorial apostrophe   61–2
authorial intent   52, 55, 56, 58–9
Averroes   118–19
Avicenna   60, 118, 135

Bacon, Roger   6
Bakhtin, Mikhail   143
Balthasar, Hans Urs von   113
baptism   3, 13, 14, 154, 155, 156, 190, 192
  renunciation   70, 71, 72, 78–9
Bargigi, Guinoforto delli   67–8, 85
Bartsch, Jakob   181
Basilica of San Petronio (Bologna)   25,
    26
  The Temptation   27–32, 38
Bayer, Johann
  Uranometria   181–2
beauty
  as evil/deception   37–8, 77
  Judith's   171, 172, 175–9
  and ugliness in music   91–3
Beccaria, Cesare   83
Bede, Saint   23, 204 n.9
behavioural iconization   75–9
Bernardine, Saint   23, 24–5
Bernard, Saint   114–15, 213 n.26
Beza, Theodore   107
Bible. *See also specific events, narratives,*
    figures, for e.g. Judith; Passion
  Augustinian reading   41
  Catholic *vs.* Protestant   96, 100, 169
  double signification   8–9
  influence on Dante   110
  metaphorical predication   51–2

and nature   181, 184, 188
paraphrase   23–4
significance of reading   160
tropological reading   68
Bloom, Harold   206 n.7, 208 n.20
Boccaccio, Giovanni   105, 114
Bonaventure, Saint   139–40, 144, 150–1
Borghini, Raffaello
Il riposo   24
Borromeo, Federico, Cardinal   153, 161

cacophony   91–3
Cajetan, Tommaso de Vio   2, 69
conception of sign   6–10
on demonic witchcraft   86–7
dissolutio signi   81
on figurative uses   50–4
Hebrew text preference   48–9
De Maleficiis   69, 87
De Nominum Analogia   51
Pentateuchum Mosis iuxta sensum quem dicunt literalem commentarii   49–50, 52, 54–7, 59, 62–3, 206 nn.2, 8
reading of the fall   47–8, 54–61
De Spasmo Beatae Virginis Mariae   132–9
on true Christian   155
on women's weakness   61–6
calendars   191–2
Campanella, Tommaso   186
Cartier, Etienne   149
cataphoric sign   50
Catechismus ex decreto SS. Concilii tridentini ad parrochos. See Roman Catechism
Catechism of the Council of Trent. See Roman Catechism
catharsis   106–7, 112
Passion plays   117–21, 129
Catholic Church/Catholicism   154, 156. See also Roman Catechism; Schiller, Julius; Vatican
and arts   97–8
and music   90, 94–103
spiritual edification   26–7, 28–9, 37, 131, 163
Cato the Younger (Uticensis)   111, 115
Caulibus, Johannes de   140
causality   4, 12, 18–19, 79

Cazzani, Pietro   168
celestial cartography. See constellations
chalice   123–5
Christian tragedy   108–16
devout representation/*devozioni*   116–29
chronotope   143–4
church. See also Catholic Church/Catholicism; Vatican
corporate metaphor   64, 190
and decorative arts   25–7, 28–9, 36–7
as earthly paradise   89
as institution and outside world   42–3
navicula as   187–8
unity of   5
and witch-hunt   69, 71–5
classicism   109–11
Clement IX, Pope   96–7, 101
Clement XI, Pope   96, 100, 101
Unigenitus (1713)   95
Vineam Domini (1705)   95
code   13, 53, 59, 77
artistic   149–50
of common spirituality   16
double-code   153–4
music as   90–1
recodification of constellations (*see* constellations)
recodification of nature   186
swoon/fainting as   132–9
Colonna, Carlo, Cardinal   97, 99
Comestor, Peter   33
Historia scholastica   23–4
communication
and arts   25–6
and conventional signs   12–13
communicational accommodation   8
conative sign   140
concept   6, 37
constellations
apostles   219 n.5
direction of curvature   196–8
Draco   187, 188
Eve   194
Magi   194
Noah's Ark   190
North Star   182, 184–5, 187, 188
Orion   194–5
recodification   181–4, 188–9, 192, 195–6, 197–9

General Index

St. Joseph   194–5
  Ursa Major   184, 187–8
  Ursa Minor   182, 184, *185*, 187
convergence   7
co-signification   50
Coster, Francois   165
covenant   7
Creation   90–1, 166–7
cross/crucifixion   112–15, 116
  defilement   82, 85
  modes   139–41
  paintings   133, 141–50
  as sacred sign   15–16
  and swoon of Mary   132–3, 136–7, 150–1
  and tree of knowledge   29, 44
cruce erecta   139–50, 151
cruce iacente   140

damnation   105–6
Danesi, Marcel   82
Dante Alighieri   29, 67–8, 108, 110–11
  Divine Comedy   105, 106, 110, 114
  Inferno (Inf.)   67–8, 85, 106, 114
  Paradiso (Parad.)   172
  Purgatorio (Purg.)   172
David, Jan
  Veridicus Christianus   153–64
Deely, John   5–6, 12
Della Valle, Federico
  Ester   166, 168–70
  Iudit   166, 167–9, 170–9
De' Sommi, Leone   107
despair   113–14
devil   218 n.16. *See also* Lucifer; Satan
  Cajetan's reading of Moses
    depiction   47–8, 54–61, 65–6
  and Christ-the-model   159
  devil's mark/physical signs   75–7
  Draco as   187, 188
  erotic union with   71–2, 77–8
  and female gender   23, 29, 31–2, 35, 37, 41, 45, 61–6, 77–8
  as female serpent   24, 29, 35, 49–50, 52–3
  and witchcraft   67, 69–73, 82–3, 85–6, 87
Devotione de Venerdí sancto (A Devout Representation of Good Friday)   121–3, 125–7

Devotione de Zobiadí (A Devout Representation of Holy Thursday)   121–5
diagram   193–5
dialogic drama   102–3
dialogue
  and thinking   47–8, 58–61
divine accommodation   7
divine grace   17–18, 95
dogmatic theology   96, 97, 98, 100–2, 210 n.10
Draco (constellation)   187, 188
drama and dramaturgy   117–18, 119–20, 127–30
  code in painting   149–50
  mimesis   17
  personification   169–70
Durand, William
  liturgical interpretation   129
  on visual signs   25–6, 28–9, 36

ekphrasis/reverse ekphrasis   147–8, 161–2, 176–7
Erasmus   133, 174, 215 n.15
erotic femininity   35, 37–8, 40–1, 45
  Judith's   175–9
  and witchcraft   71–2, 73, 77–8, 83
eschatology   174–6
Esther   166, 167–70
Eve. *See also* fall, the
  antitype   165–6
  constellation   194
  devil within   47–8, 54–61
  salvation   44
exegesis   5, 50, 63–4, 65, 110–11, 207 n.9

fall, the   1, 2. *See also* Eve
  Bernardine on   23
  Cajetan's reading   47–8, 54–61, 64–6
  Comestor's interpretation   23–4
  Jacopo della Quercia's depiction   27–32, 38
  interpretations   24–5
  Michelangelo's depiction   38–42, 177
  musical story   90–3
  Notre-Dame Cathedral panel   32–8, 177, 204 n.12
  Raffaello's depicton   42–5, 177
  visual narrative   25–6, 65

Fastidius 156, 216 n.6
fig tree 29–30, 44
flagellation of Christ/Christ at the
 Column 121, 125–7
forensic semiotics 82
fortitude 144
Foucault, Michel 83, 186
Francis of Assisi, Saint 111

Galle, Theodoor
 *Hominis vere Christiani
  descriptio* 154–9
 Orbita probitatis 154, 159–64
Garden of Eden. *See* fall, the
Gelli, Giovan Battista 85
gender. *See also* women
 and deception 29, 77
 and Glielmo's account of the
  fall 92
 and inferiority and
  libidinousness 61–6, 72–3, 77–8,
  166–7
 and messianic prophecy 34, 63–4,
  100, 173, 174–5, 176, 179
 and predisposition to evil 23–5,
  30–2, 35, 37–8, 40–1, 45, 54–61,
  86–7, 134
 social hierarchy 62–4
 and witchcraft 72–4, 77–8, 82–3, 88
gestural iconization 73–5
Giotto (painter) 114
Glielmo, Antonio
 Le grandezze della SS. Trinità 90–4,
  209 n.2
God
 ascent to 143–4
 as composer/Maestro di Cappella 89,
  90–3
Goodspeed, George 108
Gregory of Nyssa, Saint 159
Guazzo, Francesco Maria 69, 75
guilt 76, 82–5

Handel, George
 Dixit Dominus 98–9
haptic imagery 31, 40, 56
Hardison, Jr., O. B. 109
harmony 90–1
 fall from 91–3
hearing, sense of 13, 14, 15, 26

heaven 183–4
Holofernes 100, 166, 171, 174–9, 187
Holy Communion 73–4
Honorius of Autun 111, 112
 Gemma animae 108–9
humano more 7

iconicity 53–4, 159
iconization 73–9, 82, 87
idea
 as mental signs 6
 and music 15
imagination
 centrality of signs 1–2
 collective 16–18
 of crucifixion process 139–50
 and demonic magic 86–7
 sacramental imagination 18–21
 and visualization 60, 150
imitation 7, 17
 suffering of Mary 134
imitation of Christ (*imitatio
  Christi*) 153–4
 and being a true Christian 154–9
 method 159–64
immanence 1, 19, 195–9
indexicality 18–19, 75–6, 81, 157
Innocent III, Pope
 conception of sign 2–6, 11
 De Sacro Altaris Mysterio 3
Innocent VIII, Pope 79, 85
 Summis desiderantes affectibus
  (1484) 69, 70–5
intentionality 6–7, 9, 14
interpretation
 anagogical 115
 contemplative approach 153
 fourfold 129
 meditative approach 153–4, 161–2
 orientative principle 63
 rememorative 115–16
isotopy 99–100

Jacopo della Quercia
 depiction of the fall 27–32, 38
Jakobson, Roman 13, 14
Jansenism 95
Jaspers, Karl 113
Jerome, Saint 48, 49, 63–4, 102, 108, 174,
 175–6, 206 n.8

Jesus Christ. *See also* cross/crucifixion; imitation of Christ; Passion
  agony in the garden   121–5
  body   5
  church architecture as sign of   28–9
  coming of Messiah signs   8–9
  dual nature   44
  ipsum   64
  as model   154–9, 164
  witch's denigration   73–4
Job   107–8
John Damascene, Saint   136
John, the Apostle, Saint   112–13
Joseph, Saint
  constellation   194–5
Judith
  as femme fatale   175–9
  idealization   166
  as type/sign of Mary   100, 167–9, 170–3, 174–5, 179
Julius II, Pope   132

Käger, Johann Matthias   181
Kallen, Horace Meyer   107–8
Kierkegaard, Søren   158
Killian, Lucas   181
Kramer, Heinrich   69, 71, 72–3, 74, 77
  Malleus maleficarum   69, 73, 74–5, 76, 77–80, 82–3, 84–5

Lamb, Sidney   107
language   13–15, 58, 195–6
  and figurative arts   25–6, 37
  functions   131
  iconicity   53–4
  and naming/renaming   186
Lévi-Strauss, Claude
  on language   14
liturgy
  and drama script   117, 121–5, 128
  Maundy Thursday   116
  Officium de compassione Beatae Mariae Virginis   150–1
logic   19–21
Lombard, Peter   11–12
Lotman, Yury   51, 149
Lucifer   100, 179. *See also* devil; Satan
  antitype   174–5
  heavenly choir   91–3, 210 n.6–7
Luke, Saint   112–13

McNamer, Sarah   140
Magesterium   100–1
Magi
  constellation   193
malefic sign   80–1
Maritain, Jacques   2, 6–7, 9, 113
Mark, Saint   112, 113
martyrdom   114–16
Mary, Blessed Virgin, Saint
  Anomalous Woman   82
  Christological idea   173–4
  as coredemptrix   133, 144, 146, 165, 168–9, 172, 175
  Feast of the Compassion   150–1
  fortitude   144
  intercessory role   165, 172–3, 179
  Judith as type/sign   100, 167–9, 170–3, 174–5, 179
  as musical score   93–4
  and North Star   182, 184, 187, 188
  role in Passion   141, 144, 146, 147, *148*, 149, 150–1
  as serpent defeater/trampler   34, 63–4, 100, 165, 172, 173, 174–5, 177, 179, 187
  signum magnum   165–6, 182
  swoon   132–9
Mass   109–10, 111–12, 115–16, 125
mater dolorosa (Our Lady of Sorrows)   132, 133–4
  feast day   133, 138, 150–1
  representation   136
material sign   96, 195–6
  of causality   18–19
  of the fall   25–6, 47–8
  of serpent   54, 80–1, 82
  stage property   123–5
matrimony   78–9, 80–1, 202 n.21
Matthew, the Apostle, Saint   112, 113
Melchizedek   98–9
memory   7
metaphor
  Christ   64
  church   64, 190
  ocular   57–8
  serpent   47–8, 49–54, 55, 59–60, 64–6
  sky   183–4
  swoon of Mary   151
  vision   57–8
metaphysics   19–21

Michael (Archangel)
  Constellatio Sancti Michaelis 182, 184, *185*, 186, 187, 188
Michelangelo
  depiction of the fall 38–42, 177
mimesis 17
misogyny 23–4, 30–1, 72–3, 77–8, 166–7
Monastero di Sant'Antonio in Polesine (Ferrara)
  crucifixion fresco 141, 144–6
Moses
  depiction of devil 55–61, 65–6
  use of figurative language 47, 52, 54, 64–5
Muratori, Ludovico Antonio 97
music 15
  and the fall 89–93
  Mary as 93–4
mythological catasterism 193

Nadal, Jerome 154
nature 3–4, 12, 154–5
  and Bible 181, 184, 188
  and pagan superstitions 182–4
  recodification 1856
Neri, Phillip, Saint 95–6
Nicholas of Cusa, Cardinal 15
Noah 7
Noah's Ark 190
North Star 182, 184–5, 186, 187, 188
Notre-Dame de Paris 25, 26
  The Temptation, Portal of the Virgin 32–8, 177, 204 n.12
Nuzza, Angelo 210 n.6

ocular metaphor 57–8
oratorio 94–103
Origen 159
Orion (constellation) 194–5
Ottoboni, Pietro, Cardinal 97, 99

Pacino da Bonaguida
  illumination of the crucifixion 141–4, 146
painting 36, 53
  ad vivum 156–7, 163
  of *cruce erecta* crucifixion 141–50
  of crucifixion 133

interpretation 153–4, 161–2
  spiritual edification 146–7
  theatrical code 149–50
Pamphili, Benedetto, Cardinal 97, 99
Passion 102, 111–15, 158. *See also* cross/crucifixion
  dramatization 116–21, 127–30
  and Job 108
  Mary's absence 146
  Mary's role 132–9, 141, 144, 147, *148*, 149, 150–1
  supreme suffering 121–7
  visualization 131–2
  as way to redemption 150–1
passive sacrament 5
passive sign 5
patriarchal cross 141–2
Paul, the Apostle, Saint 8, 111, 117–18
Peirce, Charles Sander 138, 157, 193
Pelagian moralism 156
personification
  heaven 183
  theatrical 169–70
Peter, the Apostle, Saint 187
Plato 167
poetry 19–21
Polaris. *See* North Star
positive sign 4
probity 159–64
Prometheus 108, 211 n.9
Protestantism 96, 98–9, 100, 169, 175
Pseudo-Bonaventure
  Meditationes vitae Christi 136, 139–41, 147–9, 216 n.28
purgation 84

Queen of Heaven 165–6, 178–9. *See also* Mary, Blessed Virgin, Saint
  Della Valle's dedication 167–9

Rabanus Maurus 174
Raffaello Sanzio (Raphaël)
  depiction of the fall 42–5, 177
reality 11–12, 20
redemption 1, 106
  and Christian tragedy 107, 108–16, 118
  and church 28–9
  coredemptrix 133, 144, 146, 165, 168–9, 172, 175

and *cruce erecta* crucifixion 140–2, 145–6, 149–51
and crushing serpent's head 100
Jacopo della Quercia's representation 29–30
and Mass 98
Raffaello's representation 44
and swoon of Mary 134, 139
and witchcraft 72, 82
rememorative allegory 115–16
Renaissance 5–6. *See also* Roman Catechism
calendars 191–2
demonology 69–70
resemblance 186
resurrection 113, 115, 116, 140, 142
revelation
by imitation 7
signs 8–9
Roman Catechism 2, 10–18, 154, 190, 195, 196
authors 201 n.3
naming tradition 192
Rome 90, 94–103. *See also* Catholic Church/Catholicism; Vatican

sacrament 10–11. *See also* baptism
active and passive 5
Augustinian conception 2, 4
defilement 78–9, 85–6
indexicality 18–19, 81
and Mass 112
reversal 72
and sanctification 17–18
significance 15–17
significando causant 131
as synonym of sign 4–5
salvation 7
and celestial cartography 190
of Eve 44
and imitation of Christ 154–9
and liturgy 117, 123
Mary's role 100, 133–4, 165, 167–9, 170–3
and Mass 112, 115–16
and oratorio 94–5
and sacraments 2
sanctity 15, 17–18
San Marco Convent (Florence)
crucifixion fresco 141, *145*, 147–50

Santa Maria Antiqua (Rome) 102
Satan 183–4. *See also* devil; Lucifer
Schecks, Kaspar 181
Schiller, Julius
Coelum stellatum Christianum 181–2, 183, 184–90, 192, 194–9
metaphorical representation of sky 183–4
Scholasticism 2, 9, 87–8, 109
sculpture 36
Segni, Lothario di. *See* Innocent III, Pope
semiotic consciousness 6, 10–11
semiotics 1–2, 89
Seneca 110, 111, 114–15
sense(s) 6, 11–16, 195
and demonic witchcraft 76–7, 87
sensual empathy 32–3
serpent
cataphoric sign 50
celestial 187
gender and sexualization 23–5, 30–2, 35, 37–8, 40–1, 45, 134
and Holofernes 174–5
Jacopo della Quercia's depiction 27–32
messianic prophecy 34, 63–4, 100, 165, 172, 173, 174–5, 176, 177, 179
metaphorical reading 47–8, 49–54, 55, 59–60, 64–6
Michelangelo's depiction 38–42, 177
in Notre-Dame's panel of the fall 32–8, 177
Raffaello's depiction 42–5, 177
and witchcraft 79–81
sight, sense of 14, 15, 26
and evidence 77
sign 1–2
Augustinian conception 11–12, 16, 17–18, 41
Cajetan's conception 6–10
classical theory 136
dissolvement 81
ecclesial setting 99
in bolo and *in malo* 29–30, 204 n.9
Innocent III's conception 3–6
notion and nature 2–3
in Roman Catechism 10–18
social dimension 5, 11
Thomist conception 6–7, 8
significando causant 131, 161, 176

signification 1–2
  of book of nature 187
  of diagrams 193–5
  dual approaches 8–9, 37
  of Mass 111–12, 125
  and metaphorical predication 51
  by mimesis 17
  of natural signs 12
  of Notre-Dame panel of the fall 36–7
  prophetic and recollective 169–70
  Roman Catechism authors' conception 15
  sacramental 15–17
  spasmus 135–6, 151
signifier-signified relationship 9–10, 77, 94
  Aristotelian 17
  iconicity 53–4
  in Jacopo della Quercia's panel of the fall 31–2
  in Notre-Dame panel of the fall 37–8, 177
signum 3–4
signum magnum 165–6, 182, 184
Simplicius 118
Sixtus IV, Pope 151
sky. *See also* constellations
  metaphor 183–4
Spagna, Arcangelo 100–3
  Discorso dogmatico sugli oratori 96–7, 210 n.10
  Discorso intorno a gl'oratori (Discourse on Oratorios) 94
Speculum humanae salvationis 174–5
speech 13, 26
  serpent's ability 54, 58–9
Sprenger, Jakob 69, 71, 73, 74, 77
Steiner, George 113
subsequence 4
suffering 108. *See also* Passion
  cathartic aspect 106–7, 112, 117–21, 129
  conative sign 140
  swoon as sign 132–9, 150–1
  and witchcraft 87
suicide 105–6, 114–15
swoon of the Virgin 132–9, 150–1
symbolism 2–3
  birth of church 134
  calendar 191–2
  celestial 181, 183, 184, 187, 188–9, 191–2, 193
  and collective imagination 16–17
  denigration of Christ 74
  and drama 125
symptom 135–6

taciturnity 76, 84
Tasso, Torquato
  Jerusalem Delivered 20
tears 84–5
temptation
  ancestral 80
  Cajetan's reading 47–8, 54–5
  diabolical 176–7
  Jacopo della Quercia's depiction 27–32, 38
  Michelangelo's depiction 38–42, 177
  Notre-Dame Cathedral panel 32–8, 177, 204 n.12
  Raffaello's depiction 42, *43*, 44, 45, 177
  and true Christian 154
  vulnerability and resistance 62–3, 65
Tertullian 44, 108
Theodore of Mopsusestia 107
theology
  dogmatic 96, 97, 98, 100–2, 210 n.10
  of harmony and disharmony 90–4
  'high semiotics' 12
  and interpretation 63, 64
  and witchcraft 69, 70, 78–9
Tholosan, Claude 68, 69
Thomas Aquinas, Saint
  on argument from fittingness 51–2
  conception of sign 6, 8
  doctrine of language 13
  on Mass 111–12
  on metaphysics and logic 19
  on sacraments 131
thought 47–8, 58–61
Tilich, Paul 105
torture (judicial) 82, 83–4
touch, sense of 31, 40, 56
tragedy 107. *See also* Della Valle, Federico
  book of Job 107–8
transcendence 195–6, 197–9
Trinity 93, 94
tropology 68, 129

true Christian 154–9
  ways to become 159–64
typology 41, 63–4
  Marian 100, 165, 167–9, 173, 174–5, 179
  and Passion 115–16, 122–3
  reverse typology 44

unity of the church 5
Ursa Major 184
  recodification 187–8
Ursa Minor
  recodification 182, 184, *185*, 187

Valla, Lorenzo 137, 174, 214 n.15
Vatican 25, 26. *See also* Catholic Church/Catholicism
  Sistine Chapel's panel of temptation and expulsion 38–42, 177
  Stanza della Segnatura 42–5
verbal iconization 76
Vergil 110, 111
vestigia Dei 18–19
Vico, Giambattista 128
  on painting 36
  Scienza nuova 19–21
Viollet-le-duc, Eugene 33
virtue 160–1

visual allusion 125
visualization 9, 65
  of crucifixion 141–50
  of Gospel narratives 122–5, 129
  and imagination 60
  of Passion 131–2
visual sign 25–7, 28–9
De Vita Christiana 155–6, 159, 161, 215 n.6

Whitehead, Christiania 27
witchcraft
  and abjuration 77–9, 85–6
  confession 83–4
  crimes 71, 72, 78–9
  and devil's fellowship 67, 69–73, 82–3, 85–6, 87
  elaborate theory 69–70, 85
  evidence 79–85
  iconization 73–9, 82, 87
  and serpent 79–81
  witch-hunt 67–9, 87–8
women. *See also* gender
  role in crucifixion 146–7
  suffering 134

Zodiac sign 181, 185, 186, 191–2, 219 n.5

Index Locorum

OLD TESTAMENT

Genesis (Gen)
1.26-27	166–7
3	41, 48, 49, 52, 53, 60, 61
3-15	174
3.1-7	31
3.3	40
3.7	31
3.15	64–5, 80, 100
3.19	34
4.15-16	204 n.9
9.12-16	7
14	98
41	188

Numbers (Num)
21	3

Psalms (Ps)
19.1	2
103.2	196
109	98

Ecclesiastes (Eccl)
25	77

Song of Songs (Song)
2.13	30

Daniel (Dan)
12.3	184

NEW TESTAMENT

Matthew (Mt)
5.48	155
14.24	187
16.2-4	8

Mark (Mk)
11.12-14	30

Luke (Lk)
1.28	137, 174
1.46	159
2.34	136
4, 16-20	160
10-16	100

John (Jn)
1.50	30
10.9	28
19.25	137, 146

Acts of the Apostles

1 Corinthians (1 Cor)
11.1	163

2 Thessalonians (2 Thess)
2.9	77

Hebrews (Heb)
12.2	161

Revelation (Rev)/ Apocalypse of John
12.1	165
12.1-2	134
12.9	51
20.2	29

EARLY CHRISTIAN

Ambrose
De Isaac et Anima — 44

Augustine, Saint
De civitate Dei contra paganos (De Civ. Dei) (The City of Gods)
10.5	5, 89
	4

Confessions (Conf.)
8.12.28	30
11.20	172
12.29	159–60

De doctrina Christiana
2.1	11
	17–18

Gospel of Nicodemus
10.1	133

GRECO-ROMAN SOURCES

Aristotle
Peri hermeneias (De Int.) (On Interpretation) — 9
16a3	136

Poetics — 107, 118–19
1448b17	17

Rhetoric — 118

Euripides
Alcestis
935-61	114

Plato
Phaedrus
242b-c	61

Republic
529d	193, 195
613a	155

Theaetetus (Theae.) — 59–60

Sophocles
Ajax
430-80	114

Index Locorum

MEDIEVAL CHRISTIAN WRITINGS

Durand, William
Rationale divinorum officiorum 25
7.23-25 5

Thomas Aquinas, Saint
De Ente et essentia (De Ente) 10

Summa Thologiae (ST) 9
IaIIae.80.2 177
Ia.114.3 61
1a, q.93, a.4 8
IIIa.41.1 177
2.3.ad3 60

Summa Thologiae (ST), Suppl.
Q. 45 202 n.21

www.ingramcontent.com/pod-product-compliance
Lightning Source LLC
Chambersburg PA
CBHW072142290426
44111CB00012B/1951